Troubleshooting Men©

"What in the WORLD do they want?"

Rebecca F. Pittman

Wonderland Productions© 2014

Graphic Design by Rebecca F. Pittman

Troubleshooting Men is a copyrighted trademark of the Troubleshooting Men Website and Television Talk Show.

www.troubleshootingmen.net

Wonderland Productions, USA

ISBN: 978-0-692-27450-7

DEDICATION

To my mother Collette Wells for dedicating her life to helping thousands of women find their inner strength and happiness.

And for Ron Bueker—a man who needs no troubleshooting.

ACKNOWLEDGMENTS

I would like to thank the thousands of men who gave of their time during interviews, follow-up emails and phone conversations to make this book as inclusive and informative as it possibly can be.

A special "Thank You" to the Bull Pen from the website *TroubleshootingMen.net* for their insightful and heart-felt answers to all the women who have asked their opinions on everything from dating to marriage issues. These wonderful men are:

Ryan Pittman
Brandon Fredrickson
Todd Greene
Tom Dvorak
Henry Makowiecki
Brandon Bondie

A big shout-out to Townsquare Media and Christi Bankston for helping me create such a wonderful website that not only spawned this book and a television talk show, but continues to be an incredible forum for dating, relationship, self-esteem, image and marriage advice.

Thank you to Ray Hazen MA LPC CACIII SMC, and Casey Pittman Registered Psychotherapist, Recovery Support for their assessment of our Toad Pool candidates.

Finally, thank you to all of you who chose this book. Seeking information to enhance your life is a sign that you won't settle for ordinary, when *extraordinary* is just waiting for you!

www.TroubleshootingMen.net

CONTENTS

Coming Soon!

Upcoming books in the *Troubleshooting* Series by Rebecca F. Pittman:

Troubleshooting Women: What in the WORLD Do They Want?

Troubleshooting YOU: How to Create a Life of Abundance!

Other books currently on sale by Rebecca F. Pittman:

The History and Haunting of the Stanley Hotel
The History and Haunting of the Myrtles Plantation

How To Start a Faux Painting or Mural Business
(1st and 2nd Editions)

Scrapbooking for Profit
(1st and 2nd Editions)

T.J. Finnel and the Well of Ghosts
(Children's Novel Ages 8-Adult)

Rebecca F. Pittman

Troubleshooting Men,
What in the WORLD do they want?

Rebecca F. Pittman

Prologue-

There are many books out there on dating and relationship advice. What makes this book special? For one, the topics featured throughout this book were researched and spotlighted on my website and TV Talk Show, *Troubleshooting Men: What in the WORLD do they want?* The popularity of both forums was an overwhelming affirmation this is a huge arena where a lot of misunderstanding between the sexes still plays a role. Both men and women complained they were not only frustrated, but angry that dating was so difficult, and marriage fraught with problems and unfilled expectations.

Over the past four years I interviewed over 2,000 men in a very specific 98-essay questionnaire. What did they *really* want when it comes to a woman, a date, relationship, or marriage? Their answers surprised me, and at times I became saddened hearing how they felt about the way women misunderstood them and undervalued what they brought to the table.

Based on this information I created and launched a brand new concept…a website where women could actually ask a panel of men any questions they desired about what men wanted, about specific issues they were having with a date or husband, and receive five answers in return from men in different age brackets, income levels, and diverse interests. It was a huge hit! We were featured on *Fox 31* and asked to be on a national television talk show.

The final testament this was an area seriously needing a spotlight was when I was offered my own television talk show called, of course, *Troubleshooting Men: What in the WORLD do they want?* We featured the Bull Pen, our panel of men, who would answer our viewers' questions on anything they wanted to know where men were concerned. The panel varied from restaurant owners to CEO's, sports figures to your everyman. The show also featured experts on fashion, beauty, exercise, nutrition and self-esteem. These are still the main topics featured on the free website *TroubleshootingMen.net,* and the Bull Pen is still answering your questions.

Secondly, I grew up in a unique environment, where I witnessed first-hand some of the major issues women deal with when approaching themselves and the world around them. I was raised in a modeling agency where my mother taught not only fashion, makeup, hair, skin care and how to pivot a pretty ankle on the runway, but something I considered a lot more valuable—she taught her models the explosive power of self-esteem and the importance of knowing who you are and what you are offering the world. While my mother and her agency, Collette's Distinctive Modeling, made headlines for winning international modeling competitions, it was the behind-the-scenes victories I relished. I watched as women walked through her door with slumped shoulders, no eye contact and a general air that said, "I wish I could disappear. I have no feeling of self-worth."

A few months later I did not recognize these same women. They walked with their shoulders back, huge smiles, confidence, and an improved image. They sparkled with happiness and a visage that said, "Look out World...it's my turn!" I secretly cried over some of the transformations I witnessed. I also saw the Prom Queens, and the most-popular girls on campus take her courses, and I was amazed to find out these young women were not as confident and happy as I would have guessed. It was all very eye-opening.

I was modeling by the age of 5, and teaching modeling by the time I turned 16. After entering a few beauty pageants I was once again reminded that the women we think of as gorgeous, with an unfair advantage due to their perfect forms and flawless appearances, were actually terribly insecure under the surface. In fact many men in the survey admitted the pretty face lost its appeal if there wasn't more in the offering. They were looking for stimulating conversation, a girl who would get out and have adventures with them, a kind heart...in short...someone with substance!

At 21 I began teaching seminars on dating, personality, poise and confidence. I realized at that time how much insecurity played a gigantic part in the dating and marriage arenas, and how many women were actually sabotaging their chances at happiness by not realizing the mistakes they were making. Now, some 39 years later, I have compiled an amazing amount of information that will give you the life you've always wanted, whether you're in your 20's or 90's. Therefore, this book is special not only due to the plethora of inside information I garnered from all those men, the answers from the Bull Pen on the website and TV show, and my own personal seminars, but because the information contained here is going to show you the following:

Part I: The Reflection of You
- How to look inside and understand why you may be feeling unworthy of a great relationship
- How to improve your confidence and self-esteem
- Real ways to communicate with confidence on a date
- Etiquette in the dating world: restaurant protocol, parties, one-on-one, meeting his family
- Improving your image—inside and out
- How to recognize if you are single, or unhappy in a relationship, due to your own distorted perspective

Part II: The Male Mind
- What men are looking for on a first date, second date, on-going relationship, or marriage
- The Booby Traps men will set for you in the early stages of dating that can cancel you out
- What makes a woman irresistible so he keeps coming back
- Want to be put on a pedestal? The things that melt a man's heart

- What are the 10 stereotypes of the Toads that you want to avoid: are they treatable or toxic?
- What are the 10 biggest mistakes women are making when dealing with men at all stages?

Part III: Today's View of Romance
- Internet Dating: How To, How Not To, Writing a GREAT Profile, Dangers Online
- Today's Dating and Marriage Environments: How Our Expectations Have Changed

It is my fervent wish this book will show you that anyone can change their life for the better. You are an amazing, unique person who is SO worthy of love. That love starts with a love of you. When you realize all the incredible attributes you possess, it is then you can shine and have the relationship you are not only worthy of, but deserve. You will learn how to cancel out the negative voices you hear in your head, your experiences from the past that are not serving you today, and how to become your biggest fan. We are going to do this together. It's an amazing journey of discovering your inner secrets, and…his.

Keep in mind; I am sharing the secrets over 2,000 men confided in me about what they are looking for in a woman and a relationship. Please don't get huffy and think the information is not relevant…it most certainly is. These men did not make up what's motivating them to date one woman over another, or the things that drive them to propose, or stay in a marriage...or run for dear life! If you bought this book, I am guessing you see a need for more information on the topic of relationships. Ok. This is the true inside scoop. Most of us put more time and energy into picking out a house, an outfit, or a career than we do in understanding the most important relationship in your life...the one you have with yourself. Once that is healthy, you can decide if you want to share it with some lucky guy. If you do, this book will show you how to accomplish that. Hang on...this is going to be fun!

Rebecca F. Pittman
June, 2014

PART I:

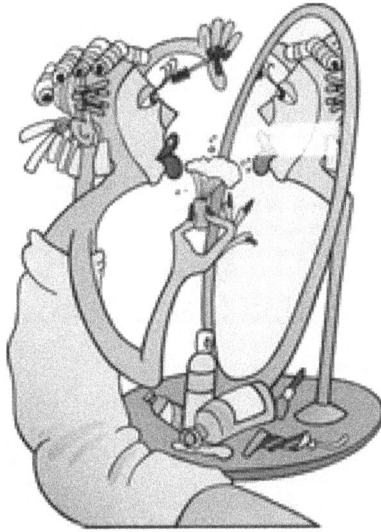

THE REFLECTION

OF YOU

Chapter One
Your Reflection is NOT Who You Are!

You may be asking, "What does this have to do with understanding what men want?" Very simply, men want a woman with confidence, who has a great life of her own, and is not looking for someone to give her one. One of the biggest complaints men have is that women complain too much, are rarely happy, and are looking for a man to fulfill them. This equates to clingy, needy and uninteresting. And believe me, that type of woman scares men off faster than an invitation to watch a Soap Opera marathon! That said, let's give you the advantage where men are concerned by giving you your best life, your best self, your best happiness.

Have you ever wondered who you really are? Do you look at yourself as the sum total of all your likes, dislikes, phobias, past experiences, school years and careers? How many of us when asked to describe ourselves start out by saying things such as "I'm a graphic designer." Or, "I'm a stay-at-home Mom." "I work part-time for the government." "I'm majoring in Microbiology." "I run an online scrapbooking store." Nine times out of ten, a person's first response to "Who are you?" will be to list their occupation. Why is that? Seriously. Think about it for a moment. Why don't we answer with "I enjoy reading about Quantum Physics, and have a talent for growing great tomatoes?" Or, "I'm really into golf and Caribbean history." Just once, I would love it if someone answered, "That depends on the moment…I'm evolving."

If you are like the majority of the homo sapiens roaming this earth, your image of yourself was created long ago. Your brain was developing at its fastest rate during your formative years of newborn to 6. In fact, by the time you were 3 years-old, your brain was already 80% developed. 80%! By 6, it was at its 90th percentile. That blows my mind…pardon the obvious pun. What that means is that during those first 6 years you were absorbing HUGE amounts of information. All those little neurons and synapses were snap, crackling and popping at an alarming rate, taking in copious amounts of information…all of which was stored permanently into memory banks. All of it! You were also getting important feedback as to how you related to the world. Your caregivers…whether parents, grandparents, foster parents, siblings, friends, teachers, aunts, uncles or cousins, were powerful influences in your life. The labels they gave you, the way they interacted with you, and the positive or negative feedback they imparted were stamped upon your nubile brain like an imprint on fresh clay. And because they were authority figures you trusted implicitly, their view of you mattered…big time!

If you were raised in an atmosphere of chaos, it may have left you feeling off-kilter. A sense of security and consistency were probably missing. Parents, who often fought, moved around a lot, had money issues, or were ambivalent in your discipline or training, no doubt left you feeling the world was not a safe place to be. On the other hand, if your environment was serene, the days flowed along harmoniously, and you felt you were unconditionally loved and cared for, you probably face the world with confidence and a sense that it will all be okay.

It is at this raw time in youth that nicknames and labels became our identities. I'm not saying they were given to us out of spite or to hurt us, but they carried a lot of weight. See if any of these ring a bell:

- Chubby
- Lazy
- Lousy at sports
- Four Eyes
- Stretch
- Midget
- Wuss
- Loud
- Shy
- Obnoxious
- Teacher's Pet
- Hyper
- "You're ALWAYS causing trouble!"
- Wallflower

- Poor student
- ADD/ADHD
- Pretty girl
- Mom's favorite/Dad's favorite
- Bed wetter
- Mommy's little helper

You get the picture. Some nicknames were considered cute in a family, and may have been innocuous, but deep inside you realized, even then, they must have come from somewhere…they must have some validity to them. And so it began, your picture of who you are, and how you fit in.

Let me give you an example: as I mentioned, I was raised in a modeling agency. Being on a runway in front of thousands of people gave me a lot of confidence when dealing with a crowd, but I struggled with one-on-one relationships.

My parents were divorced by the time I was 6. It tore my world apart due to their fighting and my mother moving us across the country to get away from my dad. I had no pictures of him at my birthdays or during holidays until I was in college. When I did spend time with him, he would teach me how to fish, sock a baseball, spiral a football, golf, bowl, and hook a basketball. So, here I was in two very different worlds. With my mother it was fashion and femininity; with my father it was sports and competing, and getting dirt under my fingernails. (Little did I realize I would later be a mother to four sons who love that I will play sports with them.) But for the most part, the father figure I needed as someone to give me a sense of self as a female was absent. The visits were few and far-between.

During these years of feeling like my family was merely pieces, especially after my brother moved away shortly after the divorce, I felt like a ship without a rudder. Life did not seem friendly or safe. To add to my feelings of insecurity, something happened during the summer before my last year of Junior High. I got an enormous growth spurt. I'm talking four inches! I was now the tallest girl in 9th grade. At a time when the boys were not growing as fast as the girls, it was a nightmare for me. I would go home crying from the cruel taunts of classmates and beg my mother not to make me go back to school the next day. I was skinny, just beginning to wear braces, and I felt like a freak. When you tower over everyone in the hallway, there is no place to hide. It colored who I thought I was in a big way. I focused on grades to compensate for not being popular. I stayed away from school dances and parties. My self-esteem was in my socks.

The pinnacle of rejection came when one day three large girls jumped me from behind a convenience store as I walked home from school. They had just found out my mother owned a modeling school, and that I was a model. They beat me up so badly that I was missing hunks of hair, and I had blood running down my arms and legs. It was not a good time to be me.

I assumed High School would be more of the same, only worse. I heard how mean that age group could be, and it was all about how pretty and popular you were. I was now 6'1 ½" tall. My Sophomore year was more of the bullying and me wishing I was home where no one could hurt me. My mother's constant support and reminding me who I was inside, and that someday I would love being tall, was all that got me through. She told me to be proud of the height, keep my shoulders back and show everyone I was glad to be me. When you're a teenager, it isn't always easy to see beyond the mirror. As we age, it still remains a daunting task.

In my Junior year of High School, things began to change. The braces came off. Instead of just getting tall, a few curves started showing up. I found I had a knack for acting and fell in love with the theater department, and then the oration classes, art, literature, science....and boys. The boys had suddenly shot up and were as tall as, or taller than me! The really bizarre part was the male teachers telling me I should try out for Prom Queen and other flimsy titles. This was my version of the Twilight Zone. The boys my age were still teasing me about my height, and not asking me out, but the grown men were telling me long legs were very cool. Yikes!

It wasn't until my Senior year that I finally came into my own. I teased back for the first time in my life instead of trying to cram myself into my locker. If someone said, "Hey Stretch, how's the weather up there?" I would retort with "Just fine Half-Pint, how's the curb working for you?" I found a new confidence that pretty much said, "Take me or leave me...I like who I am." That simple transformation changed it all. The same boys who had made fun of me were now asking me to the dances. Was it overnight? Of course not, and I still to this day feel a twinge when I walk through a group of teenage boys, waiting to see if they are going to make fun of my height. But the world has changed. Women are taller. The college volleyball girls tower over me, and long pants are everywhere. My height is now something I treasure; it makes me unique. I wouldn't change an inch of it. Mom was right.

This is a snapshot of how things in our early lives can be as indelible as permanent ink on a blank canvas. It gave me a real empathy for people who stick out and are targets of bullying. Some of us may have grown up around some pretty knee-buckling things such as alcoholism, drugs, sexual issues, or relatives doing jail time. We may have been victims of eviction, constant moving from one place to another, or other experiences that leave us feeling there is no safety net under us. Some of these things may require professional help to get past them. But the good news is, you CAN move forward. Our amazing brains are malleable, meaning they can be molded and changed at any age. It is called "neuroplasticity" and YouTube and the Internet are filled with new articles on what it is and how to use it.

I would like you to take a moment and hurriedly write down all the adjectives and phrases you feel pertain to you. For instance, words such as tall, short, slender, overweight, nice hair, good teeth, introvert, extrovert, good with people, shy, can play a musical instrument, green thumb, great cook, organized, born leader, outspoken, nervous, feisty, calm, loud, adventurous, coach potato, loves sports, loves shopping, good friend, loner, good with money, always broke, loves animals, fearful, confident, attractive, needs to work on my appearance, creative, poet, artist, photographer, sarcastic, quiet, sound sleeper, insomniac, etc. Write down at least ten descriptions. I don't care if it's "world's best nail biter," list it.

Go ahead and write down everything you can think of. How would your family describe you? What would your friends say are your pros and cons? Hubby, children, co-workers, boss, how would they describe you? Are you a morning person, or do you need four cups of coffee to open one eye? Think hard. Please don't skip this step.

Now, look at your list. Please circle all the words or phrases you have attributed to yourself since elementary school. Think back. Did you hear these adjectives and labels when you were little? Now, <u>underline</u> all the words that are more recent. Maybe your teeth weren't always great, but you've had work done and they are now. Perhaps you lost weight, took a college course, started a new sport or hobby, overcame some fears, found your voice, or changed to a career that is finally showcasing your talents.

The fact that you are evolving should become obvious from looking over the ones you circled and the ones you underlined. This proves you can change...you can grow. You are not stuck with anyone's labels, not even your own. In fact we are known to be our own worst enemies. Some of the negative self-talk I have slammed myself with I wouldn't say to someone who just ran over my dog. We drop an egg on the floor and the first thought is "Way to go, clumsy!" We're late for work and that little voice is right there saying, "Can't you get it right? How hard is it to get up on time and get here when you're supposed to? Now you're going to be in trouble!" All that does is break your spirit and bring you down. You may even recognize other familiar voices joining in, such as those of your parents, teachers, peers, etc. I still hear my father saying "Now, Becky...you can do this!" even though he's been gone for over 18 years.

Look again at your list. This is important! What negative things that you listed from when you were little are you still carrying around today that you would rather not be? Did your fear of animals then, still cause you unpleasant moments today? If you were shy in elementary school, are you still shy today? Are you still bad with money…never saving, always thinking more will come along?

Why is it important to look at this? Because it is showing you areas that are causing you unnecessary unhappiness, and they can be changed…if you want them to. You may feel stuck in these downers because you feel it is your lot in life to be painfully shy, unattractive, not good at sports, etc. I'm telling you, and every psychologist out there will tell you, that it is simply NOT true. You can change anything if you really want to, even if it's only changing how you view your situation. It starts with recognizing that those labels you still live by were given to you long ago and no longer apply. They didn't apply then, we just bought into them.

We are going to start giving you the tools to create the reflection you want. It's a simple step-by-step process and it's fun! It's like choosing from the catalogue of life all the things you want to have comprising your world. For now, please believe me that is not only possible, but happening every day. Let me be your Fairy Godmother. We'll get you to the ball and help you land the Prince. You may decide after we've given you the glass slippers that you aren't interested in the Prince after all. He may not measure up to YOUR expectations! That's just fine. It's all about the endless possibilities! Let's get started.

Chapter Two
Getting There from Here

We've all seen the maps posted at resorts, malls and other busy locations. There is a bright red box or "**X**" saying "You Are Here!" It is meant to give us a perspective of where we are and show us how to get to where we want to go. Well, let's face it...you are HERE...right here...in this stage of your life. You may like it HERE, or you may not. You may feel trapped, anxious and resigned that this is all life has in the cards for you. Possibly you are quite pleased with your location on the global scheme of things. You have the home, finances and relationships you've always wanted. Odds are, those things did not come to you without some real effort and thought on your part. And I'm happy for you!

Life is a constant series of changes. One step forward, two steps back. But once you learn life's secret, it becomes one leap forward, then another and another. You stop expecting Life to be the enemy and realize you are meant to have JOY! It's true...I promise! Does that mean there will be no more challenges? (Notice I said challenges…not hardships, bad times, sorrow or pain. Do you see the difference?) Challenges will always be a part of life, and thank goodness for that. If we weren't challenged, we would never grow or evolve. We would be complacent, boring little creatures who stayed safely in the shallow end of the pool and never experience the delicious discovery of the deep end where there is…*depth!*

So stop expecting it all to be rainbows and unicorns. Believe me, you don't want that. Your best qualities and attributes will come from going through a challenge and stepping victoriously through it with new tools to use for the next time. And the best part is it now gives you empathy to help someone else going through a similar situation. Looking back, I would not change the "hardships" that have come into my life, and some of them danged near killed me. But I am so much stronger, resilient and happy due to experiencing them. And when someone is hurting, I can honestly say, "I know how you feel. Let me be here for you."

If you are reading this and feeling you are not like everyone else who is out there dating or in a rewarding marriage, let's address that. Why do you feel that way? Is it your appearance? Past experiences with men? Something someone told you, and you believed it? Most of us feel a huge sense of familiarity when we look at ourselves in the mirror. We've been seeing that face and those features for a long time. Yep…that's me! There are the brown eyes, freckles, slightly crooked front tooth, and dark hair. There's that tummy I wish I could banish to Bora Bora and the nails that just won't grow. I wish my breasts were larger/smaller/firmer/perkier, and my feet not so big/long/stubby/wide, etc.

And then we tend to see beyond the eyes looking back at us. The negative thoughts begin about our *inner* workings. "I wish I was smarter. I should have stayed in college, or even begun it. Why can't I speak up for myself? I let that girl at work get to me again! No man is ever going to find me attractive. Why bother with dieting and fixing myself up? How come girls less attractive than I am are walking around with a nice-looking guy...or any guy at all?"

On and on the inner voices regale us with doubts, fears and insecurities. No wonder the mortals of this earth are lacking in confidence. And mark my words...they all are! No one is as confident as they appear to be, some have just learned the tricks and outer facades to pull it off. A huge percentage of today's celebrities were not popular in school. I believe many of them gravitated toward the stage as a way to find a spotlight...any spotlight. Most of the men we drool over on screen are shorter than the average male. Many female stars we deem exemplary will tell you they don't get what all the fuss is about. Farrah Fawcett said she could not understand how everyone saw her as the perfect beauty. She said her nose was odd, her lips too thin and she didn't like her jawline. Celebrities will ask for filters on the cameras to fuse out wrinkles and bags, or to be shot only from the right (or left) because they feel that is their best side. They are airbrushed and polished to perfection. And we've bought into it.

But, did you notice that many of the celebrities who are the biggest box-office draws are not outwardly perfect? Julia Roberts has said she feels her mouth is too large. Meryl

Streep's mouth is quite small compared to the rest of her face. Cameron Diaz has a wonderfully quirky face that the camera adores. Renee Zellweger's squint, Sandra Bullock's squared-off nose--the faces that are interesting are different. They are beautiful women, partly because of their unique features. Perfection becomes boring. Artists will paint their masterpieces with a touch of asymmetry, a bold blast of color in an unexpected place, or add an unusual element that keeps us wandering back to look at it again.

That is the basis for our first step in finding a new confidence and excitement about who you are and what you are offering during your time on this planet. You have a stamp to make, and it would be a terrible shame not to make it!

Step One:
It Is Not As Bad As You Think It Is!

Perspective. What an interesting word. It is the Achilles' heel of every human being. Think about it for a moment. Everything we think and feel is due to our perspective. A rainy day may be seen as a ruined picnic to one person but a God-send to a drought-infested farmer. One man may think blondes are the bomb, and another may prefer brunettes. White water rafting is exhilarating to one person, but strikes terror in someone who can't swim. Politics, religion, finances, marriage do's and don'ts, fashion sense, furniture arrangement, holiday traditions—it is ALL a matter of perspective! I can hear you now, "But that's how I was raised." And with whose "perspective" were you raised?

If a child was told from the time he/she was little that an apple's color is blue, and there was no one there to refute it, don't you think that child would grow up believing apples are blue? Based on the input he/she was given, he/she may believe 2+2=7, nice girls don't speak their minds, Christmas stockings should be hung outside, all dogs are to be feared, our family is, and never will be, good at certain things such as sports/finances/marriage/confidence...and the list goes on, and on, and on.

So, what is not as bad as you think it is? All of it! None of it is real. It's all perspective. The most-persuasive motivational speakers in the world are selling you one thing—their perspective! Does it make it correct? No. It may ring a bell with you and you feel empowered when you hear it. That's great! Adopt the parts that work for you, that make you feel better, and change your life for the positive. But the point I want you to walk away with is this: No label, no stamp, no assumption, tradition or amount of people screaming at you who they think you should be, matters at all. This is YOUR life! You write the script! You delete the parts that aren't working for you, and you tell the others that they are welcome to take their own advice but you are going to pull your own strings. Toss all of it in the trash can that is not serving you. The past is shadows. They lose their strength when you shine a light on them and strip them of their false beliefs.

Step Two:
Re-painting the Canvas

I've been a commercial artist for 35 years. I paint wall murals which means I am constantly looking at a very big, blank canvas and knowing I need to fill up every inch with a creation that will please my client. Some of these walls have been up to 60-feet long! That's a pretty daunting task.

What I learned with the thousands of murals I've created is that a blank canvas, or wall, is just that. Blank. Chuck-full of possibilities and promise. It's waiting for my imprint upon it, and it starts with the very…first…stroke of the brush.

Every day we are a blank canvas. We tend to go through the days on auto-pilot: eating breakfast at the same time, grabbing the same cup of coffee, making the bed robotically, backing down the driveway, passing the same landmarks and generally using an internal GPS system. What if we changed GPS from Global Positioning System, to mean "Gotta Plan Something!" Something new...something life-altering. It only takes that first stroke.

Let's get specific. If you are wanting to:

- **Lose weight. Then Try This:**
    1. Yoga. Pilates. Gym. Walking. Aerobics.
    2. Diet. Healthier Foods. Cutting out soda.
    3. Set a specific goal: 15 lbs. by August 5th.

- **Change Your Appearance. Try This:**
    1. New Hair Style. Coloring. Highlights.
    2. Professional Makeup Help (cosmetic counter at department store or hiring a Pro). Eyebrow contouring, shading tricks, enhancing your eyes, playing up your best features.
    3. Hire a Fashion Consultant to help you choose clothes that are more flattering and current, or ask a department store attendant to show you how to put together a great outfit.
    4. Cosmetic Surgery for something that is keeping you from being completely happy with yourself. It's your body, and your view.
    5. Change Your Posture. This is very important. If you slump, you are adding years to your appearance, and your waistline and bust. Put your shoulders back and your hips forward.

You will look and feel more confident and shave 5 pounds off your appearance.

- **More Social Life? Here You Go:**
  1. Join Meet-Up Groups in your city. Google "Meet-Up Groups" and find ones that appeal to you. There's everything from groups who eat out at different restaurants, golf, go to museums, rock climb, attend concerts, cook, attend book clubs. It's a great way to meet people and begin ramping up your confidence, and fun. As your social circle grows, so will your contacts, and those include eligible men. Many of these groups are for singles looking to meet other singles in their age brackets while doing fun things.
  2. Organize parties and get-togethers with your friends. Stop waiting for someone else to plan things.
  3. Make It a Point to Meet Different People at work or in your neighborhood. Plan a neighborhood Open House where everyone brings an appetizer. I was the new kid on the block when I moved in and threw a party for my new neighbors. They met people for the first time they had been living down the street from for over 20 years!
  4. Take Up a Hobby or Sport. This not only brings you a great deal of pleasure, it gives your life passion and depth. Men told me over and over again that they want to meet women

who have passions of their own and have interests and hobbies. There is no excuse. Many classes are free in your community. Just Google what you're interested in. As you add to your life and skills, your confidence, sense of purpose and joy will increase. I love golf. The fact that the majority of golfers are men is a bonus. ☺ Not why I took it up in Junior High, but just thought I would mention it.

These are just a few examples of how you can take control of your life and make it sparkle. You chose this book to improve your relationship skills. Books are out there on every subject! YouTube is a gold mine. Knowledge is power…use it!

Please start now if your life is not what you want it to be. Procrastination is such a waste of precious days. Men are no different from women. They are looking for someone they feel will enhance and add to their lives. Each one has a different wish list based on their specific likes and dislikes. There is someone for you, who is hoping he will meet *you.* Don't you want someone in your life who is whole and happy? Do you want a man who is dysfunctional, unhappy or out-of-shape? Then play fair. Get yourself in your best possible shape: mentally, physically, financially, spiritually and joyously. Only then will you be ready and confident to meet someone special and amazing.

There is one more added bonus to this transformation you are about to make: the people who have been holding you back and bringing you down will lose their power as you move into a healthier, happier you. You will no longer want their negativity in your life. And please always remember this:

"Never make someone a priority who considers you an option."

"The strongest factor for success is self-esteem; Believing you can do it, believing you deserve it, believing you will get it!"

Step Three:
Stop Sabotaging Your Chances!

How do we sabotage our happiness? By believing we don't deserve it. Sabotage typically comes from a feeling of low self-worth and fear. Deep inside we don't believe we are as deserving as others who seem to "have it all." And once again, those feelings tend to have their origins in our youth. True, something recent could have happened to you that left you reeling, and impacted how you see the future. But no matter what happens to us, we can ultimately choose how we process it, and how we will move forward. Sometimes a break-up is a new beginning to find something better. Not all things that bring us to our knees are bad. They can be spring boards to something amazing!

Courtney* is a friend of mine. She was head-over-heels for a guy she had dated for five years. She wanted marriage, he was happy with things as they were. Although he spoiled her with gifts, he had a problem with emotional intimacy. When they were conversing she often felt he was uninterested in her victories or dreams. He would go on for hours about his successes and something amazing that happened to him that day, but look at her blankly or change the subject when it was her turn to share her life stories. He waited until the last minute to ask her out on weekends because he knew she was sitting by the phone waiting for him to call. Finally, he met someone else and broke off the relationship. She was devastated.

No amount of her friends telling her she was better off seemed to matter. We pointed out how rotten he made her feel, that she usually left feeling empty after another non-connecting conversation with him, and how his self-centeredness was a HUGE red flag. All she knew was that she missed him and was afraid no one else would be interested in her.

So, the happy ending to Courtney's story is that she ran out and found a man that treated her better, right? Wrong!

We convinced Courtney that until she felt worthy of a

*names have been changed for reasons of privacy

good relationship, they would continue to elude her. If her sense of self-worth and self-esteem had been healthy to start with, she would never have been in a relationship, let alone a five-year relationship, with someone who treated her like crap one minute, and then gave her gifts to cover his inadequacies in the emotional department.

She sought help with a therapist and read self-help books on co-dependency and low self-esteem. She dedicated a full year to working on herself instead of rushing out to find another man to fill her emptiness.

NOW, comes the best happy ending. Courtney found all kinds of strengths she didn't realize she had. She took up classes and hobbies, met new people, and even became a culinary whiz, something she had always wanted to do. While at an advanced cooking class one evening, she was stationed next to (you guessed it) a wonderful man who took an immediate interest in her. She confided in me that she was not immediately attracted to him because he did not fit her typical taste in men. He was a few inches shorter and not an extrovert. She had always been attracted to strong personalities.

I pointed out that the guy she had dated for those 5 years had a strong personality, and it had not worked out. Why not give this new guy a chance? Which she did. He treats her like a Queen, celebrates her triumphs, and encourages her to be her very best self. I've never seen her happier. She remarked to me that "he had grown on her," a comment she made laughingly. They have now been dating for seven months and things look very bright and rosy for Courtney…in all departments. She said if the Mr. Self-Centered had not dumped her, she would probably never have discovered all the wonderful facets of herself that now make her life abundant.

Notice how Courtney became happy with herself first? A new relationship with a man who *adds* to her happiness is the bonus, but it was not the most important accomplishment. She told me that if this relationship ended, she would look at it as a stepping stone and learn from it, not fall to pieces. Having a healthy sense of herself, and a life she created on her own, is something no one can take from her. And now, a very lucky guy is sharing it.

Until we feel worthy of abundance, of love and of happiness, we will sabotage everything that comes our way. And I do mean everything! A great job, the new weight loss program, a full bank account, and a wonderful relationship will all fall beneath our negative view of ourselves. It will show up sometimes in very subtle ways: body language on a date that tells the guy you are insecure, canceling dates, playing passive-aggressive games, not calling back, making him jump through hoops to test his feelings for you, and many, many more.

Other forms of collateral damage that come with a low self-esteem are as follows:

- You'll attract the Toads. Men can sense a woman who doesn't feel good about herself from a mile away and take advantage of it. If she doesn't value herself, why should he? The great guys will pass you by.

- You will make up excuses not to better yourself, blaming it on heredity, a bad hand dealt to you, poor genes, rotten childhood, missed opportunities, and a million other non-productive situations. If not now, when? Do you want to be singing the same song a year from now? Most weight loss plans don't fail due to laziness…they fail because the dieter does not see herself as slender. She has a negative self-image that is holding her back. When you believe you are important and worthy of a healthy body, it will come to you easier than you can imagine. Your physical self is hoping you will come out and play.

- If you're a family member, mother, or friend, you are missing the chance to be a great example to someone else important to you. The Victim brand is a fashion accessory that never looks good on anyone.

This is your only shot at an amazing life on this planet. You hold all the power to turn it around completely. Talk back to the voices who tell you, you can't. Rip up the labels. Pull out a blank canvas and fill it with bold, vibrant and confident colors that show who you really are and where you're going! YouTube videos will show you everything from how to style your hair to new techniques with makeup. It is filled with exercise programs, how to pick out fashions, improve your memory, play a sport, etc. Make a Vision Board that shows the life you are creating for yourself. Mine has pictures from magazines of Italy, scuba diving, sailing, golf, Disneyland, my dream home, and book projects. Create your world not just for yourself, but for a special man to share it with you…if that is your desire!

Chapter Three
Playing the Confidence Game

Game? Are you calling "confidence" a game? In a way I am. As you recall I mentioned no one is as confident as they appear to be. Absolutely no one. People may have areas where they feel more comfortable and are therefore more at ease, but there is always a sliver of doubt. "Will this be the time I forget the words to the song?" "This presentation has to be perfect—he's our biggest client!" "I never should have eaten that birthday cake last night when I knew I had a fashion show today—in a swimsuit!" "What if his family doesn't like me?" "I can't afford another bad review." "I feel so fat." "My skin sucks!" The litany of doubt goes on forever.

I mentioned that some of the girls who took my mother's modeling classes were the Prom Queens and most-popular girls in my high school and college. From the outside they were picture-perfect: flawless skin, great teeth, hair and the latest style in clothes. But during the classes on personality, poise and dating, these girls' inner insecurities came to the foreground. I was shocked to hear their lack of confidence that bubbled to the surface.

"I have a hard time being up on a stage," one of the girls confided to my mother during a class on confidence. "I am always afraid I'm going to freeze up and forget what I was going to say, or tell a joke that no one laughs at. I've been asked to give a talk at graduation and I really don't think I can do it."

Another girl, who had more friends, and guys after her than I could count, confided that she didn't think she was pretty. Her father had called her "chubby" since she was a baby and when she looked into a mirror, that's all she saw…that chubby little girl. In truth, she was slender, athletic and gorgeous but she couldn't get past the old labels. She had a hard time accepting compliments…something my mother corrected, but it took months.

I have worked with women that seem to have it all. Great job, beautiful appearance, a body a swimsuit model would envy, friends and kids who adore them. These women have gone through painful divorces that left them feeling off-kilter, and "damaged." They fear the dating world now that they are over 40. Every insecurity they had when dating in high school rears its ugly head.

"When you're over 40, you feel most of the men your age are looking for younger women," one woman told me, looking hopeless. "I've had three kids. I'm not sure about a bathing suit, let alone letting a man see me naked. It's scary out there!"

That is a complaint I've heard more times than I can count. The dating world for divorced or single women past a certain age can be fraught with uncertainty and fear. Let's shine the light of reason on some of these issues, which should bolster your confidence. After interviewing 2,000 men in all age groups, here is their take on this issue of "older" women:

False assumptions:
- All men are looking for younger women.
- All men are looking for women with perfect bodies.
- Men are looking for the proverbial "blonde bimbo."
- All men are hoping for sex on the first date.
- Men think divorced women are "easy" and desperate.
- Intelligent, successful women are intimidating to men.
- Most guys are players or jerks.
- Men don't care about romance.
- If a guy is a "9", he'll want to date a "9".
- All the good guys are taken.

"I just started dating this great woman who is 44," Jason* told me. "She is pretty, smart, funny, has a job she loves, and two teenage sons she is really close to. I like her a lot, but I'm getting tired of reassuring her. I'm two years younger than she is and she is constantly asking me if I would rather be with someone my age or younger. It's getting old! I wouldn't be here if I wasn't interested, but I'll be honest...this is becoming too much work. I just want to relax and get to know her, not get called out every time some hot, younger woman walks by."

Mark*, a 50-year-old stockbroker in NYC, had this to say about women over 40: "I find women who are close to my age, sexy. They have life experiences that have added to their character, they've usually raised kids and are now free to go out and explore the world. They're more confident, relaxed, not into the childish head games that some women in their 20's and 30's play, and they are just more secure. Women don't look their age these days like they did 40 or 50 years ago. I've dated women older than I am that can out-hike me!"

An overwhelming 80% of the men I interviewed said that no matter a woman's age, if she likes herself, shows confidence and a little sass, she is SEXY! They listed women in their 60's who are "hot", from Christy Brinkley to Diane Keaton. "You show me a woman who has a "take me or leave me," attitude, and age falls by the wayside," Darin*, a 38-year-old marketing exec told me. "I can be out with some 20-year-old who is ditzy, has no passion in life or drive, and I will be outta there!"

So, whether you are 18 or 80, the resounding consensus is, confidence is one of the biggest traits men are looking for. Let me explain why, from their viewpoint:

"When a woman is happy with herself, she isn't needy," Bob*, a 28-year-old bartender confided. "Needy women are like Saran Wrap, they just *CLINGGGGG* to you! Every guy hates that! We want a girl who has a great life already without us. She's happy, has friends and stuff to do. You wanna hear the two words men fear most? It isn't "I do", it's "DRAMA QUEEN"! And you know what creates a Drama Queen? The girls who aren't happy, and feel the world has to make it happy for them! No thanks!"

"Women who are calm and happy with their life and the world are a joy to be with," Jason*, 42, told me. "You don't feel like you have to jump through hoops to make her smile. They have this confidence that is just intoxicating. You know she is having a good time with you, but she's also off doing her thing *without* you. Makes you want to be invited along for the ride."

Confidence comes from one place—a knowing that you are worthy of a great life. You are unique and have much to offer the world and the people lucky enough to be in your realm. You have a sense of worth, a sense of humor and a sense of pride. You can fake confidence, for a while. But I don't want the phony façade for you. You *can* have that inner core that makes you okay in any storm life throws at you; that whispers to you that alone doesn't equate to lonely; that you can change at any age and at any time; and that you are on an equal playing ground with anyone else who arrived after a nine-month gestation period.

Experts tell us we are born with two fears—only two! The fear of falling and the fear of loud noises. That's it—two! So where did all your fears, and insecurities, and erroneous beliefs come from? Yep...information you began gathering from outside sources by the time you could see, hear and touch. But that's the good news! That's terrific! Why? Because anything we learn, we can un-learn. We can create a whole new belief system with unlimited possibilities. We get a new body every 7 years. The cells regenerate, the old ones die. If your amazing body can go through those life-affirming changes, don't you think that magnificent brain of yours can reprogram your thinking? And that's all your belief system is—thoughts. I love Dr. Wayne Dyer's saying,

"When you change the way you look at things, the things you look at change." Confidence can be learned. Your self-esteem can grow and see life as it is, not the distorted filter through which many of us view it. It's a choice...and it's yours to make.

Steps To Becoming More Confident

We've defined what confidence is; now let's work on achieving it. You may feel you have a great sense of confidence. It feels good, doesn't it? Are you confident in all areas of your life, or are there certain situations that give you pause, or make your pulse race a little faster? I hope so. If not, you aren't human. Most of us feel confident in some corner of our little world. It may be making a great strawberry short cake, child care, designing a website, presenting a Power Point overview for a downtown 40-story commercial project, playing tennis, or even dating. But the odds are, there are other areas that you wish you were more courageous in tackling.

Confidence truly does come from a feeling of authenticity. A feeling you have earned your right to happiness. I feel many of the celebrities today who succumb to drugs or alcohol did so because FAME threw them; they weren't used to having all the money, accolades and adoration, and they weren't ready for it. They may have felt like a phony and that at some point the public would tire of them. Most people winning mass fortunes with the lottery are bankrupt only a few short years later. Why? I believe they didn't have the skills capable of handling that kind of money, or the belief they earned it. It was handed to them. Again, our belief system will sabotage us every time unless we work on feeling worthy.

Step One:
Own It!

We all come into this world naked and screaming. What happens after that is a toss of the dice. Where we were raised, how we were raised, our education (or lack thereof), our friends, teachers and peers. But one thing is a certainty...none of it matters NOW. Change your thoughts, and you change your life.

Step one is to take inventory of the areas in your life about which you are not feeling confident. If it's meeting people, whether it's men or women, then please understand that is an area about which everyone has some trepidation. First meetings are exciting, but they are also scary. You feel like you are back in school asking if someone will sit by you at lunch. Here's an inside secret: If you meet someone who "has it all goin' on", who is boisterous, overwhelming and too confident, be assured this is a person who is also suffering from a low self-esteem and is trying to compensate for it. In fact if you are on a date with a man who does everything perfectly, odds are this guy is a serial dater who has his act down cold. Too much polish is as bad as none at all.

Write down the areas you would like to work on, and tackle them, one step at a time. Just like painting a wall mural one inch at a time; before you know it, you have a complete picture of something lovely. Here are some common areas with which most women have trouble:

1. **Eye Contact:** Nothing screams insecurity as much as someone who will not look you in the eyes. We feel the person is either hiding something or is lacking in confidence, and it makes us feel uneasy.

     • Start out by practicing looking into your own eyes in your mirror until you feel comfortable. Once you are, begin carrying on a conversation with yourself while maintaining eye contact. Use you eyebrows to show animation during exciting or funny parts of your speech. Notice how your eyes soften to show emotion, or open wide during moments of excitement or surprise.

Actors will practice for hours in front of a mirror to gauge their facial impact during different bits of monologue.

- Now start working with other people. You don't have to tell them what you are doing. Simply approach family members, friends or even your local cashier and maintain eye contact while talking to them. It may make you nervous at first, but it will get easier, as everything does with practice. You will notice people will respond to you differently. They will become more engaged in the conversation and you will sense they feel good about being with you. This adds to your confidence. Every chance you get practice eye contact. It will boost your self-esteem and make it easier to talk to people.

2. **Conversation Skills:** Most people are nervous when it comes to holding their own in a conversation. We typically don't listen to what the other person is really saying because we are busy thinking of our "next line." Many of the men in the survey I conducted said how refreshing it was to be with a woman who really listened and asked questions, without turning the conversation back to herself or spacing out. Here are some conversation tips:

- Conversation is like a pie—the more people involved, the smaller your slice of the pie will be. Don't monopolize the conversation and tell all there is to know about you. People like to unravel a person's life, a little at a time. Let them ask you questions, and hold back a little.

- You have two ears and only one mouth…there's a reason for that. You should listen more than you speak.   When a man is telling you something, the odds are he wants to impress you or divulge something about himself without putting it out there in neon lights. The woman who can read between the lines, or ask follow-up questions is miles ahead of the game. We are typically too interested in impressing him with our own glory stories to really listen to what he is saying. We will state specific examples of this in the chapter on Communication.

- Everyone likes to feel important. They love the sound of their own name and feeling someone is truly interested in learning more about them. Ask questions, within reason. One complaint men have about women is rather than conversing, the woman hits him with a thousand questions until he feels he is applying for a job.

    Ask a question, such as "Where did you grow up?" If the person gives a perfunctory answer such as "Idaho," you are pretty much left with asking another follow-up question. Make the next question one they will have to elaborate on, such as, "Oh, really? I don't know much about Idaho. What are your favorite memories of that area?" Now they will have to use complete sentences. Listen…hard. Listen between the words. They might mention a certain river they liked...ok...what about the river evoked such great memories? Did they fish there with their father, skip rocks with friends, or listen to its water splashing at night as they drifted off to sleep? Listening to what is being said between the words is a great skill to adapt, and *oh so* flattering to the one with whom you are talking! It will set you apart more than you can imagine! Perhaps he mentions it was a hard week at work. Most people mention things for a reason. He is probably hoping you will say, "I'm sorry to hear that. Would you care to share?" Sometimes humor is a good way to open the door, as long as it isn't condescending or uncaring. For instance, "I'm sorry you had a hard week. Were the other kids not playing nice?" and smile sweetly. He will probably laugh, and go into the reasons.

- Keep confidences private. A huge complaint men have about women is that they tell their girlfriends everything, including something private he just shared with you. Men don't share or open up easily, and if you betray that trust by telling others, you can be assured he won't open up to you again. Being vulnerable to other's opinions about him is not something most men relish.

- A final big one is being too negative and fault-finding in all your conversations. You know the kind of person who can't wait to tell you how bad their day has been, how sick they are, or how awful someone treated them. If you find people avoiding you, think back to your typical conversations with them. Were they all about you, or overly negative? Men detest being around negative, habitually unhappy women. Complaining is not an art form, it is a turn-off.

Find good in others and voice it. Put a good spin on a bad event. Which way would you rather people remember you—your role as a total victim to which life is always unkind, or someone who shows strength and calm, and is optimistic that life will treat her well?

3. **Body Image:** Let's all just fact it—this is a big one! I doubt there are many among us who are totally pleased with their reflection. And that's okay. As we pointed out before, perfect is boring, and impossible. There is no such thing. Did you know that your body is never perfectly symmetrical? One hip is always higher, one nostril slightly larger, or one foot longer than the other. Any hair stylist will tell you one side of your head has more hair than the other, and usually behaves better. But our image of outer beauty is a common hot spot. In the previous chapter we detailed what to do if you are not feeling great about your weight, fashion style, or appearance. So, let's hear from the guys on this topic:

- "Women are too hard on themselves when it comes to their bodies. They focus on little imperfections we don't even notice, or we think is kinda cute." David*, 32, bank manager.

- "I get that the ladies think they are all competing with Playboy bunnies and swimsuit models just 'cuz guys like to look at that stuff. We're not dumb. We know most of those perfect bodies are air-brushed. Tell the women out there to relax. Sexy is more about how you like who you are than trying to look like a mannequin. A woman who is comfortable with her body and enjoys intimacy is the real turn-on." Rich*, 45, airline pilot.

- "Do men want someone in shape? Most do. I would think most women do too. It shows you respect your body and are willing to work to keep it in good shape. To me, unless there is a health reason behind it, overweight equates to laziness. I also know lots of guys who think plump women are sexy. It's all a matter of taste. But guys who are active and want a partner to share in those activities are going to look for someone who can keep up with them. Some women get mad about this, but you asked. Men are very visual. And in my defense I doubt most women are drooling over a guy whose shirt buttons are pinging around the room!" Jarvee*, 36, IT executive.

- "Tell the women to tone down the makeup! Men like the more natural look. If we're looking at a pair of lips with three layers of red lipstick, and an additional layer of gloss, all we're thinking is 'no way do I want to kiss that!' Women's magazines are selling cosmetics, not good dates. Men don't care about all the "smoky eye" stuff, or contoured cheeks. Keep it simple. There's a saying that the woman who is wearing too much makeup probably wakes up ugly. And stiff hair? Yuk. Too much hairspray is a real turn-off." Dennis*, 23, student.

- "Guys don't care about designer labels. Wear something that you are comfortable in and appropriate for the date. One lady I was dating wore high heels to a football game and complained about climbing all the stairs to our seats. Also, know if you are wearing revealing clothes, it's a signal to guys. Guess what that signal is? Don't slap us later if we acted on it. Be conservative, classy and don't try to copy some magazine or celebrity. Just be you." Juan*, 56, Facilities Coordinator.

- "If you're too afraid of ruining your nails if I invite you to go bowling, then your priorities are wrong. We want to date someone who will relax, and be fun and adventurous." Mitchell*, 42, real estate broker.

Long story short…if your body image is bothering you, do something about it. No one else is going to do it for you. No one else can do the crunches, pick out the clothes that fit you, learn the makeup tricks that work for you, or read the self-help books, but you. Decide now that time is too short to keep procrastinating about something that is holding you back from a life of abundance and happiness. Do it for you! One of my favorite phrases is from Don Henley's song, *How Bad Do*

You Want It? It goes, "How bad do you want it? Not bad enough!"

4. **Knowledge is Power!** A lot of women I've worked with have told me they feel inadequate in a social situation because they don't keep up with current events, have a hobby, play a sport or run a business. They are petrified someone, especially a date, is going to find them dull and uninteresting. This is the simplest one of all to fix:

- Watch the news. A mere 30 minutes gives you a Reader's Digest view of world events.
- Read the newspaper while soaking in the bath tub.
- There are phone aps to download magazines.
- The Internet is a plethora of information and sites.
- Take up a sport. It's a great way to meet people, keep in shape, and grow.
- If you know what he does for a living, or enjoys doing in his leisure time, read up on it. Nothing connects two people like common interests, or that you cared enough to learn a little about something so near and dear to him.
- When in conversation, ask "interested" questions. Most people won't notice your lack of knowledge on the subject…they will notice how good you made them feel by asking questions about their job, hobby, dog, etc.
- Find a new interest and read about it. I love Quantum Physics and read all I can about it. It has opened more conversations than I can tell you. Sailing and golf are passions of mine and it's fun

to share information with someone who is also interested in those things. Become an expert on a subject, whether it's cooking Thai food, grizzly bears, or European Travel. People are always impressed with someone who is truly conversant on a subject. It shows you find life interesting, which in turn, makes *you* interesting.

These are the main areas that will impact your life and help you to build confidence. By changing only one thing, you will find you feel empowered to go on to others.

Now, let's look at some situations that may arise which require a specific etiquette to pull them off. By knowing how to handle these situations, you will feel, and act, more confident!

Step Two:
Social Etiquette

Knowing how to act in certain situations that often arise in dating and relationships is a confidence-booster, and speaks highly of you. Here are a few of the more common situations that give some people pause:

1. **Restaurant Etiquette:** Simple but helpful rules to demystify dining out decorum:
   - Always pause at the door and step back to allow your date to open the door.
   - Wait for your date to approach the reception counter to confirm a reservation or ask for a table.
   - The woman follows the maître d' to the table, her date follows behind her.
   - Place your napkin in your lap as soon as you're seated. When you are finished with the meal, lay the napkin to the left or right of your plate in a relaxed fold. Do not refold it or wad it up.
   - Cutlery is arranged to be used from the outside in. Starting with the knife, fork, or spoon that is farthest from your plate, work your way in, using one utensil for each course. The salad fork is on your outermost left, followed by your dinner fork. Your soup spoon is on your outermost right, followed by your beverage spoon, salad knife and dinner knife. Your dessert spoon and fork are above your plate or brought out with dessert. If you work your way in from the outside, you'll be fine.
   - American style and European style for eating: American style eating requires that when cutting food the knife is held in the right hand, fork in the left securing the food. Once a few bite-size pieces are cut, the knife is laid at the edge of the plate, blade facing in, and the fork is then used in whichever hand is most comfortable for you.

European style requires the knife in right hand and the fork in the left with the prongs facing downward. Both the knife and fork are held in both hands throughout the meal. If you take a drink, you set both the knife and the fork down on the plate. At the end of the meal they are placed on the plate, fork over the knife.

- Chicken or bone-in food is never picked up with the fingers unless at a casual Bar-B-Que. Use your knife and fork.

- Liquids in a bowl are always eaten by scooping away from you.

- Never place cutlery back onto the table once you have begun eating; always rest it upon your plate.

- Never rest your elbows on the table.

- Dress code is dictated by the restaurant. If you are unsure, call and ask.

- Butter spreads or dips should be transferred from the serving dish to your plate before spreading or eating. No double dipping!

- Try to pace your eating so that you don't finish before, or too long after, your date.

- Never talk with your mouth full.

- Place your hand over your wine glass to signal you do not wish a refill.

- Do not use a toothpick or apply makeup at the table.

- Always say, "Excuse me," or "I'll be right back" when leaving the table.

- Turn cell phones off. It is not only rude to other guests, but to your date to answer your phone during a meal. Texting during a date is also very rude.
- The bill is always delivered to the table in a standing position. When you have inserted your credit card or cash, lay the bill folder flat, signaling that it is ready to be picked up.
- Proper tipping:
  Waiter: 15% to 20%.
  Wine Steward: 15% of wine bill.
  Bartender: 10% to 15% of bar bill.
  Coat check: $1.00 per coat
  Car attendant: $2.00 to $5.00.

Always thank your date for a lovely meal! You'd be amazed how many men tell me their date never even thanked them. Make a nice comment about the restaurant he chose. He put some time and effort into choosing it. Never complain about the food, the table or the service. If you have an issue with your food, handle it quietly with the waiter or staff, and always thank them. It is always safe to choose something from the middle price range on a menu, or take your date's lead. Never order the most expensive item, or send food back unless it is for some very important reason. Don't go on and on about food allergies. Remember, this date is supposed to be fun, and he is using his hard-earned money to show you a good time.

A word about doggie bags: Some experts say it is bad manners to ask for a doggie bag. Many waiters will offer one if they see you have quite a bit of food left on your plate. I feel that it is better to take food home than waste it, especially when someone else has paid for it. If it is a very posh restaurant, I would forego asking for a bag. Do not order a dessert to take home. If you are too full, don't order one.

Taboo Table Topics:
- Divorce, Surgery, Politics, Religion, Finances and other topics that can lead to negativity or are too personal.
- Gossip. As mentioned earlier, men, and people in general may look like they are enjoying a good bit of gossip, but they tend to wonder what you will be saying about them behind their backs.
- Bathroom humor, bad language, boss bashing, long-winded stories about your family, your tennis game, or anything else where you are monopolizing the conversation.
- Talking about personal things such as your weight loss program, past addictions, a family member's incarceration, your poor relationships with family members, friends or co-workers, an argument you had with the cashier—these are all poor conversation choices for a public outing. Be upbeat, discuss current events, a great movie you just watched, a concert you attended, fun things you have planned for the summer or holidays…anything that will make the occasion pleasant. The people who aren't invited out again are the ones who ruined what could have been a great evening with too much negativity or just TMI.

Wine Etiquette: We used to be safe pairing white wine with fish and chicken, and reds with meats. But today, thanks in part to wine tastings, a plethora of cooking shows and a sophisticated palette, the public is a little more wine savvy and being discriminative in their wine selection. Feeling overwhelmed when choosing what wine to pair with your meal? You are not alone. Here's a pretty safe cheat sheet:

Typically, you want to drink light-to-dark, just as when you plan a meal you start with delicate tastes and work toward heavier tastes. For this reason, Champagne tends to go very well with appetizers or opening courses in a meal. White wine is usually a match for salads and lighter dishes, such as fish or chicken, while red wine works perfectly with steaks and heavier meat sauces. A port is often the perfect end to a meal, paired with a piece of chocolate cake.

But again, it has to do with individual taste. Here is a basic pairing chart that will get you through, and give you more confidence when ordering wine:

Red Wines:
- **Cabernet Sauvignon:** Appetizers—Carpaccio, pungent cheeses. Main Course—Beef, duck, lamb, lentils. Dessert—Dark and Bittersweet Chocolate.
- **Merlot:** Appetizers—Antipasto, aged cheeses. Main Course—Veal, Sausage, Salmon, Tuna, Eggplant. Dessert—Raspberry, cherry or other dark berry desserts.
- **Zinfandel:** Appetizers—Seared Ahi Tuna, spicy chicken, or beef satay. Main Course—Barbeque,

tomato sauce, spicy sausage, duck and beef. Dessert—Dark berry desserts, carrot cake.

- **Pinot Noir:** Appetizers—Creamy cheeses, pate's, roasted vegetables. Main Course—Veal, chicken, turkey, lean cuts of beef, lamb. Dessert—Berry tart, flourless chocolate cake, crème brulee.
- **Syrah:** Appetizers—Bruschetta, stuffed mushrooms, tapenade. Main Course—Ham, pasta with tomato sauce, pizza, barbeque. Dessert—Cherry pie, chocolate mousse.

White Wines:

- **Chardonnay:** Appetizers—Scallops, crudité, hummus, mild cheeses. Main Course—Chicken, cream-based sauces, port and seafood. Desserts—Cheesecake, poached light fruit.
- **Sauvignon Blanc:** Appetizers—Oysters, crab cakes, wild mushroom and goat cheese bruschetta. Main Course—Sea Bass, lobster, langoustines, chicken, shrimp. Desserts—Sorbet, key lime pie, lemon meringue pie.
- **Pinot Grigio:** Appetizers—Ceviche, ahi tuna, tartar, antipasto. Main Course—Risotto, grilled chicken, lobster, white sauces, crab. Desserts—Petit fours, apple tart.
- **Riesling:** Appetizers—Calamari, steamed clams, creamy cheeses. Main Course—Roasted chicken, grilled pork, baked ham. Desserts—Light cakes, cream-based pies, baked apples.

These are good choices when pairing wines but the cardinal rule applies here—drink what you love.

2. **Parties/Dinner Parties:** Whether you are the host or the guest, there are some standard etiquette tips that will give you confidence when handling parties. Here are the basics:

Guest Duties:
- RSVP quickly. Follow the guidelines on your email rather than a phone call, then follow suit. **Always** thank your host for inviting you and then accept or decline. If you are asked in the invitation to furnish something, repeat the request and say you will be happy to bring so-and-so. For instance: "I will be happy to bring a fruit platter." If the invite does not clarify how many people the platter will be serving, it is alright to ask, such as, "I will be happy to bring a fruit platter. How many guests will it be serving?" If the invitation does not mention providing anything, it always a nice gesture to offer.
- It is considered rude to ask if you can bring a guest, or children. If you have usually been known for your single status, and you recently began dating someone, and you know the others are coming with a significant other, you might call your host and during the conversation mention you

are now dating someone. Leave it to your host to encourage you to bring him along.

- Mark the date on your calendar, along with anything you need to remember about the event such as special attire, food, or location.

- If you are close to the host, ask if you can be of any help with the party. Offer to run errands, help decorate, clean, prepare food, etc. Parties take a lot of prep work and it is always appreciated. Arrive in plenty of time to help. Showing up at the last minute to help vacuum or peel carrots will not be helpful. If you do help, go by your host's guidelines. Don't decorate or prepare the food the way you think it should be done. It is their party.

- It is always good etiquette to take along a hostess gift. Typically taking food or wine is not a good idea, as the host tends to feel obligated to serve it and their gift is therefore gone. It may clash with their menu as well. If you do bring wine, tell them it is to be enjoyed later for their personal use. Flowers follow the same rule. They may not match the theme of the party and if the host has to stop what she's doing to find a vase or tend to them, it becomes an inconvenience. Great gifts are music, candles, a silver frame, something specific to the host's personality, something that commemorates the theme of the party (seashells for a Hawaiian Luau, Italian music CD for an Italian dinner party, etc.). Cash is never in good taste unless it's a wedding or graduation. When you arrive, offer to help with any last minute preparations. You might offer to take coats, or greet guests if the host is busy elsewhere. Do not engage the host in voluminous conversation when they are trying to greet people and tend to their party.

- Mingle! Here is where your confidence comes in. Sit next to someone and say simply, "Hello. My name is Barbara. How do you know the host?" It's that simple. The conversation is rolling and the person will probably be grateful to have someone to talk to. Look for the people sitting alone. Be upbeat and help everyone to have a good time without monopolizing the conversation or being the party clown.

- Drink responsibly. More parties have been ruined by guests who drank too much and either got in an argument with someone, dropped their drink on the carpet or on another guest, or who were simply loud and obnoxious.

- If you are seated at a table, pass the food from your left to your right. Your bread plate is to the left of your dinner plate, your drinking glass(s) are to the right of your plate. If you need to pass the salt or pepper, always pass them together. This keeps them from becoming lost at opposite ends of the table. Place your purse on the floor behind your chair. Turn your cell phone off. Place your napkin in your lap. The same rule for cutlery applies—work from the outside in.

- If you are eating at your chair, place your plate in your lap and your beverage somewhere it won't spill. It's a good idea to load your plate lightly if you are cradling it in your lap, and have napkins ready, especially if you are placing something juicy on a paper plate that may bleed through.

- At the end of the party jump in and help. If the host is emphatic that you don't help out, then don't press it. Most are happy to have someone help with dishes and picking up cups and plates, or retrieving coats. DO NOT play host as the guests are leaving. This is the host's duties to bid the guests farewell and thank them for coming. You can say "It was lovely to see you," but save the "thank you's" for the host.
- Be sure and thank your host for inviting you and compliment them on the party and food. If there is something they obviously worked hard on such as table arrangements, a themed party or great dish, mention it.
- Send a Thank You note the next day.

Host Duties: You may be the one throwing the party. If so, here are some simple tips:

- When sending out invitations make sure you include the following:
    1. Date, Time and Place. If the location is something new to the guest, furnish directions with the invite.
    2. Mention the dress code. This is very helpful to people who are uncertain of the formality of the occasion. Some graduation parties are fancy

and some are casual. Afternoon wedding attire differs from evening. If it is a theme party, tell them everyone is to dress appropriately.

3. If a gag gift, food item, or anything else is requested to bring to the party, state it and be specific. If the gag gift is to be $5.00 or less, then put that. If you ask someone to furnish food, always tell them for how many.

4. There may be special questions you need to pose on an invitation, such as asking if the guest has any food allergies, or religious food preferences.

5. If this is an occasion where it may be misunderstood whether children are invited or not, then list your preference. It should be obvious not to bring pets, but some people do, especially if it's an outdoor party. It's fine to say, "And please, no pets."

6. List anything else they may need to bring, such as towels, bathing suits, a party item, gift, etc.

7. Ask them to RSVP by a certain date. Leaving it open-ended can leave you hanging two days before the party. A good rule of thumb for an informal party is to ask them to RSVP two weeks before the party date. A formal

event, such a wedding, graduation, etc. requires a month or more notice. Stipulate if you want them to RSVP by phone, email or snail mail. If by phone, put your phone number.

- Try to make as many of preparations ahead of time as possible so that you can relax and enjoy your guests when they arrive. Being absent throughout much of the party because you are still slaving away in the kitchen won't make it fun for anyone.

- Have a Plan B if something goes wrong, such as rain for an outdoor event, a guest of honor not showing up, etc.

- Make sure you have plenty of parking places. Tell your neighbors several days ahead of time that you are having a party and ask if they mind if cars are parked in front of their house. It is nice to take them a plate of cookies or dessert afterwards to say thank you.

- Greet each guest and introduce them around, if it's only to one person. Repeat their name at least twice and mention something interesting about them that will act as an ice breaker.

- If this is a large party, name tags are always a good idea, unless it's a formal event such as a wedding.

- Take care of their coats, purses, umbrellas, etc. and let them know where you've put them.

- Try to stage your party by placing talkative people amongst the guests that are not as outgoing. At a dining table, put your more gregarious guests in the center to help keep conversations flowing. Don't put people next to each other that you know may not get along, whether for their political views or their personalities.

- Be upbeat and fun. This is a party. Some hosts get so stressed-out over the details that the entire event has an air of tension about it. Laugh, relax and engage. If someone spills something, handle it with decorum and make them know it is no big deal. Don't bring it up again.

- End the evening at an appropriate hour so that you are neither offending your neighbors, nor letting some people drive long distances at late hours. Keep the music at an acceptable level if you are outdoors or your windows are open. Be considerate.

- Thank each guest for coming, and show gratitude to those who helped out.

3. **Meeting His Family:** Meeting your new guy's family is always a little intimidating. With today's blended families, you may be meeting parents, siblings, his children from a former relationship, aunts, uncles, cousins and favorite politicians. It can feel daunting. He is probably as nervous as you are that everything goes well. These people have no doubt heard about you through him and are curious to meet you. So, let's put your best foot forward:

- If you are going to meet someone special to your guy, for instance a parent, grandparent, or an older person who has been a major factor in his life, it is always nice to take along an appropriate gift. Flowers are always nice. Make sure they are in a vase. It not only gives the recipient a gift to keep after the flowers have died, but it saves them going in search for something to put them in. You might put some effort into baking a dessert and taking it along. Ask your boyfriend ahead of time what his family likes. You don't want to show up with walnut brownies only to find out his family is allergic to nuts. Don't buy something expensive. It looks desperate to please and too much, too soon.

- If you will be meeting his children, keep it simple. Sometimes giving a child a gift who is trying to come to terms with a divorce and missing parent can be too much. It is usually better to wait until they are comfortable with you and you know their tastes. Older kids can see early gift-giving as manipulative. Be relaxed, take an interest in their pursuits, but hang back a little in the beginning. If they bring up their Mom, smile and ask about her, or say something kind.

- Being invited to dinner or a family gathering is a big deal, for you and for him. Dress appropriately. I can't overstate this enough. I don't care what your age is, you show disrespect by showing up at someone's home in clothes that are revealing or not suited to the occasion. Leave the short skirts and plunging necklines at home! If you're invited to a barbeque, wear casual clothes. I had one man tell me his date showed up at his family outdoor grilling party in sequins and high heels. This is common sense, people!

If it's a themed party, join in! Don't be the only person who decided the Dress As Your Favorite Action Hero theme was lame, and showed up in jeans and a t-shirt. Show respect at all times.

- ALWAYS offer to help out. I have raised four sons and it was always a shock to me when they would bring a girl over and she planted herself on the couch and waited to be served. No offer of help…no thank you…no nothing. It did not make a great impression.
- Compliment them on their home, or collection of Elvis plates, trophy heads or room décor. People love to feel appreciated. Don't over-due it. Be sincere and listen.

Ask follow-up questions, like, "Did others in your family collect model trains or was this something personal to you?" Or, "I've always envied a green thumb. I even tried singing John Denver to my plants and they still died." If you're invited to dine with them, try everything unless you're allergic to it. If it's a family recipe, ask if they would share it. All of these things make you stand out as someone who they will want to invite back.

Meeting someone's family does not have to be stressful. Relax, be yourself, don't cling to your guy, kiss him in front of his family or make jokes at his expense. If his family loves board games and you hate them, you better play those cards with gusto! It's all about courtesy!

4. **One-on-one:** Meeting people face to face is a pretty simple thing. Just keep these confidence-enhancing rules in mind:
   - Maintain eye contact.

- Shake their hand with a firm, but not bone-crushing handshake. Avoid the "limp fish" handshake or the "over-pump".
- Smile. Be engaging. Make them feel you are happy to meet them.
- Repeat their name. Nothing is sweet music to someone's ears than the sound of his/her own name. Don't over-due it. Just sprinkle it around.
- Ask questions that show an interest. Don't pry or ask overly-personal things. Keep it simple.
- Stand squared-off to the person—shoulders facing their shoulders. When someone is talking to you at an angle, you feel as if they want to walk away at any moment.
- Use the 3' rule. Stand about 3' apart from the person to allow them some personal space. Don't stand too close or too far away.
- Watch your body language. Crossed arms or legs is a closed-off position that intimates you are hostile to the conversation or not relaxed. Keeping your hands stuffed in your pockets also gives the feeling of a slightly closed or defensive nature. Be relaxed with your arms at your side. If seated, lean forward during the conversation to show interest. Leaning back, again, shows putting distance between you and the other party.
- When you are ready to leave, shake their hand again, and say it was nice to meet them. Closing with their name is always nice, or mentioning something you talked about, such as, "I will have

to try that restaurant you mentioned. It sounds delicious."

Step Three:
Do What It Takes!

If you are still wondering if you can pull this off, let me reiterate that you are no different than anyone else. You are a woman with all the tools in the Universe at your disposal. Books that will teach you how. Classes, seminars, gyms, stylists and stores that will get you the body, mind, career, hobby, financial knowledge, and a tremendous sense of yourself. There really are no excuses.

You can cite lack of money for the reason you are still stuck in a rut. You can get down on the floor and do crunches and yoga moves without owning a dime. Odds are you have access to the Internet even if it's using the library computer...for free! YouTube is filled with How-To videos on every conceivable topic, from hair styling, makeup tips and fashion, to work-out routines. Information is everywhere around you. But the very first move you need to make is to let go of who you think you are, and what you think you are capable of. You can change your name, your address, your friends, your job, your weight, your fashion style, your hair color, eye color (there are colored contacts these days), and way of talking and how you walk. Sound extreme? I am making a point.

You...Nancy/Ruth/Hillary/Denise/Ashley/Debbie/Ranea/Shamikra/Jennifer/Maki...no matter your name...you can change anything in your life that is not serving you. But you have to begin. For me, that first step has always been on a blank surface, whether a wall or a sheet of paper. I love to make lists and check them off. So right now...before we go onto the next section about the guys...write down your first step that you want to work on. Write it down and list the steps it will take to accomplish it. Underline it...in red...and next to it write, "I TOTALLY DESERVE THIS!"

And you do. For no other reason than you are here on this earth, like everyone else. There was no magic fairy that wandered through the hospital nursery tapping babies on the head with a wand, saying to one, "You will be beautiful," and to another, "You will be plain." To another baby, "You will have abundance," and to another, "You will have scarcity in your life." It did not happen that way. Whatever circumstances you grew up with, use it to make you stronger, and know happiness is a choice. You are worthy. You are divine. It's your turn!

Part II:

The Male Mind

Chapter One
Male: The Urban Legend

"Homo sapiens" is the scientific name for the human species, of which there are only two genera: male and female. That's it—only two. Yet if we look at the sheer number of books, documentaries, research studies and academic focus, you would think we were looking at alien life forms. Shouldn't men and women think alike, show similar behavior patterns, and need the same things? In a word...No. Does that mean we are totally different in what drives us in the pursuit of happiness? Again, No. Confused? It is a conundrum. Let's begin by taking a look at that elusive second half of the homo sapiens species—man.

We are in pursuit of the elusive genus, the human male. He has been known to frequent locales where competitive sports are played, as well as glittering social clubs where the female species is often found. He is described as a large, dominating creature who walks upright and communicates in largely recognizable utterances. Purported witnesses have described eyes of varying colors, a pronounced muscular structure, and hair that ranges from opulent to non-existent. His tracks are often spotted in urban as well as rural territories, and can be straight forward or slightly irregular, depending on liquid diet. Most forensic casts show five toes on each foot, indicating a primate propensity. He exhibits a fierce determination to avoid extinction.

Now that we have given our subject a cursory tongue-in-cheek description, let's zoom in on fact-versus-myth about this interesting specimen.

1. **Romance.**
   Myth—Women are more romantic than men.
   Fact—Men are often more romantic than women.
   - Relationship experts state men take significantly longer to get over a break-up than women. Many state they "never got over her."
   - 58% of men say they believe in love at first sight.
   - 98% are looking for a long-term relationship, thus quelling the myth about commitment phobia.
   - 78% of men said they want a woman to be their best friend and "have their back". They listed kindness in their top three traits they were looking for.
   - 95% of single men said they were ready to balance a career and a relationship; this number was lower in men in their 20's.

- 60% of men said women who engage in sex on the first date would not be a candidate for his wife.
- 98% of men said that women who come off as too eager or desperate will send them running out the door.
- 83% said they are looking for a woman who still believes in being feminine and appreciates a man looking out for her.
- 55% of men said they have been cheated on at one time or another.
- 68% worked on saving their marriage until the last minute. Statistics show men are less likely to want a divorce than women.
- 85% of men say an independent woman who has a career she loves and a full life is sexy. The same percentage do not mind if the woman makes more money than they do.
- 87%, when asked "How do you want a woman to see you?" answered "As her HERO!"

Conclusion: Men are often given the short end of the stick in the area of romance. Their primary objective is to make the woman in their life happy, and they often jump through hoops to do so. They are just as interested as women in being in a nurturing, rewarding relationship, and will typically stay in a marriage longer rather than face divorce. It isn't commitment they are afraid of...it's giving up their freedom and taking on the responsibilities of marriage if there is a chance the woman they have chosen has the propensity to hurt them, misunderstand them, or make them feel trapped.

2. **Age.**
   Myth—All Men Want a Younger Woman.
   Fact—It Depends On The Man and His Reasons.
   - 80% of men said age did not factor in as long as the woman had kept up her appearance and was fun to be with.
   - 20% admitted to wanting a younger woman to enhance their perceived worth as they got older.
   - 76% of men said today's more mature female who was financially secure, confident and happy was a huge turn-on.
   - 90% said confidence trumped age any time.
   - 73% of men said women are more hung up about how old they are than men are. Appearance, fun and confidence came up again as huge motivators.
   - 56% of men frequenting online dating sights admitted to listing their preference in a woman's age as 10-20 years younger, but often ended up dating a woman their age or older if she had traits and interests that outweighed age.
   - 78% of men admitted wanting a woman with substance and experience, and said those traits typically come with age. "The gorgeous Bimbo doesn't last long," they stated.

- 48% of men in their 30's trying to date a woman in her 50's or 60's admitted they were looking for a Sugar Momma or casual sex.

Conclusion: Age, like beauty is in the eye of the beholder. Confidence and a healthy feeling of self-worth are more attractive than a "younger model."

3. **The Trophy Date/Wife.**
   Myth: All Men Want A Gorgeous Woman on Their Arm.
   Fact: Not ALL Men.
   - 75% of men said they were more interested in how a woman made him feel, than impressing people with her looks.
   - 92% of men said they wanted to be seen with a woman who looked nice, but not necessarily a super model.
   - 25% of single men said it was important for them to be seen with someone other men would drool over.
   - 12% of divorced men admitted to looking for a "hot babe" in both dating and marriage.
   - 48% of men said "beautiful did not equate to quality." 95% said that while beauty caught their attention, it didn't last long without substance to back it up.
   - 38% of men said they felt men who required a trophy date/wife were compensating for a

feeling of insecurity. It was basically a "Look what I was able to bag!"

- 69% of affluent men dating or marrying much younger women admitted knowing his money was a primary factor in her being with him.

Conclusion: Men, like women, who need exterior trappings to feel better about themselves are lacking in self-esteem. It all depends on the individual's needs and wants. This is not to say that these types of relationships don't work out; if it fulfills both partners' needs, it may be a match made in heaven. There are just as many men looking for a quality relationship as there are guys needing a hotter woman to validate them.

4. Professional Women.

Myth: Men Are Intimidated by Successful Women.

Fact: A Secure Man Finds a Successful Woman Attractive.

- 87% of men polled said a woman who is successful is sexy. It shows she has a life outside of the relationship which to men equated to non-needy.
- 78% said they didn't care who made the most money, as long as they felt they were still valuable in other ways to the relationship. A man has to feel needed or he will run the other way. The men in this survey said if a successful woman found ways to let him know he was indispensable to the relationship and that he could offer skills, or attributes she

couldn't get for herself, he tended to stick around.

- 90% said it depended on whether it made the woman appear too masculine or her work was her sole focus. Women workaholics were as unappealing as the male version. They wanted a woman who could switch gears and have fun outside the office.

- 89% of men found professional women a refreshing challenge. They liked their confidence, drive and varied interests. They stated professional women tended to bring more to a conversation and showed passion for their work or hobbies. (This underscores the previous chapter on creating a life of your own filled with interests and passions.)

- 92% of men said they felt the only men intimidated by a successful woman were those who had low self-esteem, or witnessed a marriage where the woman used her success to undermine her husband.

- 90% of the men polled listed today's economic uncertainty as a tipping point in valuing a woman who brings something to the financial table. Most marriages today require two incomes, making a woman in the workforce more pragmatic, and in many cases, a life saver.

- 87% said a woman bragging, name dropping or talking incessantly about her accomplishments was a turn-off.

Conclusion: The times have changed. June Cleaver's pearls have been replaced by Alicia Florrick's power suits. There are more women creating small businesses than men today. And men are aware of it. The secure male will tell you he respects and admires the entrepreneur and career woman. The insecure male will not; guess which one you show to the door. The caveat here is this: there is a difference between loving and being proud of your job, and having it become your main topic of conversation. It's a bore when men do it, and it's just as tiresome when a woman keeps tooting her own horn. If he asks about your work, answer him. Keep it upbeat, interesting and brief. And then...encourage him to talk about his work. Keep in mind. Talking about business is not going to get the romantic embers burning. Men talk about work with other men constantly. He is with you to escape the 9-5. Let your other interests take center stage, and keep it playful.

5. **Sex.**

   Myth: ALL Men Think About Is Sex.

   Fact: Not ALL the Time, But It Is Definitely On The Short List.

   - 98% of men (both single and married) said sex is very high on their list. It gives them the much needed affirmation of their masculine nature, it is a stress reliever, and he feels a bond with his partner that is not duplicated anywhere else in the relationship.

- 86% of men feel they get a bad rep in this department. They have claimed everything from being hard-wired from birth, to the Bible's premise that the sex drive was necessary for procreation. Where they feel women get it wrong is seeing men as leering, drooling maniacs objectifying women and tossing them aside when they are satiated. Secretly they are hoping for a meaningful relationship, and a very powerful factor in that scenario is the closeness that comes through sex.

- 40% of men stated that today's women are looking for one-night stands at an alarming rate. Many men on online dating sites said they were shocked at the brazen photos women sent them, and even feeling pressured on early dates to have sex.

- 78% of men said the average male will size up a woman in the first few seconds of meeting her as to whether he feels she would be a good sex partner. They take in breasts, hips, lips, derrieres, and subtle (or not so subtle) body language.

- 89% of single men said, though they may try for a tumble on the first date, if they are interested in the woman, they are hoping she will turn them down. The good guys are looking for someone who holds their interest, and that increases in value as the dates progress.

- 90% of men polled flipped the question and said they feel women objectify men, but for different reasons. Men know they are being sized up by their appearance, job status, wallet, and even by the car they drive.

Conclusion: Do men have sex on the front burner? The majority do, but they are quick to point out women hold the power as to when, or if, the sexual encounter takes place. The problem is in seeing him as a pervert because of his inherent sexual drive. Men and women are different...not right or wrong, disgusting or innocent...just different. You can be firm about telling him "No", without emasculating him. More about this in Chapter 3: The First Date.

6. Commitment.
Myth: Men Are Afraid of Commitment.
Fact: Men Are Afraid of What Commitment Might Mean.

- 62% of single men stated that the typical male sees committing to one woman as "scary." Men are inherently afraid of losing their freedom. Many see commitment as the end of all the "fun."
- 88% said the male stereotype of a single guy having sex with a different woman each night is a myth.
- 78% of males said the bachelor life can be boring and lonely. Sitting at home or hanging

out in bars becomes depressing and an empty waste of time.

- 90% said if they met the right woman who was adventurous, fun, challenging, affectionate, and gave him some space when he needed it, he would be more prone to imagine a future with her. If she was demanding, a Drama Queen, complaining and boring, the relationship typically ended at some point.

- 75% said today's media does not portray women as an incentive for men to give up their freedom. Shows about married couples are filled with strife and the wife calling the shots, often telling the husband he can't have a boy's night out. They see endless responsibilities weighing some poor chump down until he resembles a human boat anchor.

- 54% cited conversations with buddies as being a turn-off toward commitment. They hear things like, "I can't go hunting with you next Saturday…I promised Cheryl I would take her to the Home and Garden show." Or…"Yeah, I can't make the game tomorrow; my in-laws are coming in for Denise's sister's bridal shower." All the listening male hears is, "Help ME! I'm trapped! I will never have fun again!"

- 97% of the men surveyed said timing was everything. They have a check list they want to fill before thinking of settling down. Those items are financial stability, getting where they want to be in their job, sowing their wild oats, possibly trips around the world, a personal goal, and others. Once those are fulfilled they are more apt to feel ready for the next stage—a committed relationship.

- 88% said age can be a predictor. Guys in their 20's are rarely ready for that kind of financial and emotional commitment, whereas a man in his middle years may be craving companionship and stability.

- 92% said men who have been married and divorced are more likely to remarry soon after. The thrill of being free fades quickly, and they worry about being alone.

- 82% said a man's biggest fear is dying alone.

- 76% said a woman can turn a confirmed bachelor into a groom by showing him through her actions (not "the talk") that he would have an amazing life with her...one he couldn't find with anyone else. At this point he begins to fear losing her to someone else. If she is giving him plenty of space, it accelerates his desire to be a permanent part of her life. "Give him just enough rope to hang himself," is a phrase I have heard relationship experts opine.

- On the flip side, men in their 50's are complaining that women in their late 40's, 50's or 60's are happy being single. They have financial freedom, hobbies, friends, their kids are grown, and are enjoying not taking care of someone.

Conclusion: Timing is everything. If a man is not ready, no amount of persuading, cajoling, manipulating or playing games is going to convince him to lay aside his precious freedom and enter into a monogamous commitment. In Chapter 5: Nurturing the Relationship, we will cover how to spot the time wasters, and move on. We will also cover the toxic game players in our section on the Casanova Toad in Chapter 7: The Toad Pool. But keep in mind...there are just as many men out there wanting to be in an amazing relationship with his best friend, as there are those who will proudly wave the flag of bachelorhood above their man cave.

Chapter Two
Where The Boys Are!

Where the boys are! Cue the Connie Francis soundtrack from the 1960's movie of the same name. "Where the boys are, someone waits for me!" I can hear her sweet voice now. It makes sense to understand the places men frequent, but I sometimes feel we are still looking at the male species as if he were of another sub-culture.

Don't we all need to eat? Buy furniture, look at a new car, walk the dog, purchase a hose, workout for a great physique, go to the movies, hit a concert, watch the fireworks, browse a book store? I do feel we as women can overthink things. Men are human and have human needs. There are techniques that work brilliantly in approaching men so that it looks innocent and playful. Some ideas for what to say are listed in the upcoming locations, but we will go into the secrets of a great approach in the next section called, appropriately, The Approach.

That being said, here are some of the places "Where the Boys Are…"

Winging It!

- Coffee Shops. I've seen more men in a Starbucks than you can shake a mug at. Professional men are often in a hurry and grab coffee and a pastry on their way to work. Weekends will find them sitting happily with a latte near their elbow and a newspaper or laptop spread out before their face.

- Grocery Stores. We all gotta eat. The best time to find single men perusing the produce is right after office hours on their way home from work. This is typically around 5 or 5:30.

- Parties. Summer is a great time to meet new people at outdoor BBQ parties, parks, lakes and concerts. There is always a festival or party going on somewhere. This is where you can use the information provided earlier on joining Meet-Up

Groups in your area. I receive up to 12 party announcements a week through these groups, and it's all free. Throw a party yourself and ask your friends to bring along some new faces. The holidays are another party central. If you are sitting there saying, "I don't have any friends, or at least ones that throw parties," then now is the time to start meeting new people. Use the tips I gave you earlier in the section on Social Life. Fill up your Friend Cup.

- Sporting Events. This is a no-brainer. Grab your baseball cap, 7-iron, roller skates or bowling bag and get out there! Learn a new sport. Men LOVE giving advice to newbies trying to learn a new game. Ask someone sitting next to you at a ball game to explain the call the ref just made. Approach that cute guy at the tee box next to you on the golf driving range and ask what club he recommends for getting out of sand traps. Take a picnic lunch and a good book to the park and spread that blanket near a basketball court where a bunch of sweaty guys are shooting 3-pointers. A few glances their way and a cute smile might just send someone over asking if you have a spare bottle of water. Many Meet-Up Groups plan sand volleyball, hiking, rock climbing, rafting, horseback riding and other fun things men typically enjoy.

- Your Local Gym. Kill two birds with one crunch. You get the toned body and a great chance to meet the plethora of males who are grunting, groaning, and posing at these neighborhood work-out places.

- The Office. If you are in an office environment, take the opportunity to mingle. Keep it light and never bother someone who is working. Scout out the cafeteria, or notice where a lot of your co-workers go for lunch or after hours martinis. Hit the office parties.

- Classes. I love this one. There are classes out there on every conceivable subject. More men than ever before are taking dance and cooking classes. I was surprised at how many men on dating sites were looking for dance partners. The onslaught of television cooking shows has sent men scurrying for their aprons and taking culinary classes as well. Stained glass, pottery, archery, fishing, golf, painting, basket weaving (okay, probably not the basket weaving), etc. Classes are everywhere, and so are "da boys"! Plus, you get the added benefit of learning something new and fun.

- Lectures. Check your local universities, museums and libraries for lectures you may be interested in. I recently attended a lecture on European Travel and was pleasantly surprised at the number of single men attending. I learned a lot about the back roads of Tuscany, and enjoyed meeting a fascinating man who was more than happy to chat me up about Italy.

- Speaking of travel…there are cruises for singles, Meet-Up Groups that go places all over the world, airports, train stations and bus depots all teeming with men coming and going. Sitting for hours waiting for a plane is a great time to start a conversation with the bored guy sitting next to you. You may even luck out and get the Exit aisle with a nice single guy in seat D12. The point is this…if you never leave the comfort zone of your own living room, the only men you are likely to meet are the pizza delivery boy, and Eagle Scouts selling tickets to a fund raiser. Just sayin'…

- Jogging/Biking/Walking. Most cities and towns have trails that cater to the folks who feel the need for speed, even if it's a power walk. Get out and enjoy nature. Several of my girlfriends met nice guys while walking the same trail for a few weeks. If you see the same face a few times, you begin smiling at each other, and Voila.

- Single Dads frequent children's party places, parks, zoos, museums, and playgrounds. Weekends are the best time to check out these places and look for the guy sans wedding rings who are enjoying watching their kids play, teaching them sports, or taking them to a movie. It is the easiest thing in the world to make a sweet comment about a guy's child if you are standing close enough to notice how his little Susan just said the cutest thing. Keep it nonchalant and don't hover. Let him pick it up or leave it. He's got his hands full with his kids, but he may be interested enough to ask for your number, or at least ask "So, which kids are yours?" If you don't have children with you, you can simply say, "I had to drop something off/pick someone up/look for a location for an upcoming party, etc."

- Libraries and Book Stores. I am a huge fan of book stores and libraries. Men frequent these places, although online book sellers have taken a chunk out of the market. Wander over to the books on travel, home repair, sports, fiction, etc. Asking his opinion on a book in a section he is standing in is an easy opener. "I noticed you are looking at the same books I am. Which one do you feel is the most comprehensive for training golden retrievers? I'm always afraid I'm going to waste my money on a book with no real value."

- Home Depot/Lowes, etc. Let's face it. Most men like to build, repair, invent, create, and just plain buy tools. One hour walking the aisles of your local hardware store will put you face to face with more men than three years in a nail salon. (Trade in the acrylic nails for the ten penny type.) Again, asking advice is a great ice breaker. If you're like me, this isn't as manipulative as it is necessary when navigating those overwhelming stacks of products.

- Lawn and Garden Shows and Stores. Many men love gardening and outdoing Jones across the street with their green thumb. Go pick out some plants, peruse a landscaping show and "plant a few seeds" with a smile and playful opener: "I always confuse annual with perennial. Does annual mean it comes around each year, like tax season, or that

I have to plant it again every spring?" Smile sweetly.

- Bars. I am not a huge proponent of the bar scene. No matter how advanced we've become, trolling the bars still carries the same stigma and it is often the go-to place for guys looking to hook up at the last minute. If you do go, please go with friends who don't have a propensity for getting blitzed. A drunken friend is not only going to get you negative attention, but you may lose their ability to watch your back, or drive home. If a guy asks for your number, and you are interested, ask him for his number instead, telling him you prefer to not give out your number. He will respect you, and you just gave notice he will have to do some work to earn your company.

- Sports Bars give you the benefit of meeting guys who are out for a drink and to relax without the stigma of the traditional bar crawl. These bars double as restaurants where you will see family as well as singles. Old Chicago Pizza is a good example. You can sit with friends and laugh, and possibly meet someone nice. These places also offer Trivia Games which gives you an "in" to ask someone to join your group, stating "We need a wing man in the Sports arena."

- Car and Boat Shows are great places to meet men. These events give you the perfect chance to ask for a man's opinion as you stop and study some stream-lined beauty (yes, I am talking about the car or boat).

- Department Stores. Men shop for clothes. I promise. Ask his opinion on a tie you are purchasing for your nephew. Hold up two sweaters and pretend to be considering them. Then smile sweetly at him and say, "Which one of these would you buy if you were hoping to *not* lose your brother's good opinion of you?" Humor is soooo underrated. Men will see your playful side, and it keeps it from looking contrived or too serious.

- Church. Attending a Sunday Service is not only up-lifting, but if you do happen to meet a gentleman there, you will already now he has a spiritual side. If that is something on your wish list, then you can check that one off. Mingling at church services is the common thing to do, so it is so easy to simply say, "What did you think of the message today?" Many churches have refreshments after where everyone is talking and getting to know each other.

- Planetariums, Museums, Theaters, Concerts, Zoos, etc. Check your newspaper or online listing of things to do in your area. Get out and enjoy life. You will add to your joy and your list of new experiences, and bring a more fun, fulfilled and educated you to your next date—all good things where men, and women, are concerned. Many of your friends may be feeling just as stuck as you are and will be thrilled to have you come up with ideas to make life sparkle.

- Dog Parks. If you don't have a dog, you can borrow one or forego this location, but bear this in mind...diamonds may be a girl's best friend, but Fido gets top billing with his Master. These parks are brimming with dog lovers...and single guys.

I can see some women rolling their eyes and saying this makes them feel predatory, like they have to go out and hunt down, tag and bag a man. Before you ruin your mascara, here's what the men I interviewed had to say:

- David*, 45, account executive. "You women have it easy. You can approach a guy without the same fears men have. Guys know all women think we are after only one thing, so when we do approach a woman we are wondering if she is thinking we are a pervert, or Ted Bundy's long-lost cousin!"

- Markus*, 24, medical student. "Where to go to meet guys? How 'bout you tell men where we go to meet women, other than the bar scene? Pretty sure most of my friends are not dying for a pedicure. It's tougher than you girls think it is for us to meet quality women."

- Richard, 56*, retired pilot. "I will tell you this. If a woman takes the initiative, it is a breath of fresh air. A man is so grateful to have that fear of rejection taken off his plate, that he will give her major points for letting us know she might be interested. Best approach ever? I was sitting alone at a restaurant table. A nice-looking woman was seated across the room and glanced my way a few times. I noticed there were two water glasses and menus at her table so I assumed she was waiting for someone, possibly a man. But she smiled timidly once and looked away. Finally, she got up and walked past my table and lightly dropped her white napkin near my feet. When I bent to pick it up for her, she smiled, and said, "So, the white handkerchief technique is alive and well." She took the napkin from me, smiled and walked on to the Ladies Room. When she returned to her table her female friend had arrived. After the "handkerchief lady" was seated, she grinned my way as if to say, "See? I wasn't waiting for a guy."

As I left the restaurant, I dropped my napkin near her feet and kept going. As I was paying the cashier I looked back to see her smiling as she unfolded my napkin and found my business card inside. We've been dating for 8 months now."

If you are seriously wanting to be in a relationship, and let's face it, most people prefer sharing their lives with someone amazing than sitting at home watching Downton Abbey re-runs, then you need to be pro-active. (And for the record, I love Downton Abbey.) We as women need to stop overthinking this dating business, put on our big girl panties and go after what we want. The Knight in Shining Armor is great in fairy tales, but today's Sir Galahad is typically an overworked, underappreciated guy who packs his free time the way we do…finding something that equates to leisure time. Knowing where those down-time places are simply gives us a compass in that jungle out there. If this insults your feminine nature, or your feministic one, and you prefer to go on doing things the way you always have, I will use

Doctor Phil's sound bite, "How's that working for you?" This is Troubleshooting Men. I am merely loading your quiver. ☺

The Approach

The secret of approaching men is fundamentally brilliant. When the men I interviewed first tipped me off to these seemingly simple techniques, I remember smiling from ear to ear. Could it really be that easy, and that impactful? As an experiment, I went out and tried it on for size. Let me begin this chapter by giving you a first-hand example of how this "oh so" subtle technique works.

I was in a grocery store with a friend of mine and we were having fun pointing out cute guys, guessing if they were married, and generally enjoying being in a playful mood. We had been discussing my website *Troubleshooting Men, What in the WORLD do they want?* I told her about the information I had just gleaned from the 2,000 men I interviewed when I asked them the question, "What's the best way for a woman to approach a man she may be interested in?" The overwhelming response was to keep it light and then let him take over. "If you can make it feel like the whole thing was his idea, and he is pursuing YOU, all the better."

Say what??? That sounded not only daunting, but impossible. I gave it a lot of thought, and on the day my friend and I were shopping for an upcoming BBQ party, I spotted a very cute guy looking at the condiments and decided to put it into practice.

I alerted my friend that I was going to give it a try and to wish me luck. She looked at me like I was nuts, and then whispered, "Good luck! It's your butt!" *I need a new wing man.*

I swallowed hard, took a deep breath, put my shoulders back, and walked over to where he was standing. I pretended to study the huge array of fancy mustards. He glanced at me, as I was standing fairly close to him, and I looked at him and grinned. "Pardon me," I said playfully. "But would you have any Grey Poupon?" He blinked for a second, and then this huge smile came over his face. "But of course," he said, keeping in character with the popular commercial from the 1980's. He took a minute to look over the selection and then plucked a jar from the shelf. He smiled and offered it to me.

"Thank you," I said, smiling. "You're my hero." I kept it very light and prepared to walk off. I could see my friend standing there with raised eyebrows.

The gentleman turned and said, rather hurriedly, "Is there anything else I can help you find?" He was unaware I was with my friend. I stopped and turned back to him, cocking my head to one side as if I was considering his offer. I twisted my mouth, and said, "I *am* in need of bird seed." He laughed, and without missing a beat, said, "Domestic or wild?" "Wild," I answered, grinning. "I have a bird feeder in my back yard." "Right this way," he said, flagging me to follow him. As I trotted off happily behind him, I turned to see my friend's mouth hanging open. He looked up for the store sign reading Pets (something I could have done) and led me to the bags of bird seed.

"You are very kind," I said, this time in a sincere manner. "I appreciate you taking the time." "My pleasure," he answered, with a warm smile. "You should see me in the Deli department!" I laughed and said, "Perhaps another time." With that, he reached for his wallet and handed me his business card. "If you run into a shortage of sliced pastrami, I'm your man," he said. As he walked away, he glanced back at me and smiled. My friend came around the corner at that time and I showed her his business card. She hit me with the jar of Grey Poupon.

I know what you're thinking. "You lucked out that you got a guy who was that witty and spontaneous." You are absolutely correct. The whole thing could have stopped with him looking at me with an annoyed expression and saying, "I don't know anything about mustard," and walking away. It happens. Not letting it bother you that it happens is the big thing. He's a total stranger. He doesn't know you, so how can his opinion of you matter?

THIS is exactly what men risk and *fear* each time they approach a woman—the possibility of being shot down. And according to the men I spoke with, being shot down in flames was a lot more common than having their approach received with graciousness and interest. So lighten up, don't take it so seriously, and have fun with it. One word of warning, be careful who you approach, when and where. Approaching strangers is something that requires good judgment.

Now, let's take the scenario I just gave you of the cute grocery store guy and do a post-mortem autopsy on it, using some of the men from the interviews as the lecturing surgeons:

The Playful Approach

- Roger*, 42, franchise owner. "If women knew how hard it is for men to approach them, they would take pity on us. Most men would rather have a root canal, without Novocain, while listening to opera, and having their toenails removed! If a woman gives a guy the slightest hint that he won't be shot down like a pilot in enemy territory, he will already feel an inclination to like her. She just threw him a life line. If you think I'm kidding, ask any guy...and I mean *any* guy!"

- Rale*, 33, pharmacologist. "I was standing in line at a grocery store, and I casually picked up a People magazine to scan while I was waiting. A demure voice behind me said, "I didn't know guys were into celebrity gossip." I turned to see a woman about my age standing there in line, grinning at me. "Oh, I don't know," I said. "Ya gotta know what Brad Pitt has goin' on, right?" She laughed, and said, "I doubt you could learn anything new from him." It took me a minute to realize she had just paid me a big compliment.

She had this cute grin that underscored it was all being playful, but it made me feel like a million bucks. I didn't have the courage to do anything else, other than say a sheepish, "Thanks." I kicked myself all the way out of the store and across the parking lot that this woman just opened the door for me to make a move, and I froze. As it turned out, we were parked right next to each other. As I saw her approach her car next to mine, I laughed, and so did she. Then she nailed it. "Hmmm...," she said, "I doubt even Brad Pitt could have pulled off a move like knowing where to park next to me." That did it. I asked her if she would like to get coffee some time. She said, "Only if you bring your People magazine." Which I did."

- Douglas*, 56, personal trainer. "Here's the deal when it comes to a lady giving a guy the nod. If she does it in a light-hearted way, and then moves away, we're hooked. She didn't come on too strong, just enough to let me know she sees something that interests her, and moves on. Guys can't resist that. It's like a fish playing with the bait on your hook. If you don't reel it in, it's moved on to the next lure."

- Arthur*, 23, pro athlete. "I got girls hittin' me up all the time. Not bragging, it's just the way things are in my business. Most of them are too forward. I don't care how hot they are, it makes a guy pull back a little. It's like a hard sell, and nobody likes those. What's cool is a girl with all this confidence going on, who gives you a look, maybe two looks, a smile, and then heads off to do her thing. That's the soft sell, and it works. If a guy has any confidence, he's going to follow her."

- Ben*, 38, retail sales. "Coolest move a woman ever did was one night when I was out with three of my buddies at a sports bar. It was so loud in there that we were shouting at each other to be heard. I was looking around and saw this nice-looking lady across the room. She wasn't drop-dead gorgeous, just looked put together and put off this air of being happy with herself and the people she was with. She saw me look at her and smiled, and then looked back to her friends. A few minutes later she caught me looking her way again. A group in-between us were laughing really loud, the obnoxious kind of loud. She smiled at me and put her hands over her ears to signal it was really loud in there. I nodded, and flinched as another round of grating laughter came from the group of drunken guys. She was still grinning at me, so I nodded my head toward the restaurant entry area. She paused as if thinking it over, and then leaned over and whispered something to her friends. I froze, waiting for the laughter every guy fears when girls are out together and he has made a move. Instead, she got up and walked over to waiting area as I followed behind. She looked at me expectantly. Now I was going to have to say something clever. Not so much. "You looked like you needed rescuing," I said, and immediately thought how dumb it sounded. "Oh?" she said in a really sweet voice, "Do you have a spare set of ear plugs?" I thought that was cute, so I ramped it up a little. "If I give you ear plugs, you will miss out on my witty banter." She cocked an eyebrow and said, "Well, that would be a shame. I hope to sample it sometime. Right now I need to get back to my friends." What I liked was that she left the door open for me. I told her I would scribble my number on something and hand it to her at her table. All she said was, "Sounds good. Have a fun night." It was all done with class and a lot of confidence on her part, yet I still wondered if she would say "Yes" when I called her."

You'll notice in each of these scenarios that men shared with me there was a common approach that was very effective. The woman smiled, or started things off with something light and playful that fit the situation. Once she had the man engaged, she pulled back subtly, without shutting the door for further communication. In my approach with the grocery store guy, after giving him my "Grey Poupon" comment, and thanking him for handing me the jar of mustard, I turned to walk away. The smiles of the women in two of the scenarios above were just enough to indicate interest, but then they put up just enough distance by looking or walking away, so that the man felt the immediate desire to pursue.

It's the same psychology behind creating a sense of urgency at a store sale. We may have walked right by that display of handbags, glanced at them with a lukewarm interest, until an announcement is made that they are in limited supply and will be available only for the next 30 minutes. Suddenly there is a mad rush to the purse display, with women elbowing each other out of the way. Now you feel a sense of panic. You have to act now or you could be missing out on something.

This is human nature. Marketing revolves around it. We want something we can't have. The gauntlet has been tossed down and the brave of heart pick it up. Some relationship experts have called it the "rubber band theory." Pull away and he will spring back to you. It's subtle, feminine, and very powerful. It may take some practice. The last thing you want is for a man to misread you, or think you rehearsed approaching him. With some trial and error you can perfect this to where it is as natural as breathing. Isn't it just another form of flirting? Yes…but it's the "advance and then back away timing" that lands it.

The Landing

Now that I've hopefully convinced you that the old strategy of waiting for the guy to make all the initial moves is not only outdated, but ineffectual, let's take it up a notch.

You Are Cleared For Landing!

Look again at the way the women in the scenarios above handled themselves. This is gold! Men feel an instinctual need to be the pursuer. It's as hard-wired as looking at the female body. "Then why are you telling women to make the first move?" you are probably thinking. I felt the same way when men began telling me how much they appreciated women showing a subtle interest in them. But then they turned around and told me they still enjoyed a challenge and feeling they had to earn her attention. It's enough to make you run for the nearest shrink. The trick (if that's what you want to call it), is making him feel he is in control of the outcome. He will be the one to close the deal by asking for your phone number or a date. This will also work with online dating. We'll cover that in Part III: Today's View of Romance in Chapter Two: Online Dating.

If you look at what happened in the scenarios above, the man felt a challenge immediately after feeling the relief of not having to risk being shot down by coming onto the woman first. She put out the "I *may* be interested" vibe, and then immediately tossed the ball back into his court, even subtly giving him the impression she wasn't won over yet. That's psychology in its purest form. She was able to do the choosing, called the shots on when and how to approach him, and then left him wondering if he had a shot with her. Is that brilliant, or what? Please take a moment to read them again.

And by the way, you will notice in the cartoon on the previous page for *The Landing* that it is a male pilot standing there. I chose that illustration to underscore that with these techniques, the man will feel *he* landed the plane, and that's exactly what we want him to feel.

So, when you are interested in landing that nice-looking, charismatic guy you just saw in a store, a gym, a dog park, or a restaurant, remember the rules of flying:

- Gauge your approach by checking the conditions. (Make sure he looks approachable and is not involved in something that will make this an interruption. Timing is everything.)

- Lower your flaps. (Getting outside your comfort zone to approach a man will require lowering your inhibitions enough to show confidence and playfulness.)

- Alert the tower you are coming in. (Give him a soft smile or grin, or a playful opening line that alerts him to the possibility that something is about to happen.)

- Pull back on the throttle. (Immediately after "alerting the tower", pull back on the throttle. Put up some distance so that he feels a pull towards you, and even a rush of adrenaline as the sense of urgency heightens.)

- Taxi in and depart the runway. (Once the ball in his court, relax, taxi and depart leaving him wanting more. Some women kill all their hard work by talking too much, hanging on him, or appearing overly eager once he begins responding. Keep it short. He'll be intrigued enough to want to learn more and see you again.)

I would like to add two caveats to this business of approaching a man first. Men know better than anyone that it takes a lot of confidence to approach someone and risk rejection. The woman who playfully approaches him is showing a lot of confidence, and 88% of the men I interviewed listed confidence in their top three "sexy as all hell" traits they are looking for in a woman. Pretty much a win-win, wouldn't you say?

But wait! There's more! You are going to love this! It's psychology again. You may be near a man who has not noticed you, and the entire evening (or day) could go by without him noticing you. You may feel he's a "10" and that you fall somewhere in the "6-7" bracket. Let's say you catch his eye. He may just be looking around but anyone is going to notice someone who is looking at them, even if it's casual. Hold his eye for a brief second, give him the shortest of grins, and look away.

Nine times out of ten the person you grinned at will glance at you again, whether they are really interested or not, just to see if you are still looking at them. Now, you can cock your head slightly to one side, as if studying a museum exhibit, look perplexed, and then look away, as if you have lost interest. Believe me, you now have his attention. I don't care how confident a guy is, he is now wondering, "What did that mean? What's she thinking? Have I got spinach dip on my chin?"

Finally, look at him one more time, smile, shake your head slightly as if you are amused, and leave the area. Go to another room, walk to the next aisle, move on to other friends, etc. Still be where he can find you, but "put up the distance." It is human nature to want something that we had, but lost. Think of a child who owns a toy but has lost interest in it…until another child shows interest, or the toy is lost. Now it's the most valuable toy in the world and we must have it! A man who stopped dating a woman may see her out with someone else and his interest is piqued. "She was mine, and now some other guy is moving in."

So, in the scenario above, what has the man lost? He doesn't even know you. What he's lost is your attention…something he had a few moments before. There is a subtle sense that he has somehow failed to impress you. If he has any confidence at all, he will find you and get to the bottom of it. Ah yes…psychology is a beautiful thing!

It's time! Grab your goggles, scarf and helmet. Check your gauges, put a finger to the wind, and rev it up. Take a wing man if needed. You are now ready for take-off!

Chapter Three
The First Date

The First Date. You can feel the nerve endings firing as you read those three words. "Will this be "the one"? What will I wear? Which personality should I try on? Maybe I should cancel...didn't I hear there's a rare strain of the Dengue Bird Virus going around?"

If you're thinking we've skipped a step before jumping right into the first date, you're correct. He may have given you his card or asked for your phone number, but there is that tricky little area between finding each other, and going out for that all-important first date.

I call it the "Easing Into It" area. It may be an email, text or phone call, but however you communicate, you will have to get a sense of each other, and if that goes well, decide on a place to meet.

> Throughout the upcoming sections you will see a small graphic of a bomb. Wherever you see this icon, you will find what men consider the biggest mistake women make in that particular category.

Let's go to our three typical avenues for this foray into the adventurous arena called "Dating":

The Phone Call

So, he has your number or you have his. It's that dreaded first call where you get your first chance to hear his voice, his laugh, cadence and personality. You can tell a lot from a phone call—more than just the words being said. Here are some hard and fast rules about that first call, whether he calls you, or has asked you to call him. Let's start with you:

You Call Him. Let's say he gave you his phone number. You are now in the fun position of deciding when to call. It's the same fear men face with each phone call they make to a woman. "What if she sounds busy? What if I get her voice message? What if she can't carry on a decent conversation and it's all one-sided questions?" Now it's your turn. Ready? Here are the do's and don'ts, straight from the mouth of males:

- Don't ever call him during work hours. The worst first impression you can make is to call at work, even if he works from home.

- Don't call after 10 o'clock in the evening. This is etiquette for either sex. Unless he asks you to call at a certain time, shoot for the safe hours of 7-9 pm on weekdays.

- Try not to call on a weekend for your first phone call. He may have other plans and will be in an awkward position, and it alerts him you have no such plans for the weekend.

- Keep it light. "Hi Jeff. This is Nancy. You asked me to call, so I wanted to give you a quick Hello and see how your week is going." The word "quick" lets him know you have a life and that you aren't planning on turning this into a phone marathon.

- Once you've made the introduction, let him run with it. If he sounds busy, be the one to end the call. You can say, "I don't have time to talk right now. I just wanted to say "Hi" since you were kind enough to ask me to call. Let's chat another time when we are both able to focus." Keep it upbeat and with a tinge of humor. If he doesn't set up a time to call you back, or leaves it vague, let it go. The ball is in his court.

- Keep the conversation short, no matter how much he wants to talk. Ten minutes is plenty long to trade niceties and set up a time to meet. A lot of men will keep you on the phone trying to gain personal information. This backfires when you are suddenly on a date and he already knows way too much about you. It will also form a "false sense of familiarity". Here you are, finally seated across from the guy you've spent hours with on the phone, yet he is essentially still a stranger. You can't read body language or pick up those important subliminal clues when you are first meeting someone via the phone. If he keeps asking questions, simply say, "You're sweet to be so interested. Let's save it for the first date. It will be more fun in person." You've given him a compliment and not shut him down, but you've kept the conversation short. Mystery still works in creating interest early on. Let him get excited about meeting you and finding out more.

- The rule of dating for the first date is the man comes to you. This allows the woman to feel a sense of control over her surroundings that comes with being on "her turf". A gentleman will do the driving to get there on the first date. When on the phone, if he asks where you would like to go, choose something close by and mid-range for cost, such as a casual bistro, coffee or a drink. Tell him you appreciate him being willing to drive to your area.

- Do not give out personal details such as your place of business, home address or anything else that will alert him to where to find you. You still know close to nothing about this man. A man who is protective of women will understand and admire you if you tell him that some information is saved for a later time.

- Be upbeat! If you had a bad day, keep it to yourself. You are making a second impression here if you've met him before. If you met online, this is his first introduction to your personality. If you're tired or stressed, don't call!

- "Leave a message at the beep." Most people dread leaving messages on someone's phone when they don't know them very well. This is not the time to be too cutesy, long-winded or tense. Just say, "Hi Jeff. It's Nancy. You gave me your card at the party the other night and this is the first chance I've had to call. I hope your week is going great. My number is 555-5499. Talk to you later." Hang up.

"Women who giggle too much, talk incessantly, bring up personal issues, gossip, or ask too many questions during the first phone call are already losing our interest. We can only imagine what an entire evening with them would be like." Jake*, 36, architect.

One exception to the "calling him first" rule: If he made the gesture of handing you his card or phone number without you asking for it, don't call him. This is a lazy way for him to let you do all the work. If he was really interested in you, he would have asked for your number to make sure he had a way to get hold of you. If, on the other hand, he asked for your number and you replied, "Tell you what, why don't you give me yours. I don't usually hand out my number to someone I don't know," then it is perfectly fine for you to make the first call. Follow the rules listed above for keeping it light and short. Let him ask you out for a date…don't make it easy for him by hinting or suggesting you get together, or saying you just happen to have tickets to the monster truck pull. Men still want to pursue. This hasn't changed in 2,000 years and it won't change now.

He Calls You. When a man does the calling it is usually a better situation, for a number of reasons. One, he is calling because now is a good time for him. Men compartmentalize and typically do one thing at a time. Women often fail to realize this trait of the male species. We tend to do several things at once and not miss a beat. But men like to focus on one thing at a time. Hence, when he does call you, he is free to talk. Does that mean a game won't be on the television in the background? Not necessarily, but if it's a game he's interested in, he won't be calling you at that time.

Two, he is obviously interested or he wouldn't call. The catch here is "interested in what?" It won't take long to tell what the objective of the call is. If he makes small talk for a few minutes and then begins asking leading questions, pay attention to the subject matter. For example:

- Him: "So, how do like the dating site? I was surprised at a recent survey that said 33% of the women on this site have sex on the first date. Does that surprise you?" **What's He After?** He is finding out if you are one of the 33% by your answer. If he is mentioning sex in the first phone call, this guy is looking for a Hook-Up.

- Him: "How do you feel about the fact we live over 60 miles apart from each other? Do you think distance is a factor?" **What's He After?** This is his way of subtly finding out if you are prepared to meet him half-way or take turns with the driving. He might also be seeing if you mention sleep-overs as the relationship progresses to cut down on driving back and forth.

- Him: "What kind of restaurants do you like (or food do you like?)" **What's He After?** He is probably genuincly interested in your tastes to see if you are compatible when it comes to cuisine, but this also gives him an inclination as to how expensive your tastes are. If you are rattling off 4- and 5-star restaurants, or talking only about filet mignon, lobster and Baked Alaska, he sees a woman who will be making a major dent in his wallet.

- "What sounds like a fun date to you?" **What's He After?** It's pretty obvious. Does this girl prefer getting out into nature, going to a movie or a museum, sports, dinner only, will she enjoy bowling or pool...this open-ended question tells him volumes about what he can expect when dating you.

Three, notice the timing of the call. This is important. Men, who call only from work or late at night, only when driving or are away from home, are red flags. This guy is probably married or with someone else. A friend of mine mentioned to me that the only time this guy called her was while he was out running errands. I told her to ask him to call her that night around 7 when she would have more time to talk. Guess what? He never called again.

Another timing factor is the day of the week. If he calls after Thursday, he is probably not going to ask you out for that weekend, or he is waiting until the last minute to ask you out because he has nothing better on his plate. Both scenarios are no wins for you. The rule of thumb is to never accept a date for the weekend after Wednesday. If he wants to see you on your valuable weekend time, he needs to get on your dance card early in the week. Simply say, "I'm sorry, I already have plans." Don't tell him what the plans are. It's none of his business. If he asks what you're doing, or tries to find out if you have a date, just say lightly, "I tend to make plans for the weekend early in the week. It gives you something fun to look forward to, don't you think?" This puts the ball back in his court, you've given nothing away and he is now on notice that he can't wait until the last minute to ask you out. Things should improve in the next call, or if not, this tells you this guy is not long-term material.

What did our men in the survey have to say about phone calls in the early stages of dating? Here you go:

- "Women tend to treat guys like their girlfriends. This is going to sound awful but we really aren't interested in hearing about how Gale dissed you in front of Audrey at work. We're not big on gossip, non-stop complaining or hearing about your day at the stylist. Men are brief, and to the point. Keep it light, succinct and non-drama. Make us want to call you again, not look for reasons not to." Mark, 52, advertising.

- "Guys are not big on endless chatter. Period. Watch two guys talk and you'll see what I mean. It's pretty much information gathering and out the door. 'Hoops Saturday?' 'Sure. 10 o'clock?' 'Cool. See you then.' That's it! The Reader's Digest version of conversation works great with us." Palo*, 38, men's soccer coach.

- "Let us ask you questions. When women offer us all the information about themselves before we can ask, it kills any mystery about them. Let us work a little to get to know you. I know girls like to share everything but give us a chance to see the layers, not the whole onion at once." Doug*, 25, retail owner.

- "Oh man, when a woman is eating while she's talking to me, it is so annoying...and rude! No one wants to hear that. Same for an irritating laugh." Harv*, 44, banker.

- "Don't call men all the time. We feel smothered. The chase is still a big deal to us. The women I feel the most interest in are the ones where I wonder what she's doing, and if she's out with someone else. Don't make us your world early on. It's a death knoll to a guy." Paul*, 48, boat dealer.

- "If we are calling for a first date, be nice. This is a very hard move for a guy. Don't sound bored or disinterested. Hard to get is not a good move here. Be happy to hear from us without sounding desperate and don't take over the conversation. Let us get around to asking you out." Dave*, 30, marketing.

- "Say the unexpected. If I ask "How was your day?" 90% of the people out there will say, "Fine." Boring, predictable and leaves me needing to come up with another question. This girl I went out with was a genius at taking me by surprise with her answers. I asked how her day was and she said things like, "Super! I solved the national deficit, got a pedicure and designed a new marketing program for my boss, all before lunch." I loved talking to her. She was spontaneous, fun, and I find wit to be very sexy." Markus*, 42, contractor.

The consensus of the majority of men in the survey said they preferred talking to a woman who was light-hearted, breezy and let him lead the conversation. They also appreciated her showing an interest in his day, and having something to say if the conversation lagged. If they asked her where she would like to go on a date, they liked it when she had a few ideas instead of the deadly, "Oh, I don't care…wherever you want to go." A variety of ideas was always nice so that he could take her up on one that fit his budget or idea of fun.

Words of caution: Never have a man you don't know yet pick you up at your place. Meet him at the location of the date. A gentleman will expect this on a first date. Don't be too accommodating if he is vague in picking a place and time. If he is giving you a "Let me see what I've got going on and I'll get back to you" line, simply say, "That's fine. I would appreciate making plans by Wednesday evening so I can schedule my weekend." This lets him know you are not sitting around waiting for him to fill your empty days, and that you have more than just a date with him planned for the weekend. He'll take notice that this woman values her time and has a life.

As we mentioned, keep it short, no matter how much he tries to keep you talking. Some men use this as a way to find out as much as they can before meeting you, and create a sense of bonding they have not yet earned.

"Women who keep interrupting the call to do something are really inconsiderate and annoying. I've talked to women who kept stopping to let the dog in or out, take another call, check her cake in the oven, or grab something. We deserve your full attention as you would expect from us." Drew*, 56, real estate developer.

The Text

Texting a guy should be done with restraint. While it provides a quick way of staying in contact that is not as interruptive as a phone call or long email, it can be overdone, and too often, misunderstood.

We've all received texts that left us confused as to the sender's intent. We can't hear their voice or read their face to ascertain what the true intent of the message was. Even worse, auto-check will sometimes fill in a word it thinks you mean when it isn't even close. One of my girlfriends received this beauty from her boyfriend while we were all out for a girl's night:

"Having a great time. This is loads of fun. Wish you were her."

Her boyfriend was out with his siblings at a ball game. Obviously auto-check filled in the word "her" instead of "here." Unfortunately, the text came on the heels of an argument they'd had, and she spent the evening wondering if he had gone out with someone else. Double check it before you send it!

Gathering Information. Texting should be reserved for information gathering such finding a location, letting someone know you are going to be late, asking if they are on their way, etc. The other kind of texting can be effective, but again, restraint is advised.

The playful, flirty text. I don't advise being the first one to send a text. If he has your phone number and hasn't called, texting him can seem a bit desperate. If you are genuinely going to die if you don't get a feel for his interest level (that he hasn't called should be a big red indicator), you can try this:

"Hi Mike. I'm at a jazz concert with my friends at Wash Park. Knew you liked jazz. You should come."

This is effective because it doesn't sound like a date. You are already out having fun and just happened to remember he likes jazz. "You should come" shows confidence and makes it easy for him to accept. If he can't make it, the ball is in his court to answer you and hopefully offer an alternative such as, "Thanks for thinking of me. I'm tied up tonight. What are you doing Saturday?" If he doesn't pick it up and either show up or try to see you another time, you have your answer. Don't contact him again.

If you've spoken on the phone and want to send a playful text, I'd wait a day or two and then send something like this:

"I heard someone won the $6 million lotto. If it's you, I've had my eye on a cute little black dress."

This is playful and the mention of "a little black dress" gets his guy genes humming. It's subtle and fun. Or...

"Watching Master Chef. Your version of a glazed salmon is a winner. Maybe you should go on the show."

Here you've given him a compliment (always a good thing) without it being too overboard, and you're being playful. You've also shown you remembered him talking about making his famous glazed salmon. Very flattering.

Again, I would not text a man unless you have already had a few great phone conversations and you know he is interested, unless it's to get information for a planned date or to let him know you are running late. Let him do the work. Let him earn your time and attention. An exception may be to wish him "Happy Birthday."

Some texting Do's and Don'ts from the guys:

- Don't text us at work unless we initiated it, or it's important.
- Don't send us sexual content. We might have friends, parents or kids looking over our shoulder. It's not classy.
- Don't send long-winded texts, or ones with so many questions that we feel it will take us half-an-hour to answer it.
- Less is more.
- If there's a chance we could misread your intent, add something like LOL, or "just kidding." Guys are pretty sensitive about being made fun of.
- Go easy on the text slang. Not everyone knows what IMHO means. (By the way, it means In My Humble Opinion.)
- Give us time to answer. We may be busy. Sending a text, and then another ten minutes later with a "?" because we haven't answered yet is a turn-off...and desperate. The same goes for sending one before we've had a chance to answer, saying "Are you OK?" If we haven't answered by the next day, then check in.
- Too many texts = stalker. Enough said.
- Flirty is fun if it's not all the time and we already have a few dates under the belt. Something as cute as "Come play" will get a guy's attention.

"Texting after a first date to ask how he thought it went is not a good idea. Give us a chance to pursue. If we had a good time and like you, we will get hold of you. Some guys appreciate a short text later that night or the next morning saying, "I had a great time. Thank you again for dinner." This is a decision a girl can make. If the guy seems a little insecure, a text like that might encourage him. If your date was pretty confident, I'd let him take the lead." Stephen*, 33, dentist.

The Email

Emailing has become the new form of communication with online dating. We begin contact on these sites by indicating interest either through a "wink" or an email. From there it is more emails, hopefully leading to a first date. We will go into email warnings in our section on Online Dating in Part III: Today's View of Romance. For now, when it comes to the precursor for a first date, here are a few tried and trues:

- Just like a phone call or text, keep it short.
- If he asks you a question, keep your answer upbeat, unexpected and brief. Toss the question back to him, or improvise with something a little more challenging. For example:

Him: "What do you do for a living?"

You: "I help women look stunning. How about you? What imprint do you leave on the world?" This shows playfulness and it is so much more interesting than "I design clothes. What do you do?"

- Don't let emails drag on and on. Men (and women) tend to hide behind a keyboard. This is a safe place for them to gather information without putting themselves out there on a date. I will show you how to handle this in our section on Online Dating.

- Make sure your signature is turned off if you have one created on your email account that shows your place of business, phone number, etc. We sometimes forget these show up on all our emails.

- Just like a phone call or text, an email in the beginning should lead to him asking you out. If you sense other ulterior reasons, cut him loose.

- As with texting, let him make the first move, unless it's a wink on an online dating site, or a short note to say you are interested. Keep it short!

"Keep the cute stuff at a minimum. I once had a girl write me a huge poem in the first email she sent me. I know she meant it to be flattering but it was over the top. Don't put a ton of questions or show us you spent wayyy too much time on a guy you haven't even met yet. This looks desperate." James*, 31, math teacher.

The First Date Rule Guide

You only get one chance to make a first impression. We've all heard it a million times. Your mother may have whispered that to you as she gently pushed you toward the Kindergarten doors. You may have been admonished about it when you were heading out to your first job interview. But when it comes to hitting it out of the park on your first date with a man over whom you are already forming butterflies in your stomach, it's a pretty big deal.

Here is where I hit you with some pretty big stuff. I will admit, even though I have worked with women for over 30 years to help them discover their self-worth and create a life of abundance, some of the insights the men gave me on that 98-question survey were eye-opening. All this time we were putting the emphasis on how we looked in order to get his heart racing. Here is "the rest of the story".

As we learned earlier, psychology is an amazing tool. The input that sets an individual's mind reeling is complex and varied. A busty blond causing one man's synapses to fire like the 4th of July, might leave another man's neurons stuck in neutral. "Beauty is in the eye of the beholder" has never carried more weight than in the world of dating.

When 2,000 men were asked if they were all looking for a beautiful woman, their answers were mature and surprising.

- "Beauty has become a commodity. Women think of beauty as makeup, great clothes and a killer figure. Are men visual? Of course we are. So are women. We are all programed to appreciate the components that make up a pleasing appearance. But where men differ from women is how we define beauty. Women will admire another woman with her face perfectly made up, wearing the latest fashion, and her hair perfectly coiffed. Men, on the other hand, are attracted more to a smiling face that isn't buried beneath a ton of cosmetics, a feminine quality, the way she carries herself, her confidence and that she is dressed in something that compliments her frame and personality. Frankly, her behavior trumps her looks when it comes to making a guy's heart race." Devon*, 43, artist.

- "I dated two different women over the course of a month. One was what most would call "drop dead gorgeous". She had the body of a swimsuit model, a beautiful face and hair that hung in waves to her waist. We went out three times before I couldn't spend one more minute with her. She was so dull and boring that a conversation with her was like eating cardboard. She had no opinions…about anything…and her conversation usually revolved around celebrity gossip. The second girl was pleasant-looking but not a head turner in the typical sense. She was a sister of a friend of mine who was moving to my area. I agreed to take her out. From the moment she sat down at the restaurant table I felt her sense of confidence. She smiled easily, her body language was casual and she looked like she loved life. The conversation was off the chart; she was witty and really seemed interested in my hobbies and job. When I asked her out again, she made me wait two weeks to see her because her calendar was full. I felt like I was back in High School mooning over this woman." Ryan*, 39, radiologist.

What I learned from these 2,000 males was that beauty is really only perception. We've all seen celebrities that did not register a 10 on the male Beautiful Richter Scale, but had men drooling over them. Why? Because their *behavior* caused a chemical, and emotional reaction. And let me make this clear…getting to a guy's heart is all about emotion. Without an emotional connection all you have are two buddies hanging out. These behavioral qualities come through in how a woman carries herself, her conversational acumen, feistiness, playfulness, exuding that little girl charm one minute and flipping it to a subtle siren the next. It's about kindness, compassion, being adventurous and spontaneous, and above all, confident. These traits create that elusive chemistry we hear so much about.

Of course you want to look your very best for your first date. But what these men are telling you is that you don't have to be perfect or look like you stepped off a magazine cover. Odds are he has seen you already—in person, a profile photo, or a friend's picture. Unless you misrepresented yourself in your photos, he has already decided he likes what he sees and would like to meet you.

Show up in something appropriate for the date. Leave the plunging V-necks at home, and play up your best assets. This could be your pretty eyes, great hair, long legs, and beautiful smile. Wear something you are comfortable in. We've all worn new clothes that we thought would look killer, only to be so uncomfortable that we couldn't breathe. Three layers of Spanx will not allow you to relax and enjoy the date. Now that you look your best, forget about it. Men dislike women who are constantly fussing with their clothes, hair or lipstick. It's time to give him your attention, which he will remember long after he remembers what you were wearing or if your lipstick was the latest shade of Mango Passion.

Arrive on time. A dramatic entrance is over-rated. Men value consideration and not keeping them waiting.

Smile when you see him; something warm and not overdone. Some of the men in the survey said a woman beaming like a lighthouse when she saw him made him a little nervous. Keep it casual but show you are happy to meet him.

Most men said they felt a handshake when they first met a woman was a little stilted and it made them wonder if, after seeing him up close, she was not as pleased with him as she had hoped. (Guys have major insecurities too.) A casual hug is perfectly acceptable and creates an easy closeness. It adds an element of relaxation to the date, and makes it easier at the end of the meeting for another hug, peck on the cheek or light kiss. Going from a handshake in the beginning to something more at the end is an awkward jump.

In the section on Etiquette we covered the social decorum expected at most public places. If your date (and most men will admit they could be better schooled in this area) takes off ahead of you in a restaurant instead of letting you follow the maître d' to the table, let it go. Teasing him will make him uncomfortable. Men hate...let me say it again...*hate* looking like a fool. It astonishes me how many women will make fun of their husband or date in public. It is not funny, and it will see you sitting home alone on the weekend. If he makes a guffaw, allow him to save face. Ignore it, or if he comments on it, play it down.

Be flexible. Sometimes the best laid plans go wrong. Be polite and spontaneous. It may rain on a day you planned a picnic. The restaurant he chose may be sold out. He may have gotten the movie times wrong, wore the wrong clothes, left his wallet at home (be suspicious of that one), and a million other little flies that appear in the everyday ointment. Go with the flow and you will be perceived as someone who is the opposite of the dreaded DQ label: DRAMA QUEEN.

Let me give you an example of a classy woman who I saw out in public at a popular restaurant. It was shortly after Christmas and this place was packed. They did a bustling breakfast business. She was seated at the table next to me with a nice-looking gentleman. I overheard him compliment her on her beautiful blouse. She beamed and said it was a Christmas present from her mother. Just then the waiter arrived, balancing a heavy tray laden with four plates of food. He was balancing the tray with one hand while placing glasses of juice in front of this woman and her date. Suddenly, the lady behind him slid her chair back, knocking the waiter in the back of his legs. He lost his balance and the tray tipped. Two plates of pancakes and syrup came pouring down over this woman, sending food and syrup all down her new blouse. Gasps went through the room and the waiter was frozen in horror.

I watched with one hand over my mouth for what I was sure would be a total melt-down on this woman's behalf. Instead, after her initial shock, she looked down at the goo that was now dripping onto her slacks, picked up her napkin and gathered the chunks of pancakes into it. She smiled sweetly at her date, accepted a damp cloth the manager hurriedly brought over to her, and then looked up at the waiter who was apologizing profusely. "It's a shirt," she said in a soft tone. "It will wash out. Tell you what though; I think I will have the omelet." The people around her laughed, the waiter looked like he wanted to kiss her and her date had this wonderful look of admiration on his face. She excused herself and was gone to the Ladies room for about ten minutes. When she came back, you could not tell there had been an accident, except for dampness on the thighs of her pants.

I heard her date ask how she got her blouse to look like nothing happened. She said, "Water, soap and a Turbo Hand Dryer." Then she smiled at him and said, "Where were we?" Needless to say, breakfast was on the house and she made one major favorable impression on everyone around her.

Women have no idea how much men want a woman like that. They are tired to death of the histrionics, drama, and "ME ME ME" mentality of so many women today. This shows them you are a woman of value and integrity. Believe me, he will not overlook that!

So now you have gotten past the awkward first moments of meeting each other, you are seated at a table, or parked in a theater chair, or sitting by a lake. The conversation can steer into the familiar, overly traveled currents of routine question and answer, or, you can take the helm, raise the main sail, and set the compass for something that will get his attention…and keep it! This is the area where most dates die and are buried in the "What Might Have Been" cemetery. After you learn the following techniques, you won't be one of them.

Sexual Tension Is Needed

When we talk about sexual tension, we are not talking about sexual innuendo, inappropriate comments, pole dancing, or stripper clothes. We are delving into the area that either makes or breaks a date, a relationship or a marriage. With all the emphasis on the 21st century woman, we have traded in our innate feminine mystique for power suits and Power Point Displays. If you think the way to gain a man's interest is to impress him with your career, your smarts, your trophies or your name dropping, you are in for a shock.

Let me say this in advance. These techniques are not about phony behavior, manipulation or "playing" someone.

Many women shrink from using their God-given femininity and magnetic appeal due to assumptions that for some reason the rules where men and women are concerned have changed.

WHY? How does the passage of time, women's rights, bra burning, glass ceiling busting and owning our own businesses have anything to do with what makes a guy's heart pound? Evolution may have picked our knuckles up off the ground but the male/female mystique is alive, if only slightly well. One of men's biggest complaints...today...in the 21st century, is that they have no idea how to handle themselves on a date anymore.

- "I'm afraid if I open a door for a woman she will yell at me. It's as if she thinks my opening her door somehow is condescending to her as this all-powerful female." Rick*, 32, sales.
- "I'm all for women CEO's, doctors, lawyers, sport casters and trophy game hunters. They are an inspiration to all of us. But when I'm on a date with a professional woman, I still want to be with a woman who appreciates a man and his version of romance. For most of us guys, that means opening her door, pulling out her chair, and even bringing flowers. I'll tell you. A lot of women are killing off how men feel about the whole dating thing." Barkley*, 56, pharmacist.
- "I'm a scientist. I know that a magnetic attraction consists of a field that is invisible but is responsible for creating a force that attracts or repels other elements. You can't change the magnet by saying the science behind it is outdated.

Magnetic attraction is either there or it isn't and it's based on laws that have been around forever. Men are either attracted or repelled by women based on a chemistry that the sexes respond to, and have responded to since Eve made that first apple pie. If you want a man to be attracted to you, you'll need to deal with him within that perimeter. You can change the rules if you want to. Just don't blame us if you don't get the result you were after." Damien*, 42, physicist.

- "Let me show you the other side, Ladies. Let's say your hubby came home crying because Jason at work made fun of his tie in front of the other guys. He is sobbing and saying Life is not fair. He runs into your arms for consolation, still sniffling and distraught. How attracted are you to him at this moment? Your sense of repulsion at his lack of masculinity is instinctual. Men feel the same way if a woman is exhibiting traits that are not feminine. It's instinct, inbred, and God Bless It!" William*, 60, restaurant owner.

- "If I want to spend an evening talking business, or dealing with someone on a superficial basis, I've got buddies for that. If we ask a woman out, we're kinda hoping for that feminine element that only the opposite sex can offer. A woman who is at home with her sexuality and knows how to make a guy feel like a million bucks will have them lined up at the door. I'm not talking bed hopping here. I mean a lady who knows how to rock the chemistry. It can reduce a guy to a simpering idiot." Phillip*, 38, casino owner.

"I actually had a woman show up on the first date with a roll of blueprints and a portfolio for a new project she was creating. We said Hello, shook hands and she spread the designs out on the table and talked shop the entire date. The waiter actually had to find a spot to put our food down because she had turned the surface into a conference table. Hint: If we ask you out, it's a date. It's not a meeting, conference or seminar—it's a date!" Rori, *38, investor.

What are the male-melting techniques men respond to? Let's take a look.

The Words That Captivate

Do you know where most first dates fizzle? It's the conversation. Many a man will tell you that the desire to ask a woman out for a second date had little to do with her looks and everything to do with how she made him feel. It was the woman who left the mundane at the curbside and challenged him, intrigued him and basically let him know this was a lady unlike any he had ever met. Do you think a man is going to let someone like that get away, just so he can spin the bottle and go out on another first date that might be the same old deadly questions and answers? I'm thinking, NO!

A typical first date conversation goes something like this:

Her: "So, where do you work?"

Him: "Acme concrete."
Her: "Really? Cool. What do you do there?"
Him: "I mix concrete."
Her: "Wow. I've never met someone who mixes concrete."
Him: "Yeah…well, I do."

Do you feel the cobwebs filling in between the words? Can you hear the death knoll clanging overhead? And it's not just because this guy mixes concrete for a living. It's the lifeless teeter-totter of empty words. Sexual chemistry couldn't bloom in that mine field if you added 3 bags of Miracle Grow.

How do we introduce chemistry into this ubiquitous first date opener? Like this:

Her: "So, what fills your days with passion?"
Him: "Uh…passion? Well, I don't know if you would call it passion but I work at a cement plant. It's pretty boring."
Her: "Boring? Alright, if you could choose any career right now that would bring a huge smile to your face, what it would it be? And don't pick African Tour Guide…that's mine."
Him: (Laughing) "Okkk…let's see. I love working with wood and a jigsaw. I've always wanted to make furniture."
Her: (Smiling) "That sounds amazing. You must be creative."

Look at the HUGE difference between these two scenarios! She introduced the word "passion" early on, which even on a subliminal level has triggered his interest. She was playful (one of our big rules for creating sexual tension), and she got him to *dream!* It is sooooo rare to meet a person who encourages your youthful, fantasy self to come out and play. Men will love you for that. Her mention of an African tour guide showed her sense of adventure, another trait on a guy's top 5 list. Let's try another one, and add the irresistible element of *touch*. First…the wrong way:

Her: "What do you like to do on your days off?"
Him: "Oh, it depends. Sometimes work on the yard. If there's a good game on the tube, I'll watch it, or hang out with friends. How about you?"
Her: "I like to do those things too. I'm one of those rare girls who actually like football games." (Sits with hands in lap.)

Okie Dokie. First mistake was agreeing with all his interests. Men dislike a girl without a mind of her own. It also came off as a little too eager to please to point out how desirable she is since she likes football. There is no spark or challenge here. Her body language is closed off. A better way to do this is…

Her: "You sound like you work hard so I'm guessing you play hard. Do you climb 14-er's, wrestle tigers or just a big steak on the grill?"
Him: (Grinning) "I have climbed a mountain or two. Tigers are harder to come by, but I do grill a mean steak."
Her: (Reaching out and touching him lightly on the wrist as she leans conspiratorially across the table to get closer to him.) "Is there a rare secret family recipe that you use on your steak rub? You know, one you would have to kill someone after divulging it? Because I might be interested in that." (Mock serious expression)

Him: (Laughing openly) "Now why would I tell you if I had to kill you afterward? You're much too fun to get rid of."

Her: (Leaning back with a mock cocky look) "That's true. Besides, I've never climbed a mountain so this will never work out." (Coy grin)

Him: "I could teach you. It's pretty amazing when you get to the top."

Her: (Mulling it over) "I guess I could let you teach me something new, but it will cost you that secret family recipe!"

Playful! Sexy! Confident! I guarantee you this guy is "buttah!" There is also something she slipped in that is very tricky and soooo effective. She slipped in a challenge. Something men can't resist. They will always rise to a challenge. Where is it in this conversation? It's where she says, "Because I might be interested in that." Really? That little sentence raised a challenge? Yep. "Because I *might...*" In his head he's thinking, "Or she might *not*. I want her to like it. I need to pass this test." Once again, psychology at work. The subtler the better.

An even more persuasive move was when she said, "This will never work out." Not only did she throw down the gauntlet with the words, she leaned back, adding distance. This is the rubber band theory that we will discuss later. She pulled back both verbally and physically and he is now panicking, just a little. He is feeling that he could blow this, even if he knows she is being cute. Notice his next remark? He will teach her how to mountain climb. I don't know about you, but I'm pretty sure he just set up a second date. These kind of playful challenges work like magic.

In one short conversation this woman managed to be playful, sensual (with a slight, innocent touch and leaning in), challenging and fun. This guy is thinking, "This is so cool. I'm really having fun with this woman!"

I'm not advocating that every line you utter is teasing and witty, or that you continually touch him. That gets old and he will suspect it's practiced and you used it on the last guy. This is where you switch it up and add sincere interest.

Her: "I've always wanted to ask a man, is it hard to be in a work place where you feel other males competing with you? I would think it requires a lot of confidence and tact."
Him: (Thinking for a moment) "I don't know if it's competition exactly, but we do feel a need to rise up the corporate ladder. I guess that means trying harder than the next guy."
Her: "I admire that kind of drive. Women often find it hard competing in the work place as well. You don't strike me as the kind of man who would undermine someone to get to where you're going."

He will now pick up the ball and talk about being a man and competing for a paycheck. If she listens carefully to him, he will see a different side of her...a caring side that is interested in his values. This is powerful as most women (and men) are too busy thinking of something clever to say next. As we talked about in an earlier chapter, really listen between the lines. He is probably saying things he hopes you will admire. Don't overdo the flattery. She's already given him a pat on the back in a way that goes straight to a guy's heart…she complimented his masculine nature when she talked about admiring his drive.

Men love feeling admired, challenged and flirted with. This must all be done with discretion and variety. Think of it as a great movie; there are elements of intrigue, humor, passion and revelation. If a movie stayed in one element, our emotions would not be piqued. An amazing movie takes those emotions and puts them on a thrill ride with twists and turns. If you can keep a guy guessing as to what you are going to come with next, he'll keep coming back for more.

The bottom line is this. When he's out on a date with you, he is always thinking, "What would life be like with this woman?" If your conversation is boring, predictable, all business and non-stop, that's the future he'll see with you. If it's adventurous, playful, sensual (touch), unpredictable, challenging and intelligent, he will envision a lifetime of laughter, fun, great conversation, and intimacy. Which would you choose?

Your Demeanor: Confidence On Display!

Men will tell you that the way a woman walks, holds herself, surveys a room and uses her hands is very captivating. If she moves in fluid lines, with her shoulders back and hips forward, she will exude confidence and femininity.

Take a moment to look at yourself sideways in a mirror. Don't fix anything yet, just stand the way you normally do. Are your shoulders slumped? Are your breasts hanging down toward your stomach? Is your tummy pouched out, hips thrown back and knees locked? This kind of posture makes you look frumpy, tired and not very appealing.

Now, lift your shoulders up to your ear lobes in an exaggerated shrug. Roll them back as far as they can go, and drop them. This is the correct position for your spine. This gives you an erect, confident line that gets noticed. Put your chest out, and bring your hips forward. The reason models always stand with one foot ahead of the other is that it gives their figure a pleasing, curvy line. When we stand with our feet side by side, our hips and butt are squared off and sticking out. When you walk, bend your knees slightly, put your hips in front, and keep your shoulders back. You will have a more youthful appearance, and look 5 pounds lighter.

Slow down. Women who walk with quick, long strides look masculine. Take your time when you enter a room, stop and look around. It is the height of confidence to "take in" a room when you arrive. Most of us hurry to find our table or a convenient corner to hide in. Maintain eye contact. If you catch someone's eye, smile sincerely, and move on.

Men notice women's hands. Besides wanting your nails to look nice, make sure you are wearing a nice moisturizer. If he touches your hand, you don't want dry, flaky skin. As for using your hands, keep your movements light and airy. Gripping things, twisting your napkin, placing both hands palm down on the table are not feminine moves. Neither is placing your hands on your hips, unless you are being playful and showing faked anger. Don't fidget with your tableware or play with your hair or jewelry. You want an image of cool confidence; that you are relaxed and enjoying the company.

If you shake hands, keep your grip firm but not crushing. As we said, No one likes the "limp fish" handshake or the "bone-crusher". Maintain eye contact as you shake hands and smile.

If you are at a restaurant, give your waiters your full attention and smile at them. They deal with grumpy customers all day. Men notice when a woman is kind to the wait staff, doesn't ask for special treatment and is quick and decisive about her order. Extra bonus points for asking your date or waiter to recommend a fun new drink that would pair nicely with your order. Show your willingness to be adventurous and try something new.

A woman's calm demeanor soothes a man. It is the opposite of the flighty, high-maintenance façade of a woman he perceives to be a lot of work. His guy buddies are usually loud, aggressive and in his face. To be seated across from someone who shows refinement, is poised and feminine is a huge refuge for his overworked mind. When you add the playfulness, he sees you as youthful, fun and spontaneous…all good things!

Do the Unexpected!

We've talked about saying the unexpected when building that conversational bonding on the first date. Now, DO the unexpected.

- If you're at a place where there's a fountain, stop, hand him a penny and tell him to make a wish with you.
- If you're walking down the sidewalk together, playfully bump his hip and say, "Oh, I'm so sorry. I didn't see you there." Grin.

- Offer to guess a number he's thinking of, pause, screw up your face in concentration and then say, "It's no use. There's just wayyy too much going on in there!"
- If you pass a claw machine, stop, grab two quarters and challenge him to see who can get the toy.
- While waiting in line to order popcorn, a drink, an ice cream cone, etc., turn to him and ask, "What flavor would you create if you were in charge of the menu?"
- Ask him to open a jar or bottle for you…this still works. My sons love it when I say, "May I borrow your rippling muscles for a moment?" NO MAN ALIVE is going to pass up tackling that jar!
- If you are in his car, teasingly ask if he has any Barbra Streisand CD's. If he says, "No," pull a pretend pout and say, "Pity. That was your test to see if you are in touch with your feminine side." Smile at him.

We will go into more ideas for dates in the next chapter when we discuss the follow-up, *Dates 2-5*. For now, remember to relax on the first date. One thing that works for me is to take the pressure off as I leave the house to go and meet him. I simply tell myself I am going to meet a nice man, have a lovely conversation and a nice dinner. I may be meeting a new friend, business contact, or someone I would like to date again. I also put myself in the mindset of, "We'll see if I like him." This eliminates our usual concern of "Will he like *me*?" Put the ball in your court. Believe me…he is wondering the same thing as you are—"will she like me?" If you follow the guidelines laid out in this chapter, you will be way ahead of the game.

Watch Out For The Hook!

A word of caution when you are just starting out in the dating world: We have all heard the joyous exclamations from friends who come floating in the door after a first date, their hands clasped in ecstasy, eyes rolled back into their head, proclaiming, "I met him! He's the ONE! It was instant attraction…like lightning hitting. I swear I heard violins and angels singing!"

Does this sound wonderful? A once-in-a-lifetime dream come true? Psychologists will tell you that if you feel an immediate and overwhelming attachment to someone you just met, it could mean something quite different from the stuff dreams are made of.

Our subliminal mind is always on the alert, ready to send out signals based on our memories and experiences. We've all heard the phrase "comfort zone" when dealing with areas of our lives that feel familiar. We gravitate to them because they feel safe…this is something we know. Oddly enough, some of those areas of familiarity came from circumstances that could hardly be considered "safe". A perfect example is women marrying men with alcoholic tendencies even when their young lives were fraught with worry and fear from living with a father or caretaker that abused alcohol. We've all heard of the abuse cycle where abused children will often grow up to be abusers, or marry abusive men. Why is this? Because we naturally gravitate toward the known. It is often less frightening than chartering unknown territories.

"The hook" is that emotional connection that often happens on a subliminal level. We feel an instant attraction to a person's personality traits, and even physical appearance and don't really know why. We only know there is a huge spark here, and we misread it as chemistry.

Here is an example. I dated a man for several years. On the face of it he was very good to me, providing me with every material thing I could ever want. He fixed my car, cooked elaborate meals (complete with candles and music), came running if I had something break. Yet the relationship was fraught with problems. He was unable to connect on an emotional level. The conversation was pretty empty and the times I asked him for help in an area requiring emotional support, he would shrug his shoulders and leave me hanging. There were a lot of anger issues and I found myself walking on eggshells, afraid to confront him on how he was making me feel. He made fun of me in public, and in private, and found it hard to compliment my achievements. Many of my friends and family could not understand why I kept dating him.

Then one day, after reading an article on instant attraction, it hit me. He was exhibiting many of the traits my father had. My parents divorced when I was six and my father was pretty much absent in my formative years. When I was around him, he would tease me, get angry if I did something wrong or showed weakness, and if I went to him for help he would say, "Now, Becky…you can do this," pretty much leaving me hanging. I walked on eggshells around him because I was afraid he would disappear from my life again if I didn't please him. I spent all my days trying to impress him and show him I was worthy of his love.

There was the hook! In red neon letters. My unreasonable attraction to a man that was not the best choice for me if I wanted a nurturing, emotionally fulfilling relationship, was due to subliminal signals saying, "You know this. This is familiar." I think on a deeper level I even believed if I could get this man's unconditional love and approval, it would be as if I finally found what I had missed with my father; I had finally fixed it.

Just be aware that if you feel an instant, overpowering attraction to a stranger, look beneath the surface. Look into your past for similar traits. If they are reflections of a relationship that did not encourage you to be your best self—run!

On the flip side, we may meet a great guy and feel no immediate spark. He may not look like our usual preference in a man. Again, this could be that subliminal mindset whispering in your ear, "This is not familiar. Let's move along." My recommendation is to give this guy a second chance. Most people are nervous on a first date and may not be showcasing who they really are. It is surprising how many married men told me that the woman they married did not really turn their head on the first date, but she suddenly blossomed on the second, third, fourth…you get the picture. I have typically walked away from guys who on the first date didn't seem like the tall, lanky, alpha male that I gravitated toward.

I recently saw all the traits in a man I was looking for...kindness, romance, compassion, witty, smart and adventurous. Yet, he was not my tall, lanky stereotype, and he was quieter than what I usually respond to. But I saw something in him, and wanted to give this one a chance. Sure enough, on the second date he was more outspoken, challenging and a great deal of fun. I found myself letting go of the old go-to traits and opened the door to something truly life-changing. So, give that guy who seems to find you special, who makes time for you and encourages you to be your best self, *your* time. He may just surprise you!

Booby Traps!

Just when you thought your head was already exploding with information about the first date, I come along to warn you of something that is, to be honest, a little insidious. There are booby traps a man will set for a woman on the first or second date that could cancel her out. Not all men, but a pretty fair grouping of them admitted to setting these traps in an effort to find out information without coming right out and asking for it.

This question on my survey of the 2,000 guys actually met with a few hostile comments. Men said, that while they admit these booby traps aren't playing fair, they screamed that women were just as guilty of coming up with sneaky little ways to find out what they wanted to know about their date, and often the man's answers had him ruled out straight out of the gate. That being said, here are a few snares you need to be aware of:

"Are You The 'Sex On The First Date Type' Trap?"

No guy is going to come right out and ask you this, and if he does he's a slime bag and you should already be heading for the door. In an effort to find out if he has a shot at seeing your boudoir on the first date, a man might try something like this, which by the way, actually happened to a friend of mine:

Him: "I am really shocked at how forward women are these days. My buddies have even mentioned that a large number of women on dating sites are hoping to have sex on the first date."

He will now know where you stand by your comment to this statement. If you shrug and say it's "no big deal, we're all adults here," he knows a one-night stand is looking good, or, vice versa, your values are not what he's looking for. If, on the other hand, you look shocked and say you could never do something like that, he has the information he needs. If he is looking for only a hook-up, you were just ruled out from having a second date. If he is looking for a long-term relationship with a woman who is more discriminating, you just passed a test you may not have known you were taking. This next one is even more devious, and again, it happened to a woman I know:

Him: "Things have changed so much since I was dating back in High School and College. I've had women come on to me for sex on the first date. I'm old-fashioned and it kind of makes me mad that I am." (He laughs here)

This opens the door again for your comment, or in this case to ask him why that would make him mad, which my friend did. He replied, "It makes me mad because I'm a good guy and missing out on all these great opportunities." Again he laughs to keep it light, but he is watching her reaction. When my friend merely smiled and side-stepped the trap, he brought it up again 15 minutes later, repeating what he had said the first time. "Yep, I get mad at myself for being so old-fashioned."

If someone brings up the same subject twice, you can bet they didn't get the response they were hoping for the first time. My friend's response to him the second time he brought it up was perfect. She said, "We all march to our own drum beat, don't we?" She said he looked slightly annoyed at her comment. Basically he just walked away with an empty bag. He received no information, although it was obvious he was hoping she was going to enlighten him as to her sexual preferences, something that is no one's business that early into a dating relationship. Calling himself "old-fashioned" also kept him in a safe area as he could point to that if she saw through what he was doing and called him on it. As it turned out, he saw her two more times and vanished when she kept the cuddling on the couch to a minimum. So much for "old-fashioned."

The "What's Your Baggage?" Trap

I have to give credit where it's due—this is sheer genius. Here's how it works:

Your date confides something very personal about himself to you during the date, usually when the two of you are more relaxed with each other and have covered several topics. He leans in a little, clasps his hands and looks as though the next thing coming is a little hard for him to divulge. It usually goes something like this:

Him: "I guess I should probably tell you something. It's something I'm not proud of, but I like you and I want you know there was a time I struggled with alcohol addiction. It was a tough time in my life and I'm stronger now. I just wanted you to know."
Her: "I'm so sorry. A lot of people struggle with things like that. In fact, if it makes you feel better, I used to have a drug problem. I don't get near the stuff now, but for a while it really messed up my life."

Did you see how the magician did this trick? Pretty slick, isn't it? The woman is completely taken in by the confession, and flattered that he already likes her enough to tell her something so personal. She hurries to allow him to save face by sharing her own lapse of judgment. He obviously wants to see more of her and sees the potential for a long-term relationship here, right? Not exactly. By creating a sense of false security in revealing something unpleasant about himself (which may or may not be true), he has lured her into the trap of revealing something very personal about *herself* that probably would not have been discussed until later in the dating process. In this case, the lady never heard from him again, and spent the next several weeks wondering where she went wrong on the date. It seemed to be going so well.

There are many versions of the Baggage Trap. He may bring up abusive parents, siblings doing jail time, bad credit, debt, mentioning his ex is still bugging him, all sorts of things that will lull you into a sense of bonding so that you will share all your skeletons on the first or second date. If this happens, and you want to take your time telling him your personal history (which you should), just listen attentively to his tale of woe and comment in a compassionate manner without divulging anything about your own state of affairs. You can say something like, "You know, I think Life's challenges make us stronger, don't you? I'm sure you're proud of the strides you've made to have a happier life." This way, if he was just sharing with you, you've come across as caring and mature. If it was a fishing expedition to find out your baggage ratio, he is going home with an empty stringer.

The "Are You Dating Other Guys" Trap

Most men admitted they are too proud, and/or insecure to ask a woman straight out on the first date if she is dating other guys at the same time. In an effort to see how many other guys are sharing her dating locker room, he may throw this out:

Him: "So how is the Date 'Em & Mate 'Em site working for you?"

Her: "It's okay. It's not the optimum way to meet people but I work from home so I don't get the chance to meet many men and I'm not into the bar scene."

Him: "Are the guys on there pretty much what they have in their profiles? I know a lot of people lie about their age, weight and stuff like that."

Her: "Yeah, most of them are pretty truthful. How about you? Do you find the women look like their pictures?"

Him: "Oh, I just barely got on the site, so I don't have much experience with it. You sound like you've got it figured out. How long have you been on it?"

Her: "About 4 months, off and on."

Him: "How's it working for you?"

Her: "It's fine." (Starting to feel a little uncomfortable)

Him: "I'm not sure if I agree that you should date more than one person at a time. I know it speeds up the selection process but I'm more of a one-girl-at-at-time kind of guy."

Her: "That's nice. But then if you look at the question of whether or not to become exclusive with someone, wouldn't that mean that a lot of people are dating more than one person?"

Him: (Looking none too pleased.) "I suppose."

In this scenario our Hero has put several hooks in the water at the same time. He is trying to find out how long she has been on a dating sight, which might alert him to the fact that if she's been there a long time, there are a lot of guys not biting her hook. Is she weird? Is she a serial dater? The "How's it working for you?" is another way of finding out if she has had any successful relationships, possibly how long they lasted and what went wrong. His honorable good guy statement that he only dates one girl at a time may or may not be true, but his hope was to make her feel secure with him, enough to spill it. He never got his answer, although she hinted that multiple dating seemed natural or why would a couple in love decide to "become exclusive."

You will be surprised at how often men bring up the dating sites, especially if they met you on one, and ask how it's working for you. A pat answer of "It's a different world, that's for sure," is all you need to say. You will discover his motives the more he presses for information.

The "What Are You Looking For?" Trap

This one is a gray area. A lot of people who begin dating someone will eventually ask this question. It may be innocuous and information gathering. Just be careful with your answers. Less is more. Many a desirable damsel has been left at the dating threshold due to a trait she mentioned on her wish list that didn't match his. She may be looking for someone who loves extreme sports and his definition of extreme is watching two ball games at once on ESPN. Her biggest desire is for a guy who likes to travel. He interrupts that as she's looking for someone with a lot of money who can take her on endless trips. She may mention witty, and he feels his best shot at wit is repeating a joke he heard at the water cooler.

Of course there are the 5-star blunders such as mentioning marriage, kids, a big house and her parents having a loft over the garage. You think I'm kidding? 68% of the men on the survey said women brought up wanting kids on the first date. They mentioned their "biological clock" over the entrée, and their desire to "marry someone within 6 months" over dessert. The only clock the men heard was the time bombs going off all over the place.

If he asks you what you're looking for, try this: "Probably the same things most people are. Happiness and a sense of a life well lived. I have a fantastic life. If someone comes along who would be a good fit for sharing it with me, that would be nice. I assume that's why we are all out there dating." A soft smile and change the subject.

Let him discover for himself through future conversations what you are about. Don't give too much away, and I will tell you why. On a first date, most people are looking for something wrong with the person across from them. With the plethora of people on dating sites it has become a disposable society. "If this one doesn't work out, there are twenty more within 5 miles of here that will work," is the thought process.

The other reason for looking for warning signs on a first date is to save time. Men typically pay for the first date, and often the next two or three. If this woman is going to turn out to be a psycho or manifest undesirable qualities, he would prefer to find out now. While I can see the pragmatism in this, it puts a date on rather shaky ground right from the start.

There is such a thing as timing in the dating process. On a first date, as I mentioned, most people are looking for red flags. Keep it light, don't disclose too much. If you continue to date, he will become more comfortable with you and appreciate all the unique qualities that make you so great to be with. Once that starts happening, if you let him in on something that may have been too heavy on the first date, he is more apt to balance it against all the great traits he discovered about you and the happiness you bring to his life. The scale has tipped in your favor during the follow-up dates, whereas that same scale may have been precariously tipping back and forth on the first date. Finding out the negatives at the very beginning is too soon, and you will be checked off as he yells, "NEXT!"

The "Dangling Carrot" Trap

This little beauty is really devious, and sadly, effective. He will bring up something on the first date that is meant to tempt you, while at the same time giving you a false sense of commitment. Here's how it works:

Him: "Oh, by the way, I have something exciting coming up in October." (Which is 4 months away.) "I drive a Maserati and I've been invited to their VIP launch in Italy mid-October. It's for me and a guest." Here, he smiles at you and gives the impression you might be the lucky guest. He may even say, "If things work out with us, how does Italy in the fall sound?"

This works in his favor because he has now moved this relationship along faster than it normally would have. And odds are, it is to make you feel he is interested in you long-term already, and there is something really cool on the horizon line (Italy). If you don't date him again, you lose out on Rome. Other versions are mentioning parties, tickets to an event, etc. The point is, this is a false sense of security. His motive is probably to get you into an intimate relationship sooner than later. He may be legit, but just be careful with the Carrot Danglers early on!

An effective way to handle this, and give him notice you are not easily won over with enticements is to say, "How nice for you. Let's see how it goes." Keep it light and smile. If he doesn't call again, you know the carrot is now being dangled before the next victim.

The "Sooo...what went wrong with your ex?" Trap

This is such a common thing to ask on a first date that it must be in the fine print somewhere of questions for first meetings. I would hazard that this question is put forth on 80% of first dates.

Him: "Sooo, what went wrong with your marriage?" (Or your last boyfriend, relationship, etc.)

While we may feel he is showing interest in us, even wanting to validate our feelings over a painful past, odds are the question is posed to ascertain if he sees any red flags about *you*! Depending on how you answer this question he can find out quite a bit about you and the way you view men, how you handle disappointment or anger, what issues push your buttons, if you cheated on your husband, put him through a messy divorce settlement, and currently have his head mounted over the fireplace in your family room.

If you answer with hostility toward your ex, it may signal him that you still have deep, unresolved feelings. Even feelings of anger are feelings, and most men don't want to get involved in a relationship where there are still residual emotions. They want to know you have moved on, healed the wounds and are ready for something positive and nurturing.

Showing anger can also get him thinking, "This could be how she will feel about me in the near future. Maybe she holds grudges, flies off the handle, believes in revenge or is a man-hater." There are a lot of men out there who see a high percentage of women as "male bashers."

If you bring up the ex's interfering family, he may wonder if you will see his family as a nuisance. If you say money was an issue, he may think you may want things beyond his financial ability to provide them. Mentioning depriving the ex of visiting privileges with his kids will paint you as unfeeling and harsh (even if there are extenuating circumstances), and going on about how he called you fat, ugly, unreasonable, etc., will only make the new guy across from you visualize you in a way you really don't want.

Another aspect of showing unresolved anger is a man may wonder if the ex is still in the picture, perhaps stalking you or causing you problems. No man wants to saddle up and ride a horse into the enemy camp when he just met a woman. He pictures hours of you complaining to him on the phone about this guy, or asking him to come over and deal with the ex if he shows up on your doorstep.

Men will glean a great deal of information from the simple question, "What went wrong?" A safe rule of thumb is to keep it positive and short. A first date is not the time to air dirty laundry. An answer such as, "Well, we all know relationships can be complex. Things can happen where two people, for whatever reason, believe it is not a positive place to be anymore. I do wish him happiness, and I am looking forward to a great future."

This shows him a mature woman with no baggage still tagged "bad break-up." He sees someone excited about a new life. You also come across as someone who handles disappointment and conflict with calm and resolve…all good things from the male perspective.

I believe most people going out on a first date are secretly hoping they might be meeting someone special. This could be the beginning of a wonderful relationship. Dating is stressful and most people would like to find someone they are compatible with sooner than later. Just beware of the Booby Traps, rein in your desire to tell him your life story, add sexual tension and playfulness, really listen to what he is saying, and relax and have fun. Successful first dates are happening every day.

Chapter Four
Dates 2 – 5

The exhilaration of being asked out on a second date is wonderful. You feel as if you've passed a test, won a prize, measured up and done something right. Well, you could look at it that way, or simply see it as a chance to get a closer look at him, his values, personality, and the way he treats you to decide if *he* has won the prize, measured up, passed the test and done something right.

I realize we are hoping each new date might be someone special. Unless you are one of those women who use men just to get a free dinner, most of us go out on a date with high hopes. It may be summer is coming and we have dreams of doing all the fun things people do when the sun is out and water and festivals beckon. It may be the holidays are closing in and we want to share the magic with someone who makes our hearts melt. Or, it could just be wanting that wonderful relationship that adds balance to our life.

The only thing to remember is this: it's just a date. You don't know him yet. He may not be someone you would enjoy spending time with. Never put yourself in the inferior position by wanting a first date to be perfect and special too much, too soon. It's just two people meeting to test the waters. You are in control of how this goes. How are you in control? Simple. You control how you will feel if it is not what you were hoping for, or if he doesn't seem interested. If he does ask you out again, you control your answer of Yes or No. Men admitted that women control the timing and rhythm of relationships. We'll cover just what that means later. Right now, let's see what happened if he didn't call after the first date.

Why Hasn't He Called?

It was an amazing first date. He complimented your new haircut, asked about your interests, job and friends. You laughed, he touched your hand during dessert, walked you to your car and kissed your cheek. Birds are singing, colors are brighter, every song on the radio now sounds like it's being played just for you. You can't wait to hear from him and go out again. You even wrote his name with your finger in the steam on your mirror this morning after your shower.

And then...nothing...crickets. One day goes by, and then another. You are now analyzing every word and move from the date to see what went wrong. Why isn't he calling?

There are so many reasons a man doesn't call after the first date. But rather than hear from me, let's hear it from the source.

- Randy*, 39, retail owner. "I know women think it's hard for a guy to ask for that first date, and they're right, it is. But believe it or not, it's even harder to ask for the second date. Now it's personal. She's met you. She has a sense of you now. So, if she turns you down now for a second date, it is a big shot to the ego. Some of us just find it easier not to call than to risk that kind of rejection."

- James*, 45, sales. "You know, it's pretty much all about chemistry. She may have been really pretty and nice, but if the spark isn't there, there's no real pull to ask her out again. Most women make the mistake of trying too hard to please...you know, agreeing with everything you say, or ordering the same thing. In truth, guys like a girl with a mind of her own that challenges him a little. Feisty is fun, as long as it's not turned into 'man-eater'."

- Rico*, 26, finance student. "A lot of guys don't call because they thought their date was too negative. A lot of girls complain a lot, gossip or make fun of other people. When that happens, we are thinking, "What does she say behind my back?" or, "Will she be dissing my mom, sister, or friends?" Guys do think that way, believe it!"

- Norm*, 33, consultant. "Some women are just too aggressive. One lady I was out with ordered for me, made fun of my political views, shot me down for opening her car door, bossed the waiter around and talked shop all night. It's hard to feel romantic under those conditions."

- Richard*, 62. "I can feel the bullets flying, but here is the skinny. Men size up women in these terms: Do we think she will be fun (in public, in bed, around our friends, family); is she spontaneous, did she flirt with me or tease me a little, is she kind and compassionate, was she easy to be with, did she challenge me mentally? We are seriously seeing if she brings us a future of excitement and adventure, or one of drama, unceasing demands or boredom. That's how we think. If women were honest, they would admit to sizing up guys in similar ways. No one wants to be around someone who is boring and you have to pull every word out of them, or they have no interests or passions, or they give the vibe they are about as far from a romantic lover as you can get."

- Nate*30, car salesman. "Women who need constant reinforcement are so tiresome. Men love to compliment a woman, but if his compliment gets shot down with a "Oh no, I'm overweight, but I'm trying a new diet," or, "I think my haircut makes my face look fat, but thanks anyway," we finally give up trying. Then there's the begging for a compliment, like "Do you like smart women?" or, "Do these jeans make me look fat?" Bottom line, if we give you a compliment, just say "Thank you." Turning it down makes us feel like we have bad judgment and it's awkward. Don't put yourself down or ask for compliments. It looks needy and that's a real turn-off. I often don't call a girl back if she just came off as too desperate or down on herself."

- Dave*, 49, advertising. "Have you ever been out with someone that was cardboard? I mean it was like sitting across from a cardboard cut-out of a human being. No dimension, no substance, no variance of personality. Men like variety, in all departments. A girl that is just funny, or just sexy, or just smart, or just career-minded, or just athletic, becomes boring. A woman that can be serious one minute, throw in some little girl zest the next, be teasing and playful, up on current events and has a mind of her own, is a girl we won't get tired of. Bring the variety!"

- Brad*, 24, student. "I had a date with a girl who could not...could NOT quit talking about her ex. How he fixed her car, took care of her dog when she was out-of-town, mowed her lawn, etc. I finally wondered if this guy was so great, did he dump *her*? No one wants to be compared to another guy, hear about your past dates, ex-husbands or list of the traits a guy has to have to make your A-list. On the same note, if you are talking about how bad your ex's are, we are wondering if all those bad relationships may have more to do with you than them! Either way, it's a no-win. We just paid for your dinner (or movie, ice cream cone, or ice skates). Give us the courtesy of focusing on us, not the ghosts of Relationships Past."

- Mark*, 53, radiologist. "I can't stand a woman who jumps on your mistakes. If I spill something, let me save face. If I mispronounce a word, so what? If I trip in the parking lot, it happens! Guys have an innate fear of looking stupid, especially in front of a girl. Take a tip from the Disney movie *Frozen*, and "Let It Go!'" We appreciate someone who just ignores the mistakes and acts like they didn't happen.

- Franklin*, 44, attorney. "Women who complain a man did not call them back because he was intimidated by her success are fooling themselves. We men find accomplished women very sexy. Odds are she either talked about her success too much on the date, talked career goals all night or failed to show interest in my pursuits and just came off as a non-stop business Diva. We want to know you can leave work behind and just relax and are fun to be with. Sure, I want to hear about your day and your aspirations, but keep it in perspective. And big tip—let the man find out about you in stages. It adds to the mystery, and our appreciation of you grows with each new thing we find out about you."

And lastly, 33% of the men I surveyed said they didn't call back for the sheer reason they were afraid to. Some said they felt they had nothing to offer her that she couldn't get for herself, and a life of feeling useless was something they couldn't face. Many felt she was too busy to fit him into her life, and 12% said they weren't ready to be involved with a woman who had small children at home. 15% said a guy will say "I'll call you" just as a way to end the date rather than leave it hanging. He may or may not actually intend to call.

You can beat yourself up trying to figure out why he didn't call, but the bottom line is, if he didn't, you have your answer...something just didn't click. It happens to all of us.

Personalities and needs are a complex thing and we will never be everyone's cup of tea. Remember the section on Booby Traps? He may have set one for you and ruled you out. Sometimes, that's a thing for which to be grateful.

For the record, if he didn't call, you may have just dodged a bullet, which we will cover in Chapter 7: The Toad Pool.

Keeping the Attraction Going

You are going on a second date, or third or fourth... It feels nice. It may lead to something wonderful and you may have the chance to enhance another life, just as he brings new interests and dimension to yours. That's what bringing people into our lives does. So now that you have his attention, how do you proceed? Gentlemen...your answers, please.

- Ryley*, 41, tax accountant. "In a nutshell, show us what a future with you would be like. Are you fun, happy, spontaneous, adventurous, affectionate, enjoy life, have interests and passions of your own? The best date I ever had was with a woman who asked if she could plan our fourth date. I was pleasantly surprised and said, "Sure, that would be great!" She showed up at my door with a picnic basket, blanket and wine, and loaded me into her car. We drove up into the mountains to a small resort town, spread the blanket by a river, and had an amazing lunch of salmon on crackers, fresh fruit, cheeses and wine. We waded in the mountain stream, skipped rocks and made up stories of the early miners. Just when I thought it couldn't get any better, she takes me to an arcade in the town that has bumper boats, race cars and miniature golf. I felt the inner kid in me come out to play...and as an accountant, that's been a long time coming!"

- Bradley*, 24, store manager. "If a girl keeps us guessing as to what's coming next, it's amazing. I don't mean by having multiple personalities, but always up for something fun. Guys always have to plan something, so if a girl comes up with a plan, it's totally cool!"

- Mitch*, 38, oil rig engineer. "I think most relationships die off due to boredom. I'll give you an example. If you put a bunch of guys together with nothing to do, they can make a game out of tossing wadded up paper cups into a garbage can. We detest boredom. Why do you think all the TV blooper shows have all these dummies jumping off roofs, riding a skateboard down a long row of steps, blowing up cans and hanging from trees? We crave adventure, even when it means a full body cast the next day. I don't need a girl to be into Extreme Sports, but have a sense of adventure, even if it's just climbing a trail. The way to a guy's heart is through his hiking boots!"

- Denice*, 53, graphic designer. "If a woman is aware that dates can be expensive (dinners, gas, movies, flowers, etc.) and shows her appreciation of my time and wallet, it goes a long way! Someone who will make me a dinner after we've gone out several times, or opts for a hot dog stand instead of linen tablecloths, who says, "Why don't we just watch a movie tonight and eat junk food?", that shows a man you care about him and appreciate his efforts to please you. It's rare…and it's so wonderful!"

- Mike*, 21, engineering student. "No drama. That's it—no drama. I have so many friends who quit dating a girl due to the complaining, him always trying to cheer her up, her fights with her family and friends. It's a pain! If you want to keep being asked out on dates, make us want to be with you. Give us a break from work and studies and let's laugh a little."

- Carson*, 65, retired. "I like women who are kind. Women who are considerate of me and others. There are a lot of angry women out there. There are angry guys too, but we're talking about what men want in a relationship. Just relax, be yourself and show some kindness. Most of us are battle-scarred from previous relationships that went bad so our "anger antenna" is always quivering."

- Wesley*, 40, RV sales. "Simple things are cool. Board games, a movie at home, watching a game on TV, or just going for a walk around a lake. My buddies have told me, and I agree, those are the times they remember most. Not the fancy planned dates, but the ones that make us think every day with you could be easy and nice."

- Howie*, 39, physical trainer. "I like little things that say she is thinking of me. My girlfriend left a note under my windshield wiper that I found when leaving for work one morning. It said, "Have I told you lately you have amazing arms?" Most guys want great guns so this was a huge ego boost. Needless to say I cut work short that day."

- Jose*, 25, restaurant manager. "I used to hear my dad say that "If you find a woman who appreciates you, keep her." When you're a teenager appreciation isn't really on your short list for a girl. But now, I GET IT. If I do something nice for a girl, and she doesn't show some kind of appreciation, it's a pretty dull feeling. And I'm not likely to repeat doing things for her."

- Wayne*, 42, dentist. "News Flash! Guys like being admired! I know—who knew, right? We like to have our brains, our bodies, our sexual prowess, our job skills, our ability to fix your car, our lousy singing voice, our dumb jokes, and our questionable fashion sense admired. We don't want manipulation or overkill in this area—just let us know you admire us and we bring something to your life. Men often only hear about what they're doing wrong at work or on a basketball court. We get the daggers all day long. Give us a woman who makes us feel like a million bucks and we will walk a million miles to be with her."

- Josh*, 48, male nurse. "I like the little girl stuff. You know, a woman who isn't afraid to be cute and pinch my cheek, gets excited over stuff, likes me to do things for her and appreciates it. My girlfriend does baby talk to me sometimes and I like it…not all the time, but just being playful. She also makes me feel great about my body. She recently came up to me in the kitchen and put her arms around my neck, looked up at me and said, "If you get arrested for that rockin' body of yours, I can't afford bail right now." I floated around all day long!"

- Archie*, 34, fishing guide. "I think women overthink things. Men are pretty basic. Stop trying to read something into something we said or did. Most relationships self-destruct because it became too much work to please someone. Shrug it off, unless it was something we did that was hurtful. If so, then just tell us without bashing us over the head and let us know it hurt your feelings and why. If we care about you, we won't want to make you feel anything but happy. But if every step we take is tiptoeing through a land mine, it gets ugly real fast. A sense of humor over the little issues is a huge turn-on. We aren't as bad as you think."

- Winston*, wine maker. "You know what keeps a relationship going? Finding a woman who makes you feel like you're special. It can be her words, her actions, and a look. Men are just little boys with a lot of responsibility on their shoulders who wish they could set it all down for a while and feel like a Super Hero in someone's eyes. It may sound hokey but that's how we feel. We're too proud to tell you, but we would kill to find someone who thinks we are the best thing since online shopping. Don't women want that too? Someone who makes them feel like they're on a pedestal and really special? I'm not sure why we're so ashamed to admit it. It's human nature to want to be noticed, appreciated and loved."

- Ryan*, 37, flight steward. "Just because we are dating a woman doesn't mean we want her to suddenly make us her world. If a woman still pursues her own interests, hangs out with her friends and isn't available every time we call, that keeps us interested. We are still looking for a challenge. Don't make it too easy for us. I don't mean game playing or hard to get. Just let us know we still have to work a little to get your time. It's what keeps a lot of guys coming back. Be busy some nights so that we know you aren't waiting by the phone. And please!!! Don't overdue the emails, texts and phone calls! It will kill off a good thing faster than a Colorado snow melt. If we text you, call you or email you, wait a little bit before you return the message. It makes us wonder what you are doing. Jumping on a text or email makes us think you are sitting with the phone in your hand just waiting for the "ping". This is the inside scoop, ladies. ☺"

Over 80% of the men polled in the survey said that by the second or third date, they knew if this was the woman they wanted a long-term relationship with. As we mentioned earlier, men fall in love faster than women do. So the pressure is on for those first few dates. If this guy looks like someone who has potential in your book, use the guidelines we've discussed in the previous sections. Leave the drama to the soap opera characters, have fun, relax, show appreciation, surprise him by keeping him guessing as to what you might do next (challenge him to a hoop's contest, give him a fake palm reading that is playful and unexpected, ask him to help you pick a present for your nephew's birthday, take him to a build-your-own-ice-cream-cone store and challenge him to create the most original cone ever...and then give it a name), and always remember...in the back of their mind, men are gauging their future with you based on how much you bring to the relationship and whether they see a lifetime of great, memorable moments, or ones of boredom, drama, nagging, complaining and taking away his sense of adventure and fun.

.

S-E-X

Oh no...not the three-letter word that always hangs like a shadow over a relationship, whether it be the first date or a 20-year marriage. Sex. Before we take a look at how men feel about sex in the first several dates, I would like to dispel a very prevalent belief about the male species. Men are not perverts...they are genetically born to have certain centers of their brains react differently than a woman's does. Don't believe me? Let's turn to science.

According to scientists, factors related to sexual arousal are different in men and women. The conditions for women to become aroused are more complex. By studying activated areas in the brains of males and females in the response to different types of audio-visual materials, by using functional magnetic resonance imaging (MRI), scientists were able to put to rest the age-old question, "Are men more visual than women when it comes to sexual stimulation?" The answer? "Yup."

Two types of video clips were shown to a group of men and women (aged 20-28 years). The two Audio-visual films were: 1) mood type, erotic video clips with a concrete story and (2) physical type, directly exposing sexual intercourse and genitalia. The MRI images from the brains of the males and females were analyzed and compared and the results were statistically significant.

Men preferred the physical type of video to the mood type, and women preferred the mood type. The finding was that arousal and desire are interwoven and expressed in different ways in men and women and that they are hard-wired to react this way. The human sexual response cycle, sexual desire, activities, satisfaction, and physical and mental responses in men and women are different. Men usually feel sexual satisfaction during sexual activity and are more prone to physical attraction, whereas women are more affected by the environment and emotions related to the sexual partner or sexual fantasy in terms of sexual satisfaction. Men generally respond to visual sexual stimuli, such as attractive nude or erotic pictures, or erotic films. Women respond differently to the same sexual stimuli. Some women feel repulsed by muscular, erotic male photos, and some are sexually attracted by emotional or lingual (words) stimulation. In other words, men are more sexually aroused by visual stimuli, but women are more sexually aroused by concrete, auditory, olfactory (smell), touch and emotionally relevant sexual stimulation. These are gender differences. (*Gender Difference in Brain Activation to Audio-Visual Sexual Stimulation.*) WS Chung, SM Lim, JH Yoo, H Yoon. Int J Impot Res. 2013;25(4):138-142.)

Here's a fun fact. There are currently on the newsstand 42 different porn magazines catering to the heterosexual male. That's just magazines; it does not include internet venues. Guess how many porn magazines are on sale for heterosexual women? Two.

Before you point that perky nose into the air with a sense of self-righteous indignation, let's see the flip side. According to *Romance Writers of America* (RWA), more than 9,000 romance titles were released in 2012, yielding sales of about $1.44 billion (more than triple the revenues generated by classic literary fiction), making it the biggest portion of the U.S. consumer market at 16.7 percent. More than 90% of the market is women. Keep in mind this is 40 years after the women's lib movement, the pill, and women today climbing the corporate ladder with aplomb. They still revel in fantasy worlds where beefy heroes sweep in to claim the virtuous heroine and carry her away into the sunset.

"Yes, but those are romance novels, not slutty porn," you may argue. Well ladies, they are called "bodice rippers" for a reason. While many of these books go lightly in the graphic sex department, the leading man and leading lady are still rumpling the sheets, hillside, boat deck and stable. Just sayin'... With men, it's visual. With women, it's the words and emotions.

Now here's an interesting question: IF, with all the females shouting from the rooftops that we are equal with men, that we don't need our doors opened, and can fix a flat tire quite nicely ourselves, thank you very much, why are so many of today's women living vicariously through romance novels? Is there something missing in our everyday relationships, or lack thereof? One female reviewer on Goodreads.com said, "Romance novels offer an escape from daily life with the belief that true love really exists."

Has today's modern woman looked around at her accolades, hard-won freedoms and independence and felt a lack of something visceral and innate? Have we lost (and beaten out of men) the male/female mystique that brings us the sexual and emotional satisfaction captured in the prose of novels whose covers depict muscular men with flowing hair and open-shirts sweeping a bosomed, half-dressed woman into his arms? I'm not saying what women have achieved is wrong; it's wonderful to see the contributions so many talented, driven and hard-working women have made to themselves and society. I am a very fierce entrepreneur myself. But did the pendulum of independence swing too far and we now miss the old-fashioned courting and pursuit of the male species? As one man recently told me:

"Women are killing the way men think about romance...and they will not be happy with the outcome." Ron Bueker

Finally, while we are on the topic of men's hard-wired behavior in the sexual department, many experts will tell you that the male/female species are "programmed" for certain functions, responses and drives. It does not make one gender good or bad, just different, and different for a reason. Men are wired to procreate, which gives them a large sex drive. Women are not as easily aroused to allow for a certain "braking system" in this whole scenario. If men and women had equal sex drives, we would be reproducing like rabbits.

Labeling men perverts or sex addicts because they have a high sex drive is about as fair as women being labeled "moody", "PMSing" or" hormonal". We are all subject to our biological wiring. It doesn't make it right or wrong, good or bad...just *different*!

So, the next time a man brings up sex, or glances at a hot babe walking by, it does not label him a pervert any more than you could be faulted for swooning over a romantic novel or movie and secretly wishing to trade places with the leading lady. Once again, for women, it's the emotion brought out by words and scenarios. For men, the "eyes" have it.

Sex on the First Date

I will get off my soapbox now and address a huge question in the dating world: what do men think of women who have sex with them early in the relationship game?

- Harve*, 33, construction. "Bluntly, if a woman goes to bed with a guy on the first date, we figure she probably beds every guy who shows an interest in her.

While guys may have a big ego and hope we are something out-of-the-norm, we aren't stupid enough to believe we're the only guy who won this girl over in one date. She may be good for a booty call, but the desire to look at her as a long-term relationship just evaporated."

- Rick*, 43, management. "Men still want to know we earned something. Whether it's a sport we're playing, a raise at work, or a woman's affection, we like the challenge and the feeling of victory that comes with winning it. If a woman makes it too easy for us, we lose interest. This may sound shallow and self-serving, but every guy out there knows the lady holds the key to the bedroom door. We may try, but it is her choice, and secretly, if we liked a woman on a first date, we are hoping she will say NO."

- Larry*, 52, designer. "Men aren't the pigs we're made out to be. We too are looking for an emotional connection. For us, the deepest form of that connection comes through sex. Because we are Pervs? No, because for a man, making love to a woman he cares about is the utmost validation of his role as a man. It says we're accepted at our most masculine level. Women who don't get that are losing out on the deep, meaningful relationship they keep complaining they don't have."

- Michael* 48, retail sales. "A man is looking for a woman with high standards. It makes us bring our A-game, and if we finally win her heart, we feel we really earned something of value. This 3-date rule is bogus. To put a number on how many dates before you become intimate is not only perfunctory, it's a slap in the face to romance and forming a meaningful connection that leads naturally to making love. There isn't a guy out there who won't tell you sex is so much better when you have real feelings for a woman than it is with just a one-night stand. Men often feel lousy afterwards because we know any woman who hopped into bed with a guy she just met didn't see us as anything special...we were just the date at that moment. We didn't have to earn it and it diminishes the whole thing in our eyes. At that point it isn't love making, it's just exercise."

- Brandon*, 37, construction. "I have friends who are still dating someone they slept with on the first date. I know a couple of guys who married a girl who went to bed with them early on. If you want to know what the *majority* of guys are looking for long-term, it would probably be someone who held out until they knew the guy better. Not only does it show integrity, but there are such things as STD's."

75% of the men in the survey said they were looking for a woman of high standards, integrity, and someone who valued herself. And the bonus? By making him wait to get to know you better before having sex, his emotional attachment to you will be deeper because it went past the physical and he has spent time with you, enjoying your company and beginning to feel like his life is better with you in it. If a man knows that sex is in the offering at some time in the near future, he will wait if he cares about you. Don't shoot him down for trying. Let him know you find him attractive but the timing is not quite there yet. In fact, in today's age, 12% of couples are still waiting until they are married to have sex. This is a very personal decision and you and your partner will know when it is the right time.

Don't let a guy with a booty call mentality be on your radar. You can tell the ones who are only after one thing. They are the ones that when you turn them down will get upset, pressure you or disappear. Cut them loose. You are worthy of something extraordinary.

More on sex in the upcoming chapters.

Chapter Five
Nurturing A Relationship

A relationship with another human being is a complex thing. There are two personalities involved who came from different backgrounds, values, economic structures, religious beliefs, political persuasions, family traditions, and on and on. So, it constantly amazes me that we still feel the person we are linking up with should think, feel and react to situations the same way we do! In fact, if they have a difference of opinion, we act as if the relationship is doomed or they don't love us or they would see things our way. Does that seriously make sense? If you feel that a perfect meeting of the minds has to happen in order for you to be happy, then I would march right over to the Clone Factory and order up one exact duplicate of YOU.

Being in a relationship with someone who sees and reacts to the world in the precise way you do would be so boring! And believe me, there would be no chemistry. The chemistry comes from the differences, not the similarities. It would feel like walking into a grocery store and seeing only aisle after aisle of one product. One cereal selection in a green-and-white box as far as you could see. Or going to a department store and the only thing hanging on the rack is little black dresses; same style, only different sizes. Oh goody!

The way to nurture a relationship is to begin by celebrating this unique man who has entered your life. Stop trying to make him over or fix him up. How would you feel if he was telling his buddies, "Yeah, I like her a lot. Once she loses a few pounds, has that mole on her chin removed and learns how to golf, she should do quite nicely." Doesn't feel so great does it? Yet women will typically size up a guy and see his "potential" instead of accepting him at face value. I promise, this is poison and it will kill off romance and the chances for a long-term pairing quickly. He has faults—so do you. He has fears—so do you. He wants to be happy—so do you.

There is no way...and I mean NO way anyone will have the same perspective on life as you do for one simple reason—they aren't *you*! They are unique and one-of-a-kind, and to push them into a cookie press and squeeze out a shape that looks just like cookies everywhere is wrong and will not bring you happiness. A relationship crackles with chemistry when two people bring their special personalities, interests and backgrounds to it. I am certainly not looking for a man who will pull up a chair next to me and mimic my movements, conversation and thoughts. Images of The Stepford Wives enters my mind.

If I seem a little vehement on this subject it's because I raised four sons and love their unique differences. I watched them go through the dating process and listened as they commiserated about women. I actually saw girls they were dating try to change their clothes sense, haircuts, cologne choices, reading and movie preferences, cuisine tastes, and many other traits that made them who they are. My youngest son confided in me that he felt like a mannequin being dressed for a store window.

In the interview with 2,000 men, this was a hot topic and was met with some pretty strong opinions. And for the record, in my upcoming book *Troubleshooting Women: What in the WORLD do they want?* you will get your turn. In fact if you are interested in being part of my ongoing survey for that book, please email my agency at Wonderland549@aol.com and request the questionnaire. The deadline is March 15, 2015. Your real name will not be used if we choose your answers to be spotlighted in the book. It will take you roughly an hour to complete. Thank you ahead of time for sharing your insights and feelings.

Daniel*, 33, Radio DJ. "I dated a woman who made me feel like every day was jumping through a new hoop to fit her idea of the perfect man. She told me to part my hair differently, bought me golf shirts even though she knew I preferred button-downs, told me I needed to shed 10 pounds, insisted I adopt her Vegan lifestyle and even had a talk with my mother about wanting me to change to her church. It lasted one month. I returned the golf shirts, Vegan cookbooks, brochures on religion, and a DVD about Pilates in a cardboard box marked **For the Next Guy**."

Now onward. The following categories will shed some light on what men think about relationships, their needs and what keeps them coming back for more.

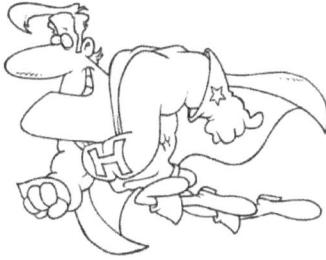

Superman and His Kryptonite

Look! Up in the sky! It's a bird...it's a plane...it's...a regular guy wishing he was worthy of a red cape and a giant "**S**" on his chest.

The thing I loved about the survey of all those men is that they knew they could hide behind anonymity and tell me about their hopes and fears without worry someone would make fun of them or know who they were. And for that reason, I was let in on some pretty startling confessions.

- Daniel, FB survey. "Most women (that I know of or have heard about) judge all men for being the same. They have had bad experiences and bad relationships, and boom, there's all this man hatin'. Not all men are the same. There are men out there that will treat women like gold. Women also need to understand that men too have had bad relationships. And we put up walls and barriers to protect ourselves. The right woman can tear down those walls and the man will put her on a pedestal and treat her as his queen. I'm thankful for my queen. She supported me through some of the toughest times and I'm ever thankful for her in my life!"

Men told me repeatedly that they will erect a wall faster than a kid with a Lego kit. Men are more sensitive than women when it comes to protecting themselves from hurtful or humiliating situations. If a woman diminishes him through blame, sarcasm, belittling or underappreciating him, he will withdraw. And once a man puts up a wall, it can be pretty hard to tear it down. His trust will take some time to come back around.

- Trey*, 31, carpet sales. "This will probably sound kind of baby-like, but men don't like their women discussing them with their girlfriends. Something we tell you in confidence already took a great deal of trust on our behalf. You may have been understanding and supportive of something we told you, but how do we know your girlfriends will respond in the same way? Men have a huge fear of being made fun of. If you run around sharing things we told you, or talking about our sex life, odds are your guy is going to quit sharing things with you. We are very vulnerable in this area."
- Markus*, 45, hot air balloon guide. "Let me put it this way. Guys are very guarded. We don't share personal stuff with our buddies. The fear of being laughed at or put down is just too terrifying. If we are close enough to a woman to confide in her, it's a big compliment to

her. If you betray that trust by laughing at our fears, putting us down or acting any way but sympathetic and encouraging, it will be the last time we come to you with something that's weighing on us."

- Randy*, 46, hygienist. "Guys put each other down for sport. You only have to eavesdrop on a locker room conversation or a typical sausage fest. That's partly why we are sensitive to putting anything out there that is deep or shows our vulnerable side. No guy wants to look weak. I think male ego is probably just another word for male vulnerability."

- Douglas*, 21, student. "A girl that makes fun of me on a date is someone I'm not asking out again. It's bad enough to have her dis you in private, but a guy's biggest fear is looking like an idiot in front of an audience. And if she does it in front of his friends??? Oh man…that's the worst!"

- Bryan*, 49, self-proclaimed Foodie. "I think if women spent a day inside our heads they would be pretty surprised. The overwhelming amount of fear a guy carries around with him is pretty substantial. We worry someone is going to beat us out for the promotion at work, we worry we will let our team down in the upcoming basketball tournament, we worry we will look foolish in front of a girl we like, we worry we won't have money when we retire, we worry about our gut, our hairline receding, our dumb jokes, our car, and most guys will admit to one of our biggest fears: dying alone."

- Paulo*, 32, equestrian trainer. "I was fixing my girlfriend's kitchen sink that she had been complaining about for a few weeks. She said the nozzle kept leaking and it was running down under the sink and that it was plugged up. I brought over my tools and got down on the floor and was working on it when she walked in. She squatted down to see what I was doing. When she saw the plumbing parts lying on the floor, she freaked. She started telling me she thought I didn't know what I was doing and that she was afraid I would make it worse. Here I am, sweaty, covered with gook that came out of the elbow joint, giving up my afternoon to fix her sink and she is making me feel like an idiot. Finally, she said, "You know what? Let's just call a plumber and get someone who knows what he's doing." I got up off the floor, wiped my hands on a towel, looked at her and said, "You know what? Good call!" I stormed out, slammed the door and haven't returned her calls. If you can't appreciate what a man does to make your life happier, then maybe you should be dating a chick."

- Jason*, 30, sports sales. "Men hate to look weak. Underline that, highlight it in orange, post it on your refrigerator. We would rather have our toenails pulled out than look weak. Women need to understand that. We want you to think we are your Hero and invincible and that we make you feel special, protected and happy. Why do you think so many men engage in competitive activities or play escapism video games where we are warriors and heroes? It's because we all wish we were. We all dream of being carried off the court on the shoulders of our teammates to the cheers of an appreciative crowd. Men get a bad rep for being players, egotists, and non-committal. There's a lot of vulnerability on the line when we let ourselves fall for a woman. Go easy on us."

- Ralph*49, mechanical engineer. "A word of caution. Be careful about putting down a guy's abilities. It isn't only that we don't like to look incompetent, but sometimes it goes deeper than that. I had a girlfriend who kept making fun of me working on her car engine. She would stand there and watch me and say things like, "My brother used to take engines apart and he didn't do it like that! Are you sure you know what you're doing?" I finally blew up. I realized later why I got so heated. She was not only putting down *my* skills, but she was also walking all over the special memories I had of my dad teaching me how to fix a car engine. Making fun of me was indirectly making fun of how he did things. He's dead now, and she was stomping on some pretty great memories I had of him. You never know how deep your cutting words can go with a guy."

A man's deep need to feel appreciated will be tackled in the next chapter. And believe me, it was mentioned over and over in a man's top 3 needs in a relationship. What I've learned from men over the years is an underlying wish to be "more". More of a man, more of a provider, more of a husband, a father, a friend, an athlete. It truly is touching to me to see how hard men try. And the area in which they try hardest is with the woman they love.

- Martin*, 61, resort owner. "At my age I can say what maybe younger guys can't articulate. Men will walk through fire for a woman that appreciates him, admires him, respects him, has his back, loves him and lets him know he is the *only* guy who could make her life so wonderful. On the other hand, if a man loves a woman, she has tremendous power to wound him at a gut level. She can cut us off at the knees and toss us into the river with cutting words, disrespect, aloofness, and making us feel we are a dime a dozen. Frankly, women can make or break us. How's that for kryptonite?"

Rubber Band Theory

Why are we talking about the Rubber Band Theory in a chapter dedicated to nurturing a relationship? For one simple reason. Men need some space; women do too. A healthy relationship requires some "me time", and the bonus is, it will keep him coming back to you.

Here's how it works. Picture an elastic band around you and your guy. When we pull away it causes the band to stretch to where it will eventually reach its expansion capability and the guy will spring toward you. Giving a man his space is vital in a relationship. Their romantic interest actually grows for you in the time apart. If you are constantly with him there is no room for the desire to grow. As one man I interviewed put it, "Give us a chance to miss you."

The reason this is hard for a lot of women is that our natural instinct when someone pulls away is to find out why. So we text him, call him, email him and basically come off as insecure stalkers. Now look at what happens when we do the opposite. We've all witnessed suddenly getting a bunch of texts and calls from friends or boyfriends who haven't heard from us in a timely manner. Our value has gone up in their eyes because we have become more elusive. One of my favorite sayings is "never consider me a foregone conclusion." We all value what we can't have. Sad but true.

Here's a perfect example: I was dating a man I was crazy about. I fell into the habit of calling him more often than he called me. I sensed his interest waning and the conversation becoming filled with more gaps of silence. I realized I was too available and he wasn't doing any of the work to talk to me. So I stopped. I didn't call, text or email. I went about my life. Four days went by! Suddenly I get a text that said, "Are you okay?" I waited an hour to reply and typed, "Yes. I'm great. Why?" He replied right back, "It's been kinda quiet over on Oak Drive (my address*)." "I've just been busy. Have a super day!" I texted.

I ended the conversation first. I could sense the confused expression on his face right through the phone keypad. A day went by and then I got a text asking if I would like to go to dinner the next night (a Friday). I thanked him for the invitation but said I had already made plans for the weekend. (I had usually assumed we would have dinner each Friday and waited around for him to let me know when and where without him having to ask me in advance.) *Now* the rubber band sprang back! "Are you mad at me?" he texted. "Of course not, why?" (Notice the ball was always bounced back to his court.) "You just seem different," he wrote. "Why?" I asked. (Bounce) "I just haven't heard from you in a while." "Oh…well the phone works both ways. ☺" From then on, he called more, texted more and asked me for a Friday night dinner in advance.

Don't answer his text immediately or return his phone call two minutes after you missed his message. Be busy with your own life as we discussed earlier. Giving him "enough rope to hang himself" is another way of looking at it. Give him some slack. Back off. "Give him a chance to miss you."

Boys Will Be Boys

While we're on the subject of giving him some space, let's look at the ever-popular Boy's Night Out. This is an area in which many women err…big time. Insecure women resent men having a night out with the boys, or playing sports, or going hunting or camping, for one reason…he is doing something fun without you. "How dare he? How can he possibly leave me behind? We're a couple. We do everything together. I don't go off with my friends and leave him to his own devices! It's the weekend…what am I supposed to do without him? This is so inconsiderate!"

If these are thoughts that have gone through your head, stop right there. You are killing off a really big chance for him to value you more, miss you, and feel even closer to you when he returns from his testosterone-filled romp. Why? Because you gave him freedom! Remember one of the main reasons men were reluctant to enter into a committed relationship? They feared losing their freedom. By happily kissing him on the cheek as he leaves and wishing him a good time you look like a confident, secure, happy woman who has a life of her own that doesn't orbit around him. You score major points.

Secondly, he gets a chance to think about you and miss you. Trust me, when a guy has been with his buddies for a few hours or a few days, the thought of something feminine, who smells good, isn't passing gas or burping, looks like…well…"a breath of fresh air."

This is a big deal to a guy. If you pull on him, throw a fit because you weren't included, remind him you had the kids all day and it's his turn to take care of them, and basically guilt him out of a much-needed respite from the working world, it will damage your relationship. You are now perceived as clinging, unreasonable, needy and the DQ word (Drama Queen).

If you're married with children don't you have a right to resent his taking off when you've had the lion's share of the responsibility with them? I do see your point. I've had similar feelings when I was raising four sons and my husband would call from work to say he was going straight to the golf course with "da boys" before coming home. "Swell. Great. Now the Calvary I was expecting to take over for a few hours in the late afternoon/early evening has just defected to the greens." I've been there. Understanding his need for some guy time to recharge his batteries took me awhile to comprehend. Once I did, we worked out a deal. He would allow me the same privilege in the upcoming days. I could go hang out with my friends, shop, attend a lecture, whatever gave me a chance to feel some balance in *my* life. Compromise works wonders. And he will get butterflies in his stomach when he thinks of being with you. It's that "rubber band" effect. Give him space and a chance to pursue or miss you. He will see a future where his freedom is still intact *and* this wonderful woman is part of the package.

Recognizing the Players

We will cover the 10 stereotypes of Toad-like behavior you should avoid in Chapter 7: The Toad Pool. For now, if you suspect the guy you are seeing may not be showing all his cards, look for these warning signs:

- He only calls when he is away from home, late at night, running errands, or on his work lunch break.
- Long-distance relationships work for him. The guy you thought was being really sweet and accommodating by driving a long distance to see you just might be doing it so that no one he knows in his area sees him. He could be married or with someone else. Ask to come to his neck of the woods and see what happens.
- He has you on his "back burner". Everything else takes precedence: his work, his family, sports, etc.

Any man who is interested in you will make time for you. Period.

- You are spending more time creating the romance than he is. You write the poems, plan nice dinners, surprise him with cards and little tokens. If this is one-sided, he's not that interested and may be giving his romantic endeavors to someone else.

- If you are both using online dating sites, you notice he seems to always be on there, even after you've had a date. More about online players in the section on online dating in Chapter 2 of Part III: Today's View of Relationships.

- He always makes sure his cell phone is with him at all times; even while going to use the rest room. He may be either texting someone else or making sure you don't get a chance to sneak a peek at his contacts or messages.

- He never asks about your kids, work, interests, something important you brought up the last time you talked, or seems interested in really getting to know you on a deeper level. He avoids your family get-togethers or other intimate events such as holiday gatherings, etc.

- He tends to vanish when you need him. A man who cares about you will bring you things when you're sick, pick up feminine hygiene supplies, call and check on you, fix your car (or arrange to have it fixed), protect you and show you he doesn't mind being inconvenienced where you are concerned. He makes your birthday special and celebrates your successes, while offering a shoulder for your hard days.

- If you've been dating for some time, say two months or more, and he still hasn't introduced you to his friends, he may not be as invested as you think. While each man is different, and he may be taking things slow, be wary of a guy who keeps you a secret. Meeting the family is a bigger deal and may take a little longer.

- Pay attention to how he pays attention. If you feel you are talking to a stump when you are sharing something with him in conversation, he may not be interested enough in you to care about what you have to say. If you repeatedly get the Zombie stare while communicating with him, toss him back into the horror flicks and move on.

I'll let Jeff sum it up for me:

Jeff*, 46, electrical engineer. "Any man who is really interested in a woman will find time to call her. We are never THAT busy. If he is interested he will be there for her, climb mountains to make her happy, and let her know he is thinking of her in a million different ways. If he is not earning your time by showing you consideration and investing in you romantically, he's a player. You deserve better."

He's Proposed!

Let's face it…this is a big deal. For you and for him. Two people are saying they are shutting the door on dating others and dedicating their lives to each other's happiness. Whether his proposal was the stuff movies are made of, or he simply popped the question over bagels one morning, as a man, he is tossing away his bachelor days and making you Number One. On the same note, you are also giving up some freedoms and looking at someone who may father children with you, or become a step-father to children you already have. It' a big deal.

Keep this in mind. Everything we have discussed so far still applies after that sparkler is on your left ring finger. You do not suddenly act as if you have him tagged and bagged. He is not your property. He is a singular human being who just so happens to want to build a nest with you. Here are some complaints men had about the engagement phase:

- Maki*, 29, carpenter. "After we got engaged, every conversation became about the wedding. I know a lot goes into planning one, and that women get really excited about all the details, but all I wanted was one night out where we just had fun, talked about something else and enjoyed being together. It felt like the wedding was now the only focus."

- Winston*, 45, furniture sales. "Most guys are scared to death about proposing. Even if we have been dating you for two years, there comes that moment when we get down on one knee and for those few moments we wonder if you will turn us down. A woman who appreciates that, and the effort we took in preparing for this moment, wins big points. Even if she picked out the ring, we put thought into this and had a little fear about the outcome. Never make a guy feel badly about how he proposed, where he did it, if it was romantic enough for you, etc."

- Terry*, 31, boat sales. "I've had friends complain that once they gave a girl a ring she changed. She started calling the shots, dismissed his ideas about the wedding details, didn't like his honeymoon plans, didn't spend as much time on her appearance (sweat pants became the dress code of choice) and basically turned into someone he didn't recognize. If anything, during an engagement you should be practicing the same consideration, courtesy and attention to things as you plan to in your married life. More guys than I can count have bailed when they felt the tides change."

- Drew*, 58, retired. "The minute we got engaged she informed me I had to cut back on golf, my church meetings and time with my family. She began picking at little habits I had, the way I dressed...even my love of Sushi. It was like I had been handcuffed and hog-tied. Sadly, I ended the engagement before the announcements for the wedding were mailed."

I'm sure these seem like extreme cases to you but a large percentage of men mentioned the women changing, or trying to change him, after he proposed. This should be a magical time of your life as the two of you plan your future together. Remember to allow him some freedom, appreciate him, and lastly, be cognizant of the costs associated with a wedding. Whether the two of you are paying for it, or your parents, it can get pricey. The memory of you demanding that $3,000 cake will linger long after the crumbs have been swept away.

Continue to have a life that isn't always revolving around him. Mystery and space is needed all the way into your golden years and beyond. We will talk about that in our chapter on marriage, but for the engagement period it is just as important to do things without him on occasion and allow some breathing room. Don't overdue the phone calls, texts and emails. Keep him excited about being with you, not wishing he could hide in a cave for a while. Go out with your friends, don't drag him to the mall for a shopping fest or insist he always do everything with you. He asked you to marry him, not to be his shadow.

Chapter Six

Marriage: Is the Fairytale Still Within Reach?

When you marry a man, how does the relationship change? In many cases, it changes a great deal. The dating phase is usually a series of dates where you do some fun and relaxing things, and begin learning about each other. It may have been simple things like dinners and movies, or you may have gone on some road trips packed with surprises and adventure. You may have even taken some pretty romantic vacations together and felt life would always be twinkling stars and violin music.

Marriage brings together two people from diverse backgrounds who are suddenly having to share...everything. It is usually fun and exciting in the beginning to choose a place to live and begin to decorate your very own home. Or one of you may have already had a place and the other person simply moves their stuff in and tries to find a way to make it fit another person's lifestyle. Either way, your life has changed and there is this other human being who you are partly responsible for. If he gets sick, it's you who is there with the tissues, soup and medicine. If his car breaks down, he calls you to come and pick him up. If he had a lousy day, you may be the recipient of a male maelstrom. You may be stepping over his dirty socks and boxer shorts, wiping toothpaste off the mirror and suddenly ESPN is on instead of HGTV.

The novelty of seeing each other naked is waning, although that doesn't mean it is any less stimulating. You are hopefully getting better at compromising on so many issues: finances, closet space, TV shows, furniture arrangement, bedtimes, eating habits, chores, etc. In-law concerns may have become an issue, or maybe not. If either of you have children from a previous relationship, that is a big area all its own.

While talking to relationship experts on my talk show I learned some very key reasons for the situations that can begin to erode even the best marriages. Here are the biggies:

- One or both of you feels entitled. Feeling entitled usually results from being an only child or being fairly spoiled during your upbringing. Your parents, siblings or other relatives may have removed obstacles from your path and generally made you feel like a princess. If you carry those expectations into a marriage, it can be a rude awakening when you are asked to be a team player and carry your weight. You may have never done laundry, cooked, cleaned or held down a job. When children are involved you may be expecting your partner to do the lion's share of the care giving. These are things that will need to be discussed between the two of you and a shared list of duties implemented. When the responsibility in a marriage is one-sided, the ship tends to capsize rather quickly.

- Communication has shut-down or is not on a mature level. Lack of communication is the main reason for most divorces. If two people can't articulate their needs, desires, frustrations or fears, there is no room to grow. One area where you or your spouse feels misunderstood or ignored can snowball into the rest of the marriage arenas. All of us knows how it feels to tell the person we love they are doing something that is making us feel badly, only to have them shrug it off or ignore it. It is numbing. How can they say they love us if our feelings don't count? Couples who engage in immature communication where there is name calling, blame and petty remarks are also in danger of having that valuable foundation of trust undermined. And when the trust goes, the foundation cracks.

- Becoming complacent. Complacency can be deadly. Many of us feel once we are married we can relax and let our dark side show. We aren't as careful about our appearance, our language, our manners or trying to make sure the other person is feeling appreciated and cared for. At the extreme it can turn into a "Yeah...well if you had fixed the sink when I told you to, it wouldn't be broken beyond repair now!" game. We stop romancing each other as we become immersed in the business of making a living or raising kids. Boredom and routine have set in and suddenly you are looking across the room at a person in droopy sweatpants and a stained shirt and wondering what you saw in him/her to start with. Boredom is like weeds. If left unattended it can destroy a beautiful garden.

- Fault-finding. It can sneak up on you. It starts out with a subtle reminder that he promised to mow the lawn. It escalates to "nagging" as we remind him over and over about it as the grass grows and now looks like a machete and map are needed to navigate through it. Finally, it becomes a war of words and blame. When it reaches this point, it is very hard for either person to feel they are being heard or understood. Picking on each other's habits and perceived faults will cause the loving feelings in a marriage to deteriorate, sometimes to the point of no return. Because we have become so familiar with this other person we are cohabitating with, we slide into pushing their buttons and picking them apart. This usually arises from our own feelings that they aren't fulfilling our needs or going out of their way to understand us and do the things that matter to us. It becomes a vicious cycle where nobody wins.

- Allowing space. We talked before about the need for space when we discussed the "rubber band theory". Everyone needs some alone time to recharge their batteries, attend to their needs and even daydream a little. Having someone invade your space 24/7 is a smothering feeling. Picture a camp fire. The flame can be warm and lovely and the air feeds it. But if you smother it with a blanket, it is turned to smoldering embers and smoke. The flame of a marriage can be extinguished in the same way. Each of you needs air and your own interests, hobbies and friends. It adds balance and allows the other person to breathe. Encouraging a man to head to the hills, go hang with the boys, or just giving him some time to work on the car, read, or watch TV uninterrupted will do wonders for your marriage. He will come to you a more relaxed and happier person. We will talk more about that in the section on the Man Cave.

The Entitled Diva

I've known a woman for years who fits the description of the Entitled Diva. She was the youngest child of three in the family and received special treatment from the time she entered elementary school. She learned at a young age how to manipulate others by appearing helpless and childlike. Her parents bought into her need to have her wants and wishes fulfilled and they began to remove obstacles from her path.

As this girl entered Junior High and High School a pattern began to emerge. She expected life to be easy. People were supposed to take care of her, admire her and clear the way for her. She tried out, and won, Homecoming Queen, university cheerleader and other high-profile roles, including going to Hollywood to follow her dreams of becoming a star. Her mother paved the way for her by paying for a penthouse apartment for her (complete with valet parking) in Beverly Hills. After years of trying to become a star, she landed only a part in a commercial. When the mother's money could no longer support the dream, the girl returned home, moved in with her mother, and waited for her needs to be provided for…which they were.

When reality dawned and the girl was told to get a paying job, she was often sick and the mother dutifully called in to her work to make excuses for her. She was fired from several jobs for lack of attendance or fulfilling simple duties. In the end she returned home and took on the responsibility of answering the phone for her mother's in-home business. If one of her soap operas was on television, she would take the phone off the hook and shove the receiver under a pillow so as not to have calls disturb her program. The fact that her mother's business was missing important phone calls did not matter to her.

As she began dating, the men she went out with quickly learned there was no substance to her. She was quick to go to bed with them, but when that became routine, they moved on. She went after high-profile men in the community hoping for a life of opulence where she would travel, have fine clothes and live a life of leisure. The fact that many of these men were married did not deter her. She often got pregnant while bedding them in an effort to trap them, believing they would gladly leave their wives for her. When these unrealistic dreams didn't materialize, she had abortions and moved on to the next victim.

Finally, a man with a good heart married her after finding out she had become pregnant with his child. She settled in and waited to have her wants and needs fulfilled. They had another child, but the marriage was doomed to failure. He caught her in an avalanche of lies as she tried to cover her spending habits and reasons for not wanting to work. He finally divorced her.

Today she is living on welfare in a friend's basement where she has created an imaginary life on Twitter, convincing strangers that she is rich and traveling the world.

This may seem extreme, but every word is true. You can see how a life of ease when one is young can become the expected norm. Unfortunately, when you take that feeling of entitlement into a marriage, it will create an unnecessary burden on the man, and feelings of resentment will emerge. No man, no matter how much he loves you, is going to keep giving and giving and getting nothing in return. Movies depicting bimbos dripping in diamonds who lead a rich man around by his sex drive are not realistic. For some men that may be the fantasy that fulfills him. But a man with integrity, who is looking for a traditional marriage where the two of them are partners who both contribute in every way, will soon tire of the Entitled Diva.

- Rix*, 34, advertising exec. "I married young. I was 22, she was 21. She was gorgeous and a lot of fun to be with, though at times she seemed immature for her age. I pictured our married life to be filled with love making, fun and hanging out. Looking back at it, my expectations were pretty immature as well. I found out after the wedding that she couldn't cook, had never managed a bank account well and had $36,000 in credit card debt. She refused to get a job, saying her father had always provided for her mother, and basically sat back to be waited on. The dirty clothes piled up until I washed them and dinner was pretty much take-out or drive-throughs. The marriage lasted 9 months. The last time I saw her she was married to a rich guy and she looked a lot older. She had not aged well, and there was a look of unhappiness about her. I've learned now to find out more about a person before I consider her wife-material."

- Jackson*, 51, real estate developer. "Women who fit the Diva role are usually pretty empty inside. Their life is all exterior: clothes, nice house, travel, fancy furniture, etc. A man who is looking for someone who warms his heart through her compassion, giving, and partnership is not going to last around a Diva. The guy quickly learns his wallet and his subservience are all she's looking for."

- Mark*, 41, sales. "My buddy married a girl that all of us warned him about. She was always holding up hoops for him to jump through and was never happy with anything he did for her. We were all like "Dude! What do you see in her? She's pretty but she's pulling you down, man!" He didn't listen, married her, and the guy is a whipped puppy. He's miserable and can't do enough to please her. It's really sad to watch him. Frankly, I can't stand to be around her. She took a good guy and beat him down. Sure, he could have had a spine and walked away. I just see way too many guys trying too hard to please a woman who will never be happy or have enough done for her."

Larson*, 45, oil executive. "If a woman can't appreciate what a man offers her, she needs to move on. These kinds of women are man-eaters. They take and take until there is nothing left of him. If she doesn't have a life of her own and just needs someone else to provide one for her, what is she bringing to the equation? Nothing! These kinds of women are like empty vessels that you keep pouring into and they are never filled."

Ladies, let me just say this. We covered in the first section of this book how you need to have a fulfilled life of your own before you can enhance someone else's. Marriage requires two people bringing their best selves to the partnership. Today, partnership has taken on a whole new meaning. Men and women are combining forces in order to have the lifestyle they both desire. Roles have evolved and are not the norm they were 40 or 50 years ago. Men have learned to embrace fatherhood and take a more active role in playing Dad, and women have found that having a career can be fulfilling and exciting. If a woman makes more money than the man, she is encouraged to "go for it." Many men enjoy cooking and have taken over the kitchen. We are not the same society where Ward Cleaver retires to his study—

the strong, remote bread winner—as June Cleaver dusts and cooks in her dress and pearls and admonishes the children not to interrupt their father.

Today's marriage is a blending of skills, talents, expertise, needs and desires. While most of this is a good thing, a wonderful thing, we are still swinging back and forth trying to define our roles as male and female. This blending has left a big question mark over our heads as to who we are. "One size fits all" may prevail in the work place, but when it comes to chemistry and sparks, the hybrid model of genders does little to ignite fireworks. Turning men into women and women into men will do nothing but let us start borrowing each other ties. Difference is good, and necessary. It takes the traits of both feminine and masculine energies to create that indefinable attraction that pulls us toward each other. Women took a look at the kinder, gentler man they created through the Women's Lib movement and found him wanting.

"Well…I didn't mean I wanted him to become wimpy," the new woman cried. "I just wanted him to be more sensitive, hands on around the house, and communicate with me like my girlfriends do. I still need him to be macho!"

And there-in lies the rub.

Men are not women. They do not come to a problem the way women do, attack a topic the way women do, process information the way women do, show emotion, worry or do tasks the way women do. Their clothes sense is simple and pragmatic; they could care less about fashion magazines touting the latest styles. Men tend to emulate the boss's attire and there's an end to it. They shave, comb their hair and are out the door. Just look into a woman's make-up kit, top drawer in her bathroom or swing open her medicine cabinet to see the array of products needed to present herself to the world. Shoes, scarves, handbags, sweaters, blouses, jackets, suits, dresses, belts and jewelry are all carefully selected and coordinated.

Does this make either sex better, smarter or more right? NO! It makes us *different*. And when women can accept that simple, indisputable truth, they will be much happier and their boyfriends and husbands will respond in ways you can only dream of.

For some reason, we feel that if another person has an opposing opinion, then they must be looking for a fight. If they love us, they should be able to read our minds, know what we want, do it without question and agree with us. WHO SAID THAT? Seriously! From the beginning of time men have been wired to be different from women in so many areas from a necessity. They had to protect, provide and shelter. Emotion could not get in the way or the saber tooth tiger would have eaten him, *and* his wife and children. Men sat facing the entrance to a cave to stand watch. Want to see 245 million years of wiring at work? Try making a man sit with his back to the rest of the restaurant. He will show you through his body language that he is uncomfortable.

Man's communication is short, direct and to the point. It is mainly for information gathering. You rarely see a man gossip. They are action-oriented and often convey their feelings through actions rather than words. Men simply don't use words the way women do. Women typically use 7,000 words a day—men use around 3,000. Big difference. If you want to know how your man feels about you, watch his actions. The way he goes out and works each day to provide for you, fixes your car, handles the debt collectors or does the heavy lifting. When women stop trying to make men behave like a woman, we will have the romantic relationship we are looking for.

Let's break it down…

Communication

We are going to see how men differ from women in the ways they communicate in the hopes of creating a more harmonious relationship for you. Isn't that the end goal? Not to keep a running tally of who didn't measure up, or who disappointed us, but to find a better way of keeping the love alive. Communication is a big area where couples feel tension and a lack of understanding. It doesn't need to be that way. And please keep in mind—this is coming straight from thousands of men; not yesterday's man, but today's. Remember the quote from Einstein? "Insanity is doing the same thing over and over and expecting different results." It's time to stop doing the same thing when it comes to communicating with men and then getting upset that we didn't get the result we wanted. To keep it fair, I am going to show you both sides of the coin when it comes to communication. Look for the male and female flipping coins graphics.

I once saw a book entitled, *Men Are Like Waffles, Women Are Like Spaghetti* by Bill Farrel. It was released shortly after the popular *Men Are From Mars, Women Are From Venus* self-help book. I assumed it was a tongue-in-a-cheek version of John Gray's book. Until I saw the cover. There was a picture of a waffle, and a graphic of a tangled mound of spaghetti. The light bulb came on over my head and I got it. Those small, square holes in the waffles represented men's capability to compartmentalize things, while women are multi-taskers, their minds often going in twelve directions at the same time—their thoughts tangled somewhat like spaghetti.

It is man's propensity to take on one task at a time and check it off. He focuses on that one compartment and feels uncomfortable if he's interrupted before he can effectively complete it. One waffle hole filled. If you will remember that, you will be leaps and bounds ahead of the communication game. Timing is everything!

A) Timing

Why is timing so important in communication between men and women? For the reason we stated above: Men compartmentalize and give their full attention to one thing at a time. It is amazing to see how well the concept of timing works with hubbies, dates and even your male children.

As a quick side note…speaking of children, you have only to look at the way boys and girls behave from an early age to realize the supreme difference in the sexes when it comes to socializing and communicating their needs. Watch any group of little girls and you will see story telling at its best. They congregate with their dolls on the floor and make up a fantasy world, complete with plot, storyline and ending. They are constantly talking, correcting dialogue that doesn't fit and creating a wonderful world of emotions and dreams.

Now peek at a group of little boys. Big difference! There is little sitting on the floor and corresponding. It is all action-driven. Trucks are smashing, balls are flying, buildings, roadways, and railways are being constructed. Anything coming from their mouths is usually sound effects:

gun fire, tractor engines and bombs. An occasional "No...no that way...put the bridge here," is pretty much the form of communication.

Psychologists have studied pre-school children to see what would happen if a small temporary wall was placed between them and their mothers at the end of the day when Mommy came to pick them up from school. It was fascinating to watch the results. The little boys would kick the wall, try to climb over it or go around it to get to Mom. Whereas the little girls, feeling thwarted by the obstacle would stand and begin crying and hold up their arms to be picked up. The girls were emotion and words, the little boys were action-driven.

So, once again...the way men and women react is hard-wired from birth. No good...no bad...just different. And men compartmentalize. When it comes to communication, it is no different. And timing is a big deal for guys:

Man's Point of View on Communication

- Derek*, 39, furniture sales. "My wife and I used to go the rounds when it came to communicating. She always seemed to pick the time I was involved in something to want to talk to me. If I was watching a close game on TV, taking the engine out of the car or going over the bills, she would plop down and want to talk about something. When she sensed my tension or that I wasn't giving her my full attention, she would pout or get mad and call me "insensitive" or that I never listened to her. Once I explained to her how men prefer to concentrate on one thing at a time and it had nothing to do with how much I loved her, she began picking the times I wasn't working on something else. It went a lot better and she was happy."

- Marlin*, 36, store manager. "I used to think women did it on purpose. You know, wait until the guy was busy with a project or watching football to come in and demand his attention. I thought they were jealous that we were doing something without them. I kinda still feel that way. I think women need to be involved more than a guy does. We like going off and working on something alone sometimes. It lets us get rid of stress from work and bills. I wish women understood that. We aren't shutting them out. We just want a chance to recharge our batteries, and then we are in a better place to give you our undivided attention."

- Rash*, 28, millwork. "I wish women would come to us and say, "I have something important I would like to talk to you about. When you have a minute could I get your opinion on something?" This works great for two reasons: 1) She is respecting we are focusing on something else right now, and put us on alert that she would like our time when we get done. No pressure. 2) She mentions asking us for "our opinion". This differs from her needing to have "the talk." Every guy loves giving advice and offering his opinion. He will come to the conversation feeling refreshed because he checked his project off his list and is now ready to give you his attention."

- Lars*, 56, operations manager. "News Flash! If a guy is watching something on TV, especially a game or movie he has been looking forward to, this is not the time to sit down and want him to chat. Would you want to be interrupted if you were watching a show you were interested in? Do you want your husband to suddenly sit down and say "Honey, we need to go over these bills now," right in the middle of the season cliffhanger of your favorite series? Sometimes, it's just courtesy!"

- Chris*, 50, restaurant owner. "I think women bring on more grief than they need to. Give us a heads up if you want to talk and we'll put it on our list. That may sound rude or mechanical but it's how men work. We are goal-oriented. When we talk it is mostly about getting the information we need to perform a task or gather pertinent details. Listen to men talk. It's pretty basic and to the point. We don't understand women's need to talk about emotions, what her girlfriend did that upset her, all the errands she ran that day, or anything that isn't designed to get to the point and get results. We're not being uncaring...we just aren't wired that way. When you talk to us we are listening for what you want from us. What are we supposed to fix for you? Men get antsy with all the embellishments and side tours simply because it's not us. It's not how we communicate. We don't know what to do with it."

- Evan*, 39, psychologist. "In a nutshell, here's what works. If he is involved with something, whether reading the paper, going over a report for work, fixing a broken door or doing yard work, wait. If it's important, simply tell him you need to talk to him now because it's important and can't wait. If it's not an emergency, you will get more from him if you wait until he is finished with his task(s). Women keep pushing men to listen to them on their terms and then feel frustrated when they don't have his full attention or he becomes tense. It's like expecting a dog to behave like a cat, or a cat to behave like a dog. No amount of telling the cat it should like getting a bath is going to keep that feline from scratching the hell out of you if you force it into a bath tub. No amount of demanding a dog use a litter box is going to work. We all need to stop trying to fit square pegs into round holes."

Woman's Point of View on Communication

On the other side of the coin is how women view communication. As we've mentioned, women use more than twice as many words as most men do. I say most because I have been with men who talked so much I felt like ordering a pizza during his diatribe. But typically women are the communicators in a relationship. Put a group of women together and they can cover every topic from political scandals to the dress sale coming up at June's Booty Boutique. They will commiserate on how awful Betty Barnes* new hairstyle is, to the price of gas. They can switch gears mid-sentence to go on to a different topic and never lose track of the flow of information. Compliments flow, shoes are extolled and weight loss programs dissed.

The major difference between a man's form of communication and a woman's is this: Women will often feel the need to talk to someone else in order to form her thoughts. Women multi-task, and with all those thoughts going 90 miles-an-hour we often need to just "get it out" so we can stop worrying about it all. When we talk, it is a release. It is a means of getting to what we are feeling and often finding a solution for something that is bothering us. The act of communicating is a means to an end. We feel better afterwards because someone has listened to us, validated our feelings, and we often have found an answer we are looking for by formulating our thoughts into words.

It's like seeing it all spelled out on a giant chalkboard in words. Ah ha! There it is! There's the answer. But, we had to "see" the words first to figure it out. That's why many women make lists and keep journals. It is a way of getting the words and thoughts out of our heads and on to paper so that we understand what's going on.

Men, on the other hand, have already figured it out in their heads before they begin talking. They have it filtered down to just the pertinent details. It's a short-hand version that works well for them. Again, not right or wrong, just different. But it explains why a woman's rambling dialogue can give them a deer in the headlights facial expression.

- Denise*, 35, graphic designer. "I think women worry a lot. We keep a lot in our minds and feel we need to just sit down and talk it out. I've found if I tell my husband ahead of time that I don't need him to fix anything, but just to let me "tumble my thoughts" for a minute, he is able to relax, and he knows I just need to formulate the things worrying me. It doesn't mean I turn him into a counselor or a girlfriend. But he is able to sit back and let me go after it. Often he will go into the fix-it mode anyway (they can't seem to help it) and come up with something I had not thought of. Either way, I feel better for talking and he has commented he didn't realize I was carrying all that baggage around in my head. I think most men would be surprised at what women worry about on a daily basis."

- Kate*, 49, advertising. "My husband and I used to fight about the times I needed to talk things out. His shoulders would sag and this face looked like it did when it was tax time. He said he didn't understand a woman's need to talk all the time. Rather than keep repeating my point of view on the topic, I found some videos on YouTube and we sat and watched experts talking about the difference between men and women when it comes to communicating. We both learned something, and things got a lot better. Having a third opinion, especially an expert opinion, takes the "I was right, you were wrong" flag from flying over a dispute."

- Maria*, 50, fashion designer. "I used to get angry when I read books about men saying a woman needed to go find a girlfriend to talk to instead of laying all this conversation stuff on her husband. It sounded shallow and uncaring. He's my husband. He should be interested in what I'm thinking and how my day is going. After talking it over with a group of my friends, both male and female, I realized it didn't have anything to do with how much he loved me. It was just men don't typically share all that stuff and he was out of his depth. We compromised. I gave him the *Reader's Digest* version and saved the *War and Peace* version for my friends."

- Maddie*, 47, teacher. "Have you ever noticed that when a man is ready to talk how much easier it is? It is all about timing. My grown son would always act a little harried when I called him. It never seemed to be the right time. I knew he had a wife, a job and little kids but I would hang up feeling hurt that he sounded in a hurry to get off the phone from me. Then I noticed that when he called *me*, he was completely different. He was relaxed, the call would last for an hour instead of 3 minutes and I felt great when I hung up. He called when he was free and could concentrate on the conversation. It taught me a big lesson on how men are. I have learned to send a text ahead of time now when I want to talk to him that says "Hey you.

Hope all is going great. Give your old Mom a call when you have a minute." This gives him breathing room and he calls when he has time without interruptions, and the calls always last longer."

- Michelle*, 27, auditor. "My wonderful grandmother gave me some great advice when I got married last year. She said "If you respect a man for his differences, you will be a happy bride." She talked to me about how unhappy women are when they try to force a man to think and act the way they do. "Who died and made you Queen?" was a quote she used a lot. I thought about that. It really is the height of conceit to expect another human being to behave as you do or else they are wrong. I value my husband's differences. I've seen what happens when a woman is always looking for his flaws and waiting for him to slip up. No wonder so many men feel like they are ducks in a shooting gallery, just waiting to be picked off."

- Gwen*, 52, retired. "It's funny. I think I have more masculine qualities than feminine ones. I have a hard time listening to some of my female friends go on and on about an endless array of topics. I find myself getting twitchy and just wanting them to come to some conclusion. I get why some men want to just shout, "Get to the point!" If you want to know if you are losing a guy during a conversation with him, watch his body language. He may squirm, lose eye contact, look around, look down a lot, lean away from you, take deep breaths, etc. Yet even with these obvious signs that he has reached his listening capacity or has become impatient or bored, many women will still doggedly plow ahead, thinking he will love the way it ends. Women, to their detriment, do tend to take the scenic route when talking about things."

B) The Scenic Route

During my television talk show, *Troubleshooting Men, What in the WORLD do they want?* I invited three of the local brewery owners on to participate in our Bull Pen. Here men would answer any questions our female viewing audience asked. As Fort Collins, Colorado is known for its micro-breweries I thought brewery owners would be a great addition to the Pen since the show was shot in this city.

The question posed to these three men was from a 42 year-old-woman who asked this: "Women constantly complain that men never listen to them. What can we do to make men pay more attention to what we are saying?"

I looked to the first gentleman seated nearest me for his answer. He looked at me in mock surprise and said, "I'm sorry...what did you say?" Everyone laughed, but he underscored the topic of the question. He grinned and answered me.

"Women tend to take the scenic route when talking. You may have a point to make but you go all over the place to get there. Say you come to us wanting to complain about the way a mechanic treated you while you were getting your car serviced. You are hoping to see if we agree that the mechanic took advantage of you. Instead of telling us that this is the crux of your issue, you start at the beginning as we sit helplessly by, waiting to hear what your point is. You might begin like this: "Oh, by the way, I took the car into the mechanic today to get it serviced. Did you know they changed the restaurant next door to it to an Asian Bistro? I thought the Italian place was really good so I'm not sure why it went under. Anyway, I had to wait 20 minutes for them to check the car. There wasn't one magazine there for women. Can you believe that? I have no desire to read about gears or race cars. You'd think they would be considerate to female customers...of course, unless, the women are stealing the magazines for the fitness sections or recipes or something like that. Oh my gosh...Alicia shared this recipe with me for White Chocolate Bread Pudding that is to die for! Maybe I should make it for Sharon's birthday party. You didn't forget about the party did you? It's next Saturday. So...where was I?...Oh Yeah...so anyway 20 minutes later the guy comes in and says I need a new air filter and shows me the one that was in the car. It looked OK to me but he says it needs a new one so I said "Go ahead" and then he comes back a few minutes later to tell me I need a new windshield wiper blade on the back window and I say maybe I should check with you first because all this is starting to add up. I mean...it's crazy how much all of this stuff costs. Speaking of costs, did you get the estimates for the house painting? The HOA has a deadline to get that done, you know. I wish we could pick our own color instead of using their palette. Wouldn't a nice sandstone color with sage green trim be perfect?"

"Here she pauses," my brewery owner says, as everyone in the studio is laughing. The other two owners are doubled over, nodding their heads in agreement. He continues, "She looks at him waiting for an answer. He is now hopelessly lost. Does she want to know if he is disappointed the Italian restaurant is now Asian, that he should advise the mechanic to stock more women's magazines, that he should double check to see if he has Sharon's birthday on his calendar, that he should look at the windshield wiper blade to see if it needs replacing or that he should comment on the house painting schedule and colors? Finally, he sighs and says, "What did you want to ask me?" She gets upset, crosses her arms and says, "This is exactly what I mean…you never listen to me. I want to know if you think the mechanic was taking advantage of me because I'm a woman and he was trying to sell me all this stuff I didn't need!" *That's* the scenic route!"

I thought his answer was perfect. As a female who has gone "off-roading" myself, I recognized a woman's tendency to tell a story. But men feel as if they just underwent dental surgery. What are men looking for in a conversation? In a word…brevity!

- Malcolm*, 29, sales. "Pleeeaassseee! Just the facts, ma'am, just the facts! Less is more. Tell us at the beginning what you need from us, so we can be paying attention as you speak. This way we can pick out the pertinent information in order to give you a concise answer to your problem. If you don't have a problem, tell us up front you don't need us to fix anything and that you just have a cute story to tell us about something that happened to you today. Men are geared to listen for things they are supposed to fix. It's what we do all day and the only people who come to us usually need something done. We have to shift gears if you merely want to share and not have us do something for you."

- Matt*, 58, retired. "If you had a fight with the neighbor and want to know if we think you were in the right, just say "I feel badly. John ran over my plants again with his lawn mower and I "lost it". This happens a lot and it feels like he is doing it on purpose. Do you think I'm overreacting or would you be mad too?" It's direct and to the point. If we feel you are in the right, we will probably take on John for you. It's when you go off on all sorts of things before getting to the point that we tend to lose focus…and patience."

- Brad*, 43, landscaping. "Just tell us the main point *first*. "I can't get the sprinklers to work." Or, "Would you help me figure out why I can't get the bank to return my calls?" Straight to the point. If we need further information we will ask for it. I promise you will get more out of your man and feel less ignored if you will tell us up front what the topic of the conversation is. It's a guy thing. If it is going to be a long-winded thing, try this: "Honey, there is something happening at work and I need your opinion. My boss is complaining about my power point displays. It's rather complicated so I need to tell you a couple of things first so you can give me your viewpoint, okay?"

This way, we know the problem (boss not happy with your displays) and that there are some key points coming that need to be considered. We can now look for those points and formulate some helpful feedback. This is how men handle situations and it's what we are used to."

If you know your guy has plans for something in the next few minutes, don't start a conversation with him that you know will require more time than he has right now. It isn't fair to him and it will be met with frustration on both your parts. 82% of the men polled said their wives picked inopportune times to talk to them about something that would take 30 minutes or more to hash out. Here, brevity is key. If you know he has to run or a big game is coming on TV, just tell him you have something to talk to him about when he has 15 or 30 minutes. Letting him know how much time will be required of him helps him plan for it. Since women do take the scenic route in a lot of their discourse, a lot of men will hesitate to sit down and talk to you as they're not sure how long this is going to take. Tell them in advance how long you will need his undivided attention. Remember, men are goal-oriented, and they like the direct approach.

C) The Deadly Blame Game

When we share a space with another person we get to know all their habits, quirks, short-comings and doubts. Their vulnerabilities become obvious. This gives us tremendous power to hurt our partner at a very visceral level. The sad truth is that the person we swore to love and honor is often the person we destroy little by little with unfeeling words and actions.

This is where blame comes in. Blame in itself is an interesting action. Why do we feel the need to point the finger at someone else for something that displeases us? Perhaps it is partly due to our own feelings of insecurity. "This can't be my fault. If I find out it is because I am lacking or made a bad decision I won't be able to handle it. I can't be wrong! Wrong is bad. Wrong says I'm not perfect."

Many people will take on the Victim role rather than admit they messed up. They may have been raised around perfectionistic parents or have an innate fear of others seeing them fail. Whatever the reason, blaming others for misfortunes can be a controlling maneuver to keep ourselves looking spotless and perfect. We are the Victim here. They need to feel badly for our misery and suffering and make it right. It *has* to be someone else's fault.

If these thoughts have run through your head, ask yourself these questions:

    a. Why is it important to me that the other person is to blame?

    b. Do I feel better when I blame someone else rather than taking responsibility for a problem?

    c. Did I see my parents use the Blame Game to get out of admitting their part in an issue?

    d. By playing the Victim (or wronged party) do I feel a sense of control? Am I using this ploy to get him to grovel, apologize or make it up to me?

    e. Has blame become a habit instead of looking at a situation fairly?

    f. Am I using blame to punish him for not fulfilling my needs?

If you answered these questions fairly you may be surprised to find that what you saw as a flawed partner may just be your perspective and your need to avoid consequences, or avoid seeing yourself as fallible and human. People who constantly point the finger of blame at others are usually people suffering from a low self-esteem who lack the confidence to say "I messed up on that one. I'll do better next time." It takes maturity and a healthy self-esteem to admit we made a mistake. And you know what? We all make mistakes…every day…every year. It makes us human.

Constantly looking for your partner to make a mistake says more about you than it does about him. Why is this so important to you to catch him in the act of being just like you…susceptible to error? This is the man you are supposed to love above all others. Yet we as women constantly nag them, belittle them and make them feel like they are walking on egg shells to please us. This is a huge area of contention in a marriage. Please go over the questions again on the previous page and see if perhaps the problem lies with your need to make him feel small, or to make yourself look bigger.

Once blame becomes a habit, it is hard to fix. It will take you reconnecting to him on a loving level and appreciating him as he is, with all his imperfections and silly quirks. You need to realize you have the power to ruin another human being's life by the way you treat him. Men who are belittled and criticized at home go out into the world bent and beaten down. Why would any of us wish this on another person? On the other hand, you can build him up, appreciate him and let him know how proud you are of him, and that same man will feel he can conquer the world. It's pretty powerful stuff!

If we look at the times we get into playing the Blame Game, I will bet you money it is during a period where we are not feeling connected to our spouse. There are usually negative feelings flowing from somewhere just before the incident occurs that causes us to begin blaming and criticizing. It is hard to put someone down you are feeling good about. If you are both nurturing each other with positive actions, blame is usually absent from the equation. If you wake up in the morning feeling negative, or a series of negative events happen, this atmosphere spawns fights and blame takes center stage.

Here's what the men in the survey had to say about this insidious trait:

- David*, race car driver. "My wife and I work hard to keep the blaming to a minimum. We both realize that when we start pointing fingers it's a signal that something else is wrong. Usually it means one of use let the other one down somehow. We may not even be aware we did. So we have learned to nip it in the bud and ask the other one why they are feeling negatively about us at that moment. This is very powerful because it takes the focus off the incident in question for a minute (which could be totally insignificant) and places it where it belongs...on the other person's feelings. Once we get to why the other one feels badly, we are able to correct it, see their point of view and apologize if necessary. It keeps it from blowing up out of proportion. Nine times out of ten the problem wasn't that I didn't take the garbage out; it was because I didn't comment on her new dress she was wearing last night and she is feeling unappreciated."
- Wayne*, 62, professor. "I have found that I can defuse a potentially bad situation by listening to my wife when she starts blaming me for something. Often it isn't the incident I just "mismanaged" but something else that is bothering her. After I let her talk it out, I

show that I heard her and validate her hurt feelings. I ask if there is also something else on her mind where I may have let her down. It almost always comes spilling out and I find out that there was other things I was doing that made her feel "less." This is a great tool for pulling the wick out of the dynamite before it blows up. Our first inclination is to get defensive and fight back, which never works. Listen... ask... clarify...and fix it."

- Darvin*, 38, IT tech. "I wish women knew what it does to a guy to get picked at all the time. All the loving feelings we have for you go away. How can we feel close to you or want to please you when you keep letting us know we are failing you? A guy's fear of failure is a really big thing! To go home and be told over and over that you're a Dud and a mess is like ripping into him with barbed wire. No wonder men finally leave or end up with a woman who makes him feel like a great guy."

- Mike*, 43, car dealership owner. "Men put up walls when their women constantly berate them. That's when our wives accuse us of shutting them out. There comes a time when we are so shell shocked that we just retreat from the marriage."

- Dennis*, 29, tennis pro. "You know how you hear guys complain that every time they get in a fight with the wife that she brings up everything he did wrong for the past five years? Well, it's true. Women do this a lot! Why can't we keep on the topic instead of bringing all this other crap in? It only makes us more leery of confiding in you or trying hard. What's the point? We are only going to get shot down for it."

- Braden*, 21, student. "I don't care if you're dating or married, when your girl nags at you all the time you just want to get the heck out of there. If she isn't happy with anything you do, let her find someone else. Seriously…men hate this side of women. It's a turn-off and will ruin a relationship. If we did something that made you unhappy just say so without all the name calling, labeling and put-downs. Why can't you just say "You just hurt my feelings by saying I wear too much makeup." Odds are most guys don't know we messed up. We want you to be happy and we will jump through fire to keep you smiling. I guarantee if you tell your guy in a loving way that he messed up, and *what* he did, without all the daggers, he will fix it."

- Mark*, 39, firefighter. "Men are simple and direct. If we did something one of our friends didn't like they will point it out. It's usually something like "Dude! Don't put your sweaty gym socks on top of my water bottle!" That's it. The socks are removed, a parting shot may be taken by the water bottle owner, and it's over. We are laughing over a beer three minutes later. Women drag it out. They are still pouting 6 months later over something their girlfriend said about them. Guys are just simple, basic creatures who want everyone to be happy."

- Marshall*, 38, interior designer. "One of my favorite comedians is Bill Engvall. He has this joke about women always looking for a guy to mess up. He says it's like a "grassy knoll" following him around taking sniper shots at him all day. Ping! Ping! Ping! No matter what he does, she is there to take a shot at him."

A large majority of the men I interviewed commented on the difference between men and women when it came to the blame game. They mentioned that men don't typically criticize women over small details. It's just not important to them that the dinner is perfect, the refrigerator is spotless, etc. They admitted some guys are neat freaks and controlling and may point out those kinds of things, but if a man is in a loving relationship, he is more interested in keeping her happy than telling her she is slipping up. They tend to reserve their comments for important things like car maintenance (she never gets the oil checked and the car could blow up), finances ($300 for a purse is not reasonable), or allowing little Johnny to watch too much television (the kid is getting D's in every class).

The next time you feel the urge to criticize him, stop and look at the mood of the day. Did it start out on a negative note? Think about the importance of the thing you are about to attack him over. Is it really that important, or is it just a safe harbor for your venting when the issue is actually something bigger.

I have a male friend that confided in me he couldn't understand why his girlfriend always picked a fight with him in the mornings. He had just spent the night and gotten up early to fix her breakfast in bed. When she came downstairs later she lit into him for the mess he made in the kitchen while fixing her breakfast. He was dumbfounded and hurt.

I asked what happened the night before. He looked at me with surprise and said, "What do you mean? What does that have to do with it?" I told him to "humor me" and I asked if they had made love the night before or cuddled. He thought about it for a minute and said, "No...I am having trouble in that area and the sex hasn't been as frequent. My ex is going after me in court and I'm stressed a lot."

"You told me most of the fights she initiates are in the morning after you spend the night," I pointed out. "I think she is finding a safer subject, such as a dirty kitchen, to vent her anger at you. My bet is that she is feeling your lack of intimacy is tied to your issues with your ex and she is feeling left out. Why don't you bring that topic up and see what happens?"

They did have a discussion about his ex's interference in his life (and hence in their love making) and things improved. It had nothing to do with dirty dishes—it was all about unfulfilled needs.

Often a fight is picked over something insignificant. It can flag there is something much bigger festering on the back burner. If you do feel your partner is doing something that is causing you stress, let him know in a loving, non-judgmental way. And again, men like directness, not hinting, belittling or name calling. Something like:

"Sweetie, I tried winding up your socks to see if they could march themselves off the floor and down to the washer, but the wind–up key is missing. Can you help me out with that?" (Humor is huge when you need something done. It takes the sting out and men enjoy it. Women do as well.)

"Dave...would you take the garbage out for me please? I think I hear the truck coming." (Simple, uncomplicated and time-sensitive.)   Hint: Use the word "would" instead of "could". "Could" implies there is some doubt he may be capable of carrying out the task; "would" shows confidence in him that you know he can do it. Sounds trivial? All I can say is it works wonders, with teenage boys *and* their Dads!)

"I don't mean to criticize what you have on, but I'm pretty sure most people going to this party are going to be wearing slacks instead of shorts. While I appreciate those masculine legs of yours, they may be the only ones on display this evening." (Give him a peck on the cheek and leave the room. This allows him space. He will love the compliment and you didn't come off as a know-it-all. When he gets to the party and sees all the slacks, he will probably feel grateful to you for saving him from looking like an idiot.)

The major point is to take a long look at your need to criticize and blame, and to remember you hold a lot of power over how this guy sees himself. You married him because you love him and wanted to share a life with him. Our need to blame comes from a feeling our needs are not being met. This can stem from insecurity and a low self-esteem. Do the homework needed to have the confidence and feelings of self-worth necessary to rid you of the need to always be right. This is your husband. At what point did he become target practice?

Curtis*, 47, engineer. "I will tell the ladies out there one thing. If you attack a guy on a subject that he is especially vulnerable about, he may never trust you again. If he is insecure about his beer gut, his receding hairline, his job loss, stutter, shyness, lack of mechanical knowledge, or any myriad things, and you aim at that target during a fight, you probably lost any loving feelings he has for you, and it can take a long, long time to get them back. Play fair. No name calling or labels. Those memories have long shadows."

D) Hints vs Direct Statements

Oh boy, is this a big one with men! The complaints about women dropping hints instead of just asking them to do something in simple, clear-cut directions were brought up over and over again. Hinting does not work, never has, never will, and yet women continue doing it. We feel it is a better way to gently remind a man of something we would like him to do for us. So why is this approach so ineffective? Simple…it doesn't work.

- Barkley*, 42, DJ. "Here it is -- period. Guys don't hint to each other. We don't say things like "Hey Gus, did you hear they added another hamburger to the list at Burger Barn*?" in hopes Gus will get the hint and ask if we should go get a burger. We just say, "Hey Gus, let's hit Burger Barn. They've got a new burger I'd like to try."

Done deal. We are pretty simple people. Just tell us, point us in that direction, and we are happy to do it if we are capable of doing it."

- Don*, 56, furniture sales. "Hinting is frustrating for men for the simple reason we don't communicate that way. With us it's just grunts and groans. Listen to men talk sometime and you will see what I mean. Women get mad when we miss their hints. We aren't being obtuse; it's just not how our auditory system is set to receive signals. Just ask us...without the sarcasm or criticism, please."

- Richard*, 51, teacher. "Simple is better. You don't need to justify your request, embellish it or remind us we keep forgetting to do it. "Honey, I know you have a lot going on but I'm feeling stressed over the tires. Would you take the car in for new tires today please? I APPRECIATE how you always take care of us." Unless the guy is a total jerk, he will take care of it, pronto. If he doesn't, don't bring it up again. Take the car in yourself and I guarantee he will feel badly about it and not make the mistake of waiting again. I have a female friend who did just that and when her husband got mad and said she spent too much on tires, she didn't say a word. She just walked away. The silence underscored her disappointment in him a lot louder than mean words could have. Don't bring out the machine guns. Actions speak louder than words with guys. Your action just put him on notice that he is not stepping up to make sure you are safe."

The bottom line is this: Don't hint. Tell. Don't play a song with your message in it, leave a magazine article lying around, plug in a movie depicting your current grievance, or drop hints hoping he will catch on. Use your big girl words. Hinting only leaves both of you frustrated.

E) Nonverbal Communication

Pay close attention to this topic. Underline it, highlight it in pink and put three stars next to it. Nonverbal goes a long way with men. Touch and action are the way to his heart.

My co-host on *Troubleshooting Men* is a man who operates a counseling and coaching camp for men. He works with husbands and boyfriends who are feeling out of their depth in relationships, or have self-esteem issues. His advice on the show to women is gold. He brought up the very important component of touch.

"When a woman grabs her husband by the belt and pulls him up close to her, it is dynamite! Every nerve ending in this guy is going to go off and whatever she is saying to him at the time was just highlighted in neon! When a woman touches a man, his body and mind react and he feels an instant connection to you. It is an art too many women forget to employ."

Typically women are too busy using their words to communicate and forget how powerful the sense of touch is to men. Running a finger along his neck while he is cooking, putting your arms around his waist, nibbling on his ear are all short-cuts to his feelings for you. It can reconnect the two of you faster than words for the simple reason men respond more to action. It's partly why sex is so healing for men. It is a physical act and carries more weight than words. Women tend to respond more to romantic phrases or having him tell her how beautiful she is. Again...it's the difference between the sexes.

The next time your guy is engrossed in the newspaper, IPad or television, don't say a word, just walk past him and trail your fingers lightly over his shoulders, maybe adding a light squeeze at the end. Watch what happens. He may look up in surprise, or ask "What's that for?" Just smile in a flirtatious way over your shoulder and keep going. Silence can be powerful when touch does the talking. Touch his wrist when talking to him. It will draw his attention back to you if his mind has wondered. Lean over in the car and nibble his ear or kiss his neck. A playful swat on his backside sends a signal that you like his body.

- Mark*, 34, accountant. "One day my wife walked into the kitchen where I was making a sandwich. She grabbed me by my shirt collar, pulled me in close to her face, and looking me directly in the eyes said, "Have I told you today I think you are drop-dead sexy?" She kissed me hard, let me go and walked off saying, "Bye-bye. I'm off to get groceries," and headed out the door. I about fell over. It was an amazing feeling, and so unexpected. I waited on her the rest of the day and night."

I know what you're thinking, and you may be right. There is a good chance touching him can get his motor racing. If you are not in the mood for sex, be careful where you touch him. Teasing is not nice if you have no plans to follow through. If he becomes more aggressive, and you are not ready to advance things along, whisper in his ear that "patience is a virtue", and "good things come to those who wait". Kiss him lightly, and whisper, "Later." He will be buzzing all day.

When two people are connecting on the levels that are important to them (men with action, women with words) they form a bond. Keeping the flirting going in a marriage will keep the romantic fire burning. When a man feels you desire him in a physical way (like grabbing his belt and pulling him towards you) he will literally climb mountains, swim piranha-infested waters and take on 12 burly linebackers to make you happy. Denying him that affirmation that you love his masculinity and his male needs, will find you ending up with crumbs. Doesn't a banquet sound so much better?

Appreciate Him

Appreciation. Is it as rare as great customer service these days? Or even mediocre customer service? I think all of us crave appreciation in some form or another. How many of us have felt let-down when we've gone the extra mile to make a holiday special, or cook a great dinner, or take extra time looking nice for an evening out only to have not one single comment made about our efforts. It's pretty deflating. All of us crave a well-earned compliment, and even those we didn't earn.

Men listed feeling appreciated as a huge need of theirs in a relationship. When you look at how often men receive criticism, put-downs and trash talk in the real world, it's no wonder a compliment feels like manna from heaven. And when that appreciation comes from the woman who makes a man's heart beat faster, it carries even more weight.

So, what is it men want the women in their lives to appreciate? This doesn't take rocket science to answer this one. They want the things that make them uniquely masculine to be uppermost in the appreciation department. Men may appreciate you complimenting him on his haircut, or his chipping in to do the dishes after dinner, but the kudos extolling his masculinity are the ones he craves.

- Anthony*, 43, store owner. "When my wife feels my biceps and says something cute, like "Nice guns...are they loaded?" I just melt. It makes me feel so manly and I just want to carry her off to a cave somewhere. It may sound corny, but men will never change when it comes to needing that reinforcement that we are all man. The rewards to the woman who gives us that will come straight from our heart."

- Davis*, 51, restaurant owner. "I was bent over trying to fix a leg on the couch when my wife walked up behind me and said, "You know, a butt like that should be illegal." She swatted it and left to run errands. By the time she got home I had vacuumed, mopped the kitchen floor and taken the trash out. When she looked surprised at all my efforts, I said, "Just thought I would get some of these chores out of the way in case you needed more time to appreciate my rear view." Men crave appreciation. We won't admit it, but we lap it up like honey."

- Winston*, 60, limo driver. "Guys take heat all day. We're told constantly when we screw up at work, at sports, jibes from our buddies, etc. When we come home to a woman who can't wait to see us, grabs us at the door and says she's happy to have us home, that is the best! It builds us up to go out and face it all again the next day."

- Balki*, 23, student. "When my girlfriend tells me how much she appreciates all I do to make her happy, it just makes me want to do more. Something as simple as putting a nail in the wall for her to hang a picture, or checking the oil in her car, is always met with a big hug and Thank You! Guys want their women to be happy and we will do anything to make that happen, especially if we feel it's appreciated."

85% of the men in the survey listed appreciation in their top 3 needs. 12% put it as number one! So many of them commented on how hard they try to make their woman happy. It was a source of joy to see her smile. One man put it in perspective:

"When my wife is happy it is a direct reflection on my role as a husband. If what I am giving her is making her days happier, there is no better feeling for a man. We take our roles as provider and protector very seriously. It may not make sense to a woman, but when she is unhappy, we feel at a deep level we are not measuring up, and have let her down. When we marry someone, that person becomes our sole purpose for getting up in the morning and going to work. It's a responsibility we feel keenly."

The ongoing refrain throughout the survey was men wanting to be the Hero in their women's eyes and to feel she appreciates what he brings to her life. I can't underscore this enough. This is a very real need for men. When it is taken away by his wife nagging him, belittling him and criticizing him, something inside a man dies, and at some point, he will withdraw to avoid the pain her words and actions cause him. Most men will tell you that men don't cheat on their wives for sexual gratification. It was to find a way to feel needed and appreciated again. I'm not condoning affairs...far from it. I am merely passing along the information.

Have His Back

As we've talked about, men are often whipped around like a sail in the wind in the world outside their front door. They are supposed to be tough, so people feel justified in letting the bullets fly feeling the poor guy can probably take it. There are no velvet gloves or restraint used when dealing with men in the corporate or sports worlds. Trash talk runs rampant on the courts and fields, and undermining and downsizing are prevalent in the business arena. No wonder he is sensitive to slights and recrimination when he pulls into the driveway of the only sanctuary he has...his home.

The recent economic downturn took the world, drop kicked it and slammed dunked it into a tailspin. No job felt secure and many people found themselves suddenly on welfare. While women were hit hard and felt the sting of being dismissed and in need of security, men felt it at a deeper level. Their hard wiring to be the provider was severed. This is a terrifying event for anyone, but for a man, it is a nightmare.

Whether a husband loses a job, a championship, his hair or his self-respect, the one person who is in the seat of the greatest power to lift him up again is the woman he loves. It is at this most vulnerable time in a man's live that his wife can either make him or break him. If he is met with her lack of faith in him, blaming and pressure, he may never recover. On the other hand, if she shows him she trusts him to spring back, and shows her love both verbally and physically, he will find the will power and drive to climb out of the abyss. Some of the stories shared with me concerning this topic were truly moving.

- Doug*, 53, computer tech. "My company got hit hard in 2009. They laid off over 450 people. I went from having a consistent paycheck to looking through the classifieds for a job. With so many people out of work, the jobs were scarce and they were looking for younger guys. I panicked. I felt like a failure even though the reason for my unemployment had nothing to do with me. I looked around at the lifestyle my wife and I had become accustomed to and could see it vanishing within the next few months.

  My wife sat down with me, took my hand in hers and said, "You know what? I believe things happen for a reason. I've wanted to help my sister with her floral shop and you've wanted to make furniture in your woodshop out back. We have enough money to get us through the next six months. Let's both go after our dreams and see what happens! It will be an adventure!"

I'm not ashamed to say I cried. She turned the entire thing around with her faith in me. Her sister made her a partner in the shop and she is making great money and I am living my dream of designing and creating furniture. I have never been happier to be out of an office cubicle. As of this writing we are together making more than I did alone in the corporate world. I married an angel. I am one blessed man."

- Markus*, 40, personal coach. "I was in a bad motorcycle accident. My left leg was so mangled I was told I had to give up skiing and basketball, two things I love more than life. It was a really bleak period for me. My guy friends tried to cheer me up with lame jokes and finding me information on Wheelchair Olympics which did nothing but make me feel worse. Then one day my wife came in from the store with two bags filled with odds and ends. She plopped them into my lap. One bag was books on coaching basketball. The other was filled with t-shirts, a whistle and a clip-board. I looked over at her and she smiled. "You've always wanted to coach basketball...go do it. There are enough shirts in there for a kid's team. No excuses, Hamlin* (my last name), go change some kid's lives!" I pulled one of the shirts out of the bag and the team name was emblazoned across the back: Hamlin's Heroes. That moment has never crossed my mind without my throat swelling shut with emotion. She knew me...better than anyone else, and turned what had been a huge downturn for me into an opportunity of a lifetime. And the rest of the story? Hamlin's Heroes won the district championship! She showed me a detour can lead to a road you might have missed. And she showed me her unconditional love and support. It's those "make or break" times that a wife can truly be your lifesaver. I couldn't play the game I loved anymore, but I could coach it…and make an impact in those young lives."

Stories like these were replete throughout the survey. It was inspiring and heartwarming. There were also stories from men whose wives abandoned them emotionally when the times got hard. We will never have a chance to show our husbands our unwavering faith and support as when he is suffering a set-back of some kind. Be sensitive to his need to be masculine, a provider and protector and you will have a strong male willing to slay dragons for you.

Keep the Mystery & Adventure Alive

This is the fun part. As some of the men mentioned earlier in the book, boredom in a marriage (or dating relationship) can be deadly. This should be an area both of you keep interesting, and I will alert the guys in *Troubleshooting Women*, but for now, let's see how you can add to the cauldron and keep it bubbling.

Men love adventure and the unexpected. It appeals to their sense of freedom and achievement. Role playing with video games, and living vicariously through football games on TV are all popular past times for the average male. Keeping his life interesting by suggesting or implementing exciting diversions will keep your marriage fresh, spontaneous and fun.

Coming up with ideas to keep him guessing are easier than you think. You will need to offer activities that appeal to his particular likes, but here are some tried-and-trues:

- Head for the hills (or beach, desert, or backyard). Getting out into nature replenishes the soul and vanquishes the routine of daily living. Grab a picnic blanket, basket filled with his favorite nibbles, a bottle of wine or his beverage of choice, and go somewhere off the beaten path. If you're by a stream, take his shoes off and put his feet in the water. There is something rejuvenating about water, and the cold mountain stream will feel like a shock to his system. Take along a card game, or simply lay back and watch the clouds. This can also be done in your back yard with candles, twinkling lights in the trees and a telescope.

- Take him bowling, to the archery range, shooting range, tennis court, miniature golfing, toss a Frisbee around in the park, play horseshoes or buy a cheap ring toss game at the dollar store and put it outside. Have a water balloon fight, chase each other with squirt guns, or play touch football. Men love to play. And they will love you for remembering that.

- Create a themed dinner and surprise him. Cook an Italian meal of lasagna, complete with garlic bread, oils, a salad and a bottle of wine. Buy an inexpensive red-and-white checked tablecloth, some matching napkins and light the candle tapers you've screwed into empty wine bottles. Find some gondola music on YouTube, or find a Pandora station on your phone that plays romantic love songs. If you're feeling really creative, make some menus on your computer with your last name as the restaurant logo—for instance *Bailey's Bistro*. List your dishes along with some graphics of Italy you Googled. Under Dessert, you can list Tiramisu, and beneath that a dessert called "Between the Sheets." See which one he chooses. ☺

- Have a special movie night where you have two of his favorites waiting, his favorite snacks, lit candles and drinks. Have him put his feet in your lap and give him a foot massage during the movie. He won't know what hit him.

- Leave love notes around the house telling him the things you admire about him.

- Throw him a surprise Guy's Night. Invite his best buddies over for a night of cards, food and drinks. Put everything out on the table and when the doorbell rings, kiss him on the cheek, tell him to have fun and disappear to have a Girl's Night Out with your friends.

- Buy some sexy lingerie, get creative with some mood lighting in the bedroom, put on the soft music and call to him that the smoke alarm is chirping and to please bring up a new battery. When he comes into the bedroom, be draped across the bed with a playful look on your face and say, "Oops, I guess it's my battery that needs recharging."

- Variety in the bedroom is something most men feel is lacking. The same routine, same time, same station…Creating some role playing, coming to bed in something other than the PJ's with feet your Grandma gave you when you turned 16, getting creative with sexual positions, toys and music all add a spark that will benefit both of you. The adage that says "If the sex is good, the marriage is usually in good shape" was founded on solid principles. If you feel inadequate in this area due to naiveté about sex, there are tons of books and videos out there from conservative to red hot Siren! If it's your body image that's holding you back, work on it, but remember, women tend to obsess about their tummies more than men do. If you are bringing the excitement, the last thing on his mind is your less than perfect figure. And keep in mind…sex is not just for the bedroom. Surprise him with some innovative locations, and times.

You get the idea. Change it up. Surprise him. Pay attention to things he mentions. Take him to that car show, indoor sky diving, rock climbing, a new play, the planetarium to look at the stars, the zoo…just get out of the house! There are classes on things he might love to learn, from stained glass to glass blowing. White water rafting, zip lining, an Asian dinner on the floor with pillows and you in a Kimono.

Keep the fun and adventure in your marriage alive and he will run home from work. Plus, you will be teaching *him* how to ramp it up. It may surprise you to see him take over and come up with some great ideas of his own!

Along with keeping the mystery and fun going is to also create a special "you and me against the world" bond. This can be done with nicknames for each other. A cute nickname can cause an immediate sense of connection when your partner hears it. It immediately reminds him of the relationship and the special bond between the two of you.

When my ex-husband and I were first married he began calling me "Grudge." At first I didn't pay much attention to it, but after a few times of him calling me that, I asked him where the name "Grudge" was coming from. "It doesn't sound like a good thing," I said to him. He smiled and said, "I call you Grudge because I like holding you." It took me a moment to realize he was referring to the saying, "Holding a grudge." My face lit up and it is still one of the sweetest nicknames I've heard. He also called me Cricket Lighter (after the popular lighter in the 1970's), and said he loved it when I "sparkled." Both comments were his way of saying he loved it when I was happy and effervescent. He still remains a very dear friend of mine.

Create traditions with him, no matter how small. Watching a favorite sit-com together each night at the same time, reading a book together, cooking together, date nights, etc. all add special bonding that we remember for years. Having theme nights like Murder Mystery Night where you turn off all the lights, light a candle, set out treats, pop in a scary movie and cuddle on the couch is a lot of fun. Creating a dish together you just saw created on your favorite cooking show is a bonding experience.

A marriage that plays together stays together. Who wouldn't want life to be filled to the brim? Complacency is so insidious. "Familiarity breeds contempt," is unfortunately true. So do the "unfamiliar." Life should be joyful, experienced and enjoyed. If you bring to your relationship a constant sense of adventure, you will reap rewards beyond your imagination.

At the time of this writing, my boyfriend showed up with his Jeep and two river rafting tubes in the back of it. I have lived in Colorado for 36 years and never tubed its gorgeous rivers. I cannot tell you how invigorating and refreshing it was to float down a river with my feet dangling in the cold water of the Rockies on an August day with the sun shining down on my shoulders. The rapids found me screaming with delight. I felt reborn. He brings so much adventure to our relationship. We take turns coming up with surprises for each other and it makes life "sparkle."

So come on people! You only get one chance at this life. There is so much to see and do. Bring out the little kid in you and your guy and go have some fun! That's how memories are made.

The Man Cave

Ah, the man cave. That elusive, often misunderstood haven for the male species. What can he be doing in there, and why is there such a need for one?

Have you ever come home from work or shopping and found the house empty? No loud television, kids pulling on you, or someone demanding your immediate attention? Isn't it delicious to have those few, rare moments all to yourself? Just to plop, run a bath, raid the frig or read a book?

We all need space to recapture a part of ourselves. We have shared ourselves until the tank is pretty much empty.

And while family life is rich with rewards and we would miss all the chaos, everyone needs a chance to recharge their batteries. For women, it may be to sit down with some girlfriends and just talk...about anything and everything. It might be a long bubble bath with candles and soft music, or a good book or movie. We feel reborn and we are ready to face it all again.

Men are no different, with one exception. Rather than have a gab-fest with their friends, they crave some solitude to regain a sense of themselves. They do this by going off to do something, or nothing, that takes their minds off work and responsibilities. Remember how men compartmentalize? Tinkering on the car, adding to his model train collection in the basement, working out, shooting hoops, are all things that he can focus on and leave the hectic world behind. If women allow their men to do this, you will have a happier husband who is now ready to go back into the fray. One woman's bubble bath is another man's drip pan.

- Brian*, 33, bartender. "I think some women get miffed if a guy needs some space. They take it personally, as if he is trying to get away from her. I know women that will follow him and nag him to come back to the family. How good would it feel if your husband encouraged you to take some time for yourself? Wouldn't you feel he really appreciated you and cared? Stop seeing a man's need for some privacy as a direct cut to you. It's his way of sloughing off the day and being more open to you when he finally pokes his head out again."

Roger*, 45, technician. "If you deny a guy his right to some space, you are opening up a can of worms. It's like backing a moose into a stand of trees. Eventually he will charge. A guy can hit the boiler point when too much is put on his plate and he has no way to release some steam. We aren't saying women don't reach that saturation point as well. Guys just aren't as good as using words to release the pressure. We need to do something with our hands or just sit for a while and decompress. Give us a chance to do that and you will be glad you did."

Chapter Seven
The Toad Pool

Here at *Troubleshooting Men's* "Toad Pool," we take a look at the warning signs that you may just have landed something you might want to toss back! We will also show you the traits that create a very desirable Prince. So, without further ado, let's take a peek at the local gathering pond and see what's perched on those precarious lily pads!

And for the men who may "croak" at our stereotypes, or use of the word "toad", we are merely identifying toad-like behavior, not labeling men as amphibians.

We will also give you our *Troubleshooting Men* website's psychologists' viewpoint on each toad-like personality to see if he is "toxic" or "treatable".

Ten Stereotypes of Toad-Like Behavior

"As we discuss these "Toads," it is important that we simply do not respond to just their outward behaviors, but also take into consideration what inner workings (thoughts, emotions, beliefs, values, and the like) perpetuate those behaviors. With that said, a lot of the behaviors presented by a Toad are usually some level of over-compensation for their own brittle and elusive self-concept.

Historically, personality traits and characteristics have been deemed "untreatable." However, with three ideas in mind (time, patience, and a willingness to change) as a foundation, some relationships are indeed salvageable. The most confusing of the foundations is the willingness to change – it is not gauging YOUR willingness for the other to change, but the desire of the OTHER person to change that is brought into question.

In order to facilitate change, there are a lot of considerations to be made. For example, are there any genetic predispositions? What environments and role models were experienced that made someone who they are today?

So, as we look at each of these toads, there rests an argument as whether or not they maintain "personality defects" versus merely having "difficulties of adaptation." As a defect, one focuses on the negative components; as a difficulty of adaptation, one emphasizes the positive efforts to improve (again, with a greater focus on the Toad presenting the characteristics). It is important to remember that people do maintain the innate ability to change over time, and if they do not (or cannot) change, it is often due to their lack of knowledge in who they are, what they want to be, or where they truly are at in their life. So, to some, these characteristics can be responsive to treatment (with the foundations in place) rather than a permanent fixture in a person's repertoire.

As a vessel for change, you simply cannot "push" someone to change, or "pull" them in your direction to change, but be able to walk side-by-side with someone during their "journey" of change. However, with that said, and recognizing that there are two individuals inside of a relationship, and that the relationship as a couple takes on a life of its own, a warning goes out that one should not be a victim of a toxic relationship introducing drama (rather than opportunity), depression or anger (rather than joy), or fear and anxiety (rather than excitement)."

Ray Hazen, MA LPC CACIII SMC

Here are our 10 Toad Stereotypes…

Super Toad

"Look! Up in the sky…it's a bird, it's a plane, it's… Super Toad!" He is amazing—always regaling you with stories of his incredible feats. He saved the project at work, made the winning touchdown, or corrected a professor in front of an awe-struck classroom. He is always there for you, telling you how to run your life. Women all want a Hero, right? However, there are certain traits to look out for, if that red cape seems to pop up too often.

Toxic or Treatable Toad:

"When it comes to picking a partner, some women will fall under the whole "I need someone to rescue me" mentality and that's when in walks the man who will not only do just that, but is more comfortable with someone who needs rescuing; we call them Rescuers. Most Rescuers are not doing this to necessarily help the women but more because they think they have the answers in order to make her life better and do not think that the woman has the ability to solve her own problems. This bond that forms from the "rescuing" or care giving can give the woman a sense of instant intimacy. To the one doing the "rescuing," they will receive a sense of control over the woman, giving him a feeling of both value and importance. This creates a problem when the woman starts to think for herself or becomes "healed." The Super Toad will become defensive and may even resort to belittling to get the woman back to a "broken" state. These guys most likely have felt alone and lost in the past and need to control a relationship to feel more needed. It can even give him a sense of fulfillment. Woman who have found themselves in relationships like this, have said they have turned to this man to make even the smallest decisions. These types of relationships normally do not last long for two common reasons: one, because the woman abandons the "rescuer" once she is "healed", and two, because he sees nothing else in the relationship and finds someone else who is more "broken" at which time he will replace the woman.

The Super Toad can also exhibit heroic behavior due to a low self-esteem. He feels if he can constantly tell her how he saved the day at work, during a sporting contest, rescued a child from being run over, was the only one to answer a hard question, etc., he will be a Hero in her eyes. In an effort to corral his excessive need for reassurance, try building him up before he asks for it. If he can feel like a Hero in small ways, he may begin to lose the need to brag about grandiose behavior.

For women who get caught in the victim role in a Rescuer relationship the best thing to remember is that you need to be independent and be able to make decisions for yourself. A healthy relationship consists of two people not telling each other what to do, but being supportive when needed. Look for the signs of a Rescuer, or Super Toad, and be able to tell if a guy is in the relationship for the right reasons, or is he just simply looking for a "wounded bird" to "fix."

Treatable if he merely needs some reinforcement for a low self-esteem. His tales of daring may be masking someone really needing someone to be proud of him.

Toxic if he is only looking to be the Rescuer and requires helpless people to feel good about himself.

Casey Pittman, Registered Psychotherapist, Recovery

Shamrock Toad

Shamrock Toad is that wonderful amphibian that we all know and love. His mantra is "You are so LUCKY to have me in your life!" What are the warning signs that the ego in your guy is a harmless *ribbit* and not a narcissistic *croak*?

Toxic or Treatable Toad:

"As this toad looks into the horizon, he truly appreciates the fact that all the world and universe truly rotates around him, and if he were to pass, an apocalypse of darkness and disease would spread across the earth and life as we know it would be no more. This fantasy is usually incorporated with a lack of ability to recognize other's feelings and needs, as well as a tactless need to be admired by others. With this inflated sense of self comes an inability to recognize another's viewpoint; therefore, should someone disagree, an incredible wound is created, taking a significant amount of time to heal, as well as emotional instability (such as increased anger, depression, embarrassment, and anxiety), that may lead to aggressive (or passive-aggressive) behaviors. As a victim of themselves, they can be dangerous and unpredictable.

Specific behaviors you can look for is this toad's preoccupations with his own beauty, brilliance, power, or success. Look and listen for any belief he has of his own existence as being "special," "unique," "exclusive," or "irreplaceable."

With these beliefs, in his mind, he can only be understood and admired by persons of high status, and, as a result, could very easily make you feel as if you are undeserving. With this toad come expectations that can often not be met by you, as well as an expectation that you will automatically comply to his wants, needs, and desires due to his greatness. Should you disagree with this toad, he will simply blame you and identify it as your envy of what he has."

Toxic. This one will probably require professional help.

Ray Hazen, MA LPC CACIII SMC

Workaholic Toad

Telltale signs of the Workaholic Toad are a well-worn briefcase, loosened tie, bags beneath the eyes, clinched jaw, and an expression that changes from determined to bone-tired by the end of the day. His cell phone beeps so often that people near him wonder if he is backing up. The Rocky Theme Song plays in his head as he tackles the corporate world or his new venture. He is determined, he is focused…he is too busy for a relationship!

Toxic or Treatable Toad:

"As with any job focus, having a relationship with a Workaholic Toad has benefits: money, vacation time, money, health benefits, and more money. However, the greatest downfall is the attention that should be focused on a relationship is geared toward *individual* prestige, fame, and fortune. Although the short-term benefits may abound, the long-term losses, if unrestrained, are riddled by a person who accepts nothing less than perfection, and is relentless with inflexibility. These traits cause the toad to be preoccupied with uncontrollable thoughts and actions that can definitely interfere in the relationship, causing extreme levels of distress in the other person's ability to function.

There are certain traits you can look for beneath the white shirt and striped tie, the patent leather loafers, and clean-shaven smile. Their self-esteem is often hinged on their ability to mask youthful fears of failure or inadequacy with charisma and a need for orderliness, perfection, and interpersonal control. This toad may have lists (and a list of lists) and is focused on details, order, organization, rules, and schedules. These guys have an unrelenting standard that is both time- and task-driven, with a great focus on completing tasks in an efficient manner (which may not speak well of intimate performances). Similarly, although they are deemed as devoted by peers, their devotion is to the job and the relationship is often viewed as if in a rearview mirror – this allows the toad to become "comfortable" in the relationship, therefore taking it for granted. In his mind, the relationship "will always be there" – if not, well, there is always work to do. Because they are so in tune with the logical part of their brain, no emotion is required, desired, warranted, or needed.

Unless you want to give up your individual goals, dreams, and desires, and you want to be propped on a mantle as a "trophy," your best chance of bringing about change is to make it his idea that his future (especially after retirement) rests with you and not the job...the one thing that can be a constant is YOU...a job can very easily come-and-go."

Treatable if he can relinquish the need to excel at all costs. He may need someone to help him take some of the financial burden off his shoulders so he can slow down a little.

Toxic if his drive has more of an underlying personality disorder where he cannot balance relaxation and work. There may be narcissistic tendencies here where his need for success and accolades outweigh his need for a positive relationship.

Ray Hazen, MA LPC CACIII SMC

Sleepover Toad

Beware the Sleepover Toad! His mission is to get you to his lily pad as quickly as possible. Every movement is orchestrated to skip 1st, 2nd, and 3rd base and simply slide into home! If you are fine with the one-night stand type of toad, you may skip this section. If not...read on for the warning signs that he is "lily hopping"!

Toxic or Treatable Toad:

"There are different names for this type of guy: Player, Flake, and Mr. None-Commitment. There are different ways of spotting this particular type of toad, which we are going to briefly go over. Distance can be a key sign in many different ways for this man; such as when he is conversing with you. This type tends to not disclose too much about himself or really encourage too much conversation from you (he will only want the basics; name, where you work, etc.). This is a clear sign that he is not really into you or interested in getting to know you. Social invitations will also start being shot down, unless the invitation is to go to your place; if it is with a group of people, this guy will want nothing to do with it.

There are different types of toads in this category; some will come off as amazing at first and romance you and treat you like you have never been treated before. He can't see enough of you, calls or texts every day, makes dinners and takes you to movies. Do not be fooled. Sometimes these gentlemen can be a classic neophiliac, meaning he likes anything new and once he has "had it" he throws it to the side. This guy loves the "chase" and once he has "caught" you, he no longer is interested. These are typically the "full court press" type. You will be flattered that he is asking you out several times in one week. There is a reason for this. It fast forwards the relationship so that you are at an advanced stage much sooner than usual. He has only invested a week or two but suddenly you feel like you are in a tail spin of activity with him and the race to the bedroom has begun.

Another type of Sleepover Toad is the guy who is already promising great things in the future, even though you have only gone out a time or two. This provides false security and a sense he is really interested if he is already planning events with you down the road. Very often these special activities vanish after he has gotten what he wants.

One way to protect yourself from this type is to not be fooled right away by the perfect lines, romantic behavior, and frequent dates. Set up boundaries and really make sure you "interview" this guy for a while to see what his intentions are. The best way to weed out men likes this is time; these guys are not looking for long term and after a while the romantic mask will slip away. Do not settle for someone who will disrespect you or has no interest in you whatsoever. Truly get to know the guy and make sure all is as it seems before making any leaps."

Toxic. The need for "quickie" relationships that offer nothing in the way of substance or durability is a bad sign. There are underlying issues that will require professional help.

Casey Pittman, Registered Psychotherapist, Recovery

Spotlight Toad

"Look at me! Look at Me!" He has to be the center of attention, whether it's one-on-one with you, at work, or at a

party. Here are the warning signs that you may be dealing with a spotlight stealer who has no real interest in your accomplishments, dreams, or needs:

Toxic or Treatable Toad:

"Unlike some of the others, this Toad likes to express his emotions, and he does so in a very exaggerated, inflated, and embellished manner. Their emotion is often larger-than-life, sometimes very inappropriate, and often occurs at inopportune times. Because of an ill-feeling of not being the center of attention, if one emotion does not work, they will try another, and then another, until they find one that gets the desired response from others. They can be recognized simply by appearance, for they will dress or do things that make them stand out (from clothing, to the car they drive, to the people they hang out with) – WHATEVER will draw attention, often no matter the cost.

Although they are entertaining at times, sometime in the future this becomes an annoyance. You will find this toad can be easily influenced. They are often naive, suggestible, and willing to do things "on a dare."

Their character is one in which they have an extreme need to draw the admiration of others. Because of this, this Toad finds difficulty in being independent. They are also extremely indecisive and clingy. There is often an intense fear they may be alone and will have to take care of themselves. These are the guys that find great difficulty in accepting accountability for what they have done in the past, and have equal difficulty in defining and following through with the responsibilities they have in the future. They are often going to do the opposite of what YOU want, for often, negative attention is better than no attention.

Because of their playful nature, they will often confuse any casual relationship as one of increased intimacy. So, if you happen to be "just friends," can you say, "Stalker!"?"

Toxic. Rarely can the Spotlight Toad be "fixed" with the simple means of offering him more attention or trying to understand his need for it. There are some deep-seated issues here that a layman cannot obliterate or heal.

Ray Hazen, MA LPC CACIII SMC

Poor ME Toad

See that amphibian in the corner who has been going on and on for over an hour about how awful life is? The poor toad seated next to him is praying for a trap door to open and swallow the Poor Me Toad into the abyss below. We all know the type. Their life is so hard, all the bad things happen to them, nobody loves or understands them. They drain the sunshine out of the day and rain on everyone's parade. Do you want to walk around with this guy constantly holding an umbrella, or leave him to drop green teardrops into his pond of doom?

Toxic or Treatable Toad:

"When it comes to being around someone who is suffering from self-pity, it can be hard to understand them or get why they are like this. This is typically a "victim" mentality. They will "handle" the victimization by indulging in self-pity for many different reasons; to hide away, comfort themselves, or just wait until someone else comes along to "save them" or do the comforting for them. Some of the outward signs are depression and a lack of energy along with being unmotivated. This type will, at times, avoid other people and react to what would be to anyone else an easily handled situation as if it were a crisis or traumatic event. A fear of taking on normal responsibilities is sometimes obvious as well. These toads will complain about *everything*...from their job, lack of money, perceived unfair treatment from others, their car breaking down...you get the picture. Typically, these were coddled toads when they were smaller. Their parents probably removed all the obstacles in their path and came running each time the toad was upset or feeling defeated. They made it "all better." Now into adulthood, they are still looking for someone to make everything bright and shiny. Typical everyday occurrences that happen to us all set this toad into a world of despair.

For someone dealing with this person, you will start to feel yourself having to "rescue" this person on a daily basis. What makes things even harder for the person dealing with the self-pitying individual is that this toad may refuse to be helped at first, so you will find yourself being stuck in a revolving door. To complicate matters, if you refuse to help or point out that things aren't that bad, they will go into victim mode, not always consciously. They can do this unconsciously as well, and will justify their reasoning for being the victim. If you try the other route and ignore them while they are having a "pity party," they will have the tendency to become upset and angry with you for the lack of empathy being shown. If there is a goal for this self-pity individual, it is manipulation by getting into "victim mode" and trying to get you to feel sympathy for them, which will then allow them to continue their victim-stance. If you commiserate with him in an effort to show you care, you have become the "enabler" and this lop-sided Merry-Go-Round will keep on spinning. You are not helping him...you are continuing to enable a crippled adult.

It is very energy draining, annoying, and frustrating to deal with someone who fits the self-pity individual. When someone goes into a relationship with the Poor Me Toad, it is usually out of some form of guilt or sadness for their plight. Your feelings of guilt, or empathy, are then used by the self-pitying individual so they do not have to take any form of responsibility for their own problems and situations. You are now "stuck" in the relationship. Does this sound healthy at all? I hope not, because self-pity cannot play a healthy role in any kind of relationship and should be avoided. If you find yourself in one of these relationships, do not fall into the mind set of "I can fix this" or "he will change." When someone is living life as the victim, there is nothing anyone can do to change this except the individuals themselves. And unless they see a reason to change, they won't. You walking away and letting them deal with life on their own could be that reason. Try saying, "I realize this seems difficult, but the only way to handle situations like this is to tackle them yourself. If I take it over for you, you won't have the tools to deal with it in the future. I care about you enough to walk away and let you be the strong person I know you are." In cases of clinical depression or a total inability to handle life, they will need a professional's help.

Self-pity can be categorized as a form of abuse by some professionals and so it is important to be able to look for the signs and not be the person holding the other up. Find someone who can stand on their own two feet. If those feet are webbed to start with…toss 'em back!"

Treatable if you can show some initiative and let him solve his own problems by removing yourself as the Rescuer. Poor Me Toads have responded to finally seeing the need to change and be responsible for their circumstances.

Toxic if he refuses to see his hand in the negative things occurring in his life and cannot overcome the need to blame or deny.

Casey Pittman, Registered Psychotherapist, Recovery

Santa Toad

Ah, yes! The clever disguise of the Santa Toad. How could a toad bearing gifts be a bad thing? Isn't he spoiling you rotten with all these presents, fancy dinners, and unrelenting text messages? What could possibly be bad about that???!!! It's all about timing. Read on, dear Froglet, read on!

Toxic or Treatable Toad:

"As we look at the inner workings of this toad, we see great insecurities and his concerns regarding power and control. These gifts are usually an apology for something gone wrong, a guilty conscious, shame, or coercion to get their way. Too many gifts can mask an insecure nature where he feels he is inadequate in some area and is masking it by all the *outward* displays of generosity. The danger of a relationship with a Santa Toad is confused and erratic. Over time, an onlooker can recognize a cycle of calmness, tension-building, a storm (usually a scary time for those around him, that can lead to physical, emotional, mental, spiritual, or sexual abuses), and making-up (hence, the gifts).

A toad of this character has a general disregard for another's emotions and sense of being. In most relationships, there are marked times where they get along with everyone, as well as marked times where they get along with no one. There is a continued repetition of doing things for their own good, often stepping on the toes of others. Any relationship is one built on negative manipulation, in which this toad generally cons another for profit or pleasure. Specific things to look for with this toad is lying repeatedly, failing to plan ahead, and acting impulsively to get his own immediate needs met. When in conversation, he generally degrades others (so, if he is talking about you to his co-workers, it will probably be negative), but to your face, can be very kind and complimentary. Although appealing at times, this toad is extremely dangerous to be around for there may be a general lack of care for safety, maintaining long-term relationships, and placing you in a victim role.

If abuse is not an indicator, then he may just be dealing with a feeling of insecurity and hence offers gifts to hide it. Depending on the depth and nature of those insecurities, he may just need to know he is accepted for himself without the need of presents. This may take some time to build him up. Only you can decide if his other qualities make him worth the time invested to help him recover his self-esteem."

Treatable if his desire to bring gifts is only masking a low self-esteem. This trait can be resolved if the person is lead to believe he does not need to constantly buy another's affection through gifts, and can relax and believe he contributes to the relationship in none-material ways.

Toxic if this is an abusive relationship where the need to punish another and control them is prevalent. Buying them gifts afterwards is a means to keep the victim in the relationship through a false sense of "he must really love me or he wouldn't be nice to me afterwards." It is a deadly game.

Ray Hazen, MA LPC CACIII SMC

Peter Pan Toad

These are the toads that refuse to grow up. There comes a time when a tadpole must become a full-grown toad. Here are the warning signs that you may be reading bedtime stories to your toad instead of the Wall Street Journal:

Toxic or Treatable Toad:

"The Peter Pan Toad can best be described as a tadpole trapped in a Toad's body. This toad's character is one that has yet to develop into an "adult" identity, and is accompanied with rapid changes in mood, love-hate relationships, impulsive behaviors, and a fragile self-image.

The delicate and tenuous self-concept of this Toad is generally due to an imagined, but real (to them), chance of being abandoned in life. Because of their desire to control a relationship (much like that of a rebelling adolescent), there will be times when the relationship is idealized, and then there will be times where it is devalued. Idle threats are often stated, but over time, can become dangerous, should the tadpole decide to actually follow-through with those threats. Again, this technique is extremely powerful in keeping another entrenched and entwined through the use of shame, guilt, and joy. If in this type of relationship, you may find yourself confused and misunderstand what emotions you have regarding the relationship.

So, if it sounds like you are dating a juvenile or adolescent, you are. As you attempt to work on and navigate through a relationship with the Peter Pan Toad, the most effective question you can ask regarding your future is: Do you want to be the wife or mother of this person?"

Treatable if the person can learn to be responsible at an adult level. It may require you walking away until he can stand on his own two feet.

Toxic if he refuses to address life as a grown-up. These toads are the ones living off their girlfriends and wives with a pretense of being somehow unable to find a job/care for themselves/behave like an adult.

Ray Hazen, MA LPC CACIII SMC

Angry Toad

The Angry Toad is pretty easy to recognize. His fuse is usually half-lit. He is the disgruntled guy in the check-out line, huffing and puffing at the delay. The last person that flipped you off in traffic was probably Angry Toad cleverly disguised as a businessman late for work. This can be a dangerous species, and here is why….

Toxic or Treatable Toad:

"Angry Toad will shut you down just as quickly as he lifts you up. This toad can sometimes be very hard to spot right off the bat but once you start to get to know him it becomes very obvious that you have in fact encountered the Toad of Anger.

Dealing with someone with anger is no laughing matter. People who have anger issues are also called Abusers. There are three types of Abusers when it comes to relationships: emotional, verbal, and physical abusers. It's becoming more and more common to find someone with these problems, which makes the risk of falling into an abusive relationship even higher. The different signs to look for are someone who is controlling, possessiveness, and jealous. Violent behavior is an obvious trait and falls under physical abuse. The biggest problem about abusers is that they are very good at masking all of these characteristics, especially in the "getting to know you" phase and most likely will not show any of the following signs to you right away, so be warned.

One sign in the early stage is this guy will blame all negative feelings and events on anything or anyone but himself. He might even use you as a comparison and make you look great while calling his last girlfriend an "evil fat cow". Do not assume that this guy just needs some form of understanding, or someone who cares, because once you get close to him, the blame will shift onto you. Verbal abuse is very demeaning and results from the abuser's low self-esteem. Another term for this is Victim-stance; it's never his fault—always yours or someone else's.

Another sign to look for is he thinks he deserves special treatment and consideration, not just in the relationship but in all forms of life. This can also be called "Entitlement" and it can be shown as rebelling against rules such as smoking wherever they want, saying whatever they like, and just doing anything they choose without any regard for everyone else. Road Rage is a huge red flag in this area. The rules of the road do not apply and other drivers are seen as threats to his fragile ego, especially if they cut him off in traffic or make a careless move. The "entitled" guy will be disappointed and offended a lot of the time because of his high standards for how things should go and how people should treat him. Others signs are pettiness (either making something big out of nothing, or continually bringing up past arguments, and focusing on negative aspects), and of course there is the sarcasm. When it comes to sarcasm it can range from just being innocently insensitive, to poorly timed humor, but more often than not, the sarcasm comes in a hostile and harmful way.

Last but not least of the signs, is the fact that most Abusers need to make themselves feel better by putting someone else down. This is sometimes called having a "hierarchical self-esteem" as well as the aforementioned Victim-stance. They will do everything from pointing out what you are doing wrong, to how they are better or smarter than you are. This man will even mask it sometimes by immediately pointing out how you are superior right after he just shot you down. Emotional abuse is very similar but can be something totally silent, such as ignoring you, or facial expressions that show condescension, mockery, hate, or amusement. It can come in the form of sabotage, such as ignoring requests you've made, deliberately being late for an important event you have planned, not returning phone calls, emails or texts for lengthy periods of time in an attempt to control you, and any of the passive-aggressive behavior these traits exhibit.

Abusers are not anyone's top choice to date but many find themselves falling into this trap and even worse will find themselves *continually* falling into this trap. The reason for this repetition of going for someone who is an Abuser usually comes from women who have been mistreated in their past. They are susceptible to being abused or mistreated in their next relationship. You hear women all the time say that no matter how hard they look, they always seem to fall for the "wrong guy." This is not because these women have some magical magnet in them that attracts abusive and angry men. It has to do with gravitating toward men who feel familiar to her, even if it is in a negative way. We tend to recreate our "comfort zone," even when that zone is fraught with problems. This can be on a subconscious level, which makes it harder to detect. Women from an abusive past tend to walk right past the "good" guys. That "edge" is just not there that provides the hook. If someone has been mistreated in the past, they will put up barriers and the "good" guys will respect these barriers and tend to back off while the "bad" guys will disrespect these barriers, or not even recognize them, and will continually try to break down your walls until it finally falls and he moves in for the kill, so to speak.

Be able to put up healthy barriers and also be aware of the signs discussed in this article. Ask yourself if it's worth settling for. When you are with them, if you have to hide and conceal yourself, or find you are altering your personality to sidestep a possible tantrum, this is a major sign to walk away. Walking on eggshells to keep from being yelled out, demeaned, or physically hurt is no way to live. You want a relationship where you can disclose, expand, and more importantly grow as two individuals who respect each other and can, most of all, communicate in a healthy way."

Toxic. This person will require professional help to get to the bottom of his anger. Until the basis of his problem is addressed, and solved, no amount of love or support is going to put a dent in his distorted view of the world.

Casey Pittman, Registered Psychotherapist, Recovery

Casanova Toad

Casanova Toad is what we might affectionately call the "multi-tasking" species. He believes if one is good, five is better! The term "serial dater" was invented by this tireless hopper and he has made juggling toadettes an art form.

Toxic or Treatable Toad:

"Dealing with a "Casanova," (also known as Tom Cats, Seducers, Predators, and Womanizers) is like trying to capture smoke. These gentlemen are masters in the art of manipulation. Womanizers are normally charming, curious, and attentive and they know how to make a women feel like she is the only woman alive. These types of guys are addicted to the feeling and "power" they get when seducing a women. One of the easiest ways to recognize a Womanizer is by their addiction to the actual chase and the challenge of getting the girl.

These toads are very well informed in the arenas of women's emotions and feelings and will manipulate those areas. It's obvious what a womanizer's main objective is: to get the women in bed and move on. They focus on the woman's professional and personal problems and show empathy towards them. This creates a sense of comfort, and that's when he will make his move. Most Casanovas suffer from low self–esteem (contrary to the belief that they are full of confidence), and seduce multiple women in order to get a sense of fulfillment. (Their need for many women at one time differs from the needs of the **Sleepover Toad**.) But for these guys it's only a temporary fix. They manipulate women for selfish reasons and will either ignore guilt feelings from these actions or not feel any guilt whatsoever. Narcissism and sociopathic tendencies are often involved. Other traits that these guys may have are flirting with unavailable woman, even friend's wives, and sleeping with inappropriate women. They tend to have many secrets about their romantic life that they will not divulge, and they often resort to lies.

When it comes to resisting a Casanova, it all comes down to boundaries and not allowing yourself to be easily manipulated. A real Casanova will only try so many times before giving up and, unlike the **Sleepover Toad**, he will easily give you the cold shoulder once he realizes you are a "waste of time." If a guy is coming on strong and you get the impression his intentions are not "pure," play into that and take it easy, and try to find out his motives. Most of all, have guidelines or rules for yourself; such as no sleeping with someone on the first date or no going over to a guy's house that you just met. It might sound simple and even ridiculous but having your own rules that you abide by can be the first step to developing healthy boundaries."

Treatable if he finally grows tired of this empty lifestyle and need to feel like the conqueror. Some men will grow out of this phase but it usually requires time and understanding their underlying need to feel attractive and desired.

Toxic if the desire to "date and dash", or have multiple women adoring him is from a very unhealthy need to discard women. Some men in this category may have had dismissive mothers or other female relationships where he felt he did not measure up. Those issues will need to be resolved before he can contribute to a healthy relationship.

Casey Pittman, Registered Psychotherapist, Recovery

Those are your 10 stereotypes of toad-like behavior. There are many others but these encompass the most-prevalent. We reserved the **Predator Toad** for the section on online dating in Part III. If you have a toad-like quality candidate for us, please let us know and if we agree it's a prevalent problem, we will post him on our website, *Troubleshooting Men, What in the WORLD do they want?* You can send us your thoughts to Wonderland549@aol.com.

Is He Prince Material?

I thought it would be interesting to ask the men I surveyed what they thought constituted a Prince—a man worth keeping. You may find their answers revealing, and some, a little surprising. Here are the traits they recommend looking for:

- "He's a step-up kind of guy. He is there for you when you need him."
- "He takes a big interest in what makes you happy. He listens and then does what's necessary to help you fix a problem or just to enhance your life."
- "He may not be the handsome Prince you always envisioned. Some of the best men out there are not "head turners". They can be reserved, average-looking and not the life of the party. But they may have the

real stuff that makes a man worthy of your love. Many women have ruled a guy out on the first date because he wasn't dashing, handsome or built. Give him a chance. I know a lot of guys who were just too nervous on a first date to bring their best selves to the table. He may surprise you on the second date and you just might start to see him as attractive in an entirely different way."

- "He remembers the important things: anniversaries, birthdays, presents that were thoughtfully chosen based on your wants and needs."
- "He feels protective toward you. He "has your back"."
- He is a good provider. He works hard, is not afraid of responsibility and shows maturity."
- "He never does things that are belittling, mean, sarcastic or hurtful to you or others. Those are signs of a guy with a big ego problem and some pretty big self-esteem issues."
- "He helps around the house."
- "He is respectful of your friends and family and enjoys being included in your activities with them. If you have kids, he makes an effort to be part of their lives."
- "He isn't drowning in debt from poor purchasing or loan decisions."
- "His past relationships are in the past. This Dude isn't still arguing with ex's on the phone or trying to patch holes from a previous marriage or relationship."
- "He makes an effort to enjoy your interests. He may not like them all, but he respects your pleasure in them."

- "He gets along with the neighbors, friends, etc. A guy who is usually in a fight with someone or another has anger problems. You don't want that."
- "He plans for the future and isn't reckless with money."
- "Obviously good hygiene is a big one. Avoid the guy who usually smells like a herd of dead goats or wears the same clothes three days running."
- "Romance is a big deal. How does he show his romantic side? Not every guy brings cards and flowers. Look for other ways he lets you know he cares about you. It could be just the fact he works his butt off to provide for you. A real Prince will be able to show some signs of romance, such as making you a meal, taking you to a movie he knows you will like (but one he would rather skip), cleaning the house so you can relax, etc."
- "In an argument, does he let you save face? A guy who always has to win has an inferiority complex. Would he rather win, or actually find constructive ways to fix the issue, while keeping the lines of communication open? Beware the guy who withdraws from a conflict, blames you, and uses name calling, labeling or other demeaning behavior."
- "What is his relationship like with his mother, sisters, female co-workers, etc.? How a man gets along with women in general shows you if he respects them or has some underlying issues that need to be addressed."
- "Do his friends, family and co-workers respect him? If you keep getting warnings from the people closest to

him, you may be looking at him through rose-colored glasses. "Where there's smoke, there's fire" is a good safeguard here."

- He compliments you. He tells you look beautiful, your hair looks nice, you're a great cook, mother/wife/girlfriend. He lets you know, if not always with words, then with actions, that he is proud of you. Men who withhold compliments are usually insecure or trying to control you through the "you have to earn my approval" game. If he can't throw you a crumb, perhaps you need to throw him a ticket out of your life.

- "He handles disappointment well. A mature man with a healthy self-esteem will handle life's pitfalls with calm and bounce back. If he deals with let downs with depression, anger, panic, blaming and other negative emotions, he may fit more into the toad category than a Prince."

How does your guy measure up? Most women know at a gut level if they are being treated right. Again, perspective plays a huge role here. It's all subjective. If your past relationships (and this includes family members) were not so hot, a guy who is merely throwing you crumbs may look like a step up from what you had. Is that all you feel you are worthy of? Change your yardstick. You are worth so much more!

Chapter Eight
Your Troubleshooting Tool Box

If you are troubleshooting anything you are going to need the proper tools. Attempting to understand or get inside a situation requires strategy and knowledge of what makes the object of your attention "tick". Since we are troubleshooting men, these are some of the tools you should have in your toolbox. These traits were listed by our men as the top 10 most-desirable characteristics a woman can have:

1. **Femininity**: Accentuating the differences between a man and woman was high on the list. A feminine nature and dress was something that appealed to most men. A t-shirt, levis and a ball cap was also

mentioned as the cute tomboy look men love. If heels were added, it was a home-run.

2. **Kindness**: Mentioned in the top 3 was kindness. I found that especially compelling. Men were tired of the Drama Queens, rude dates and unappreciative natures. Compassion and a kind heart were mentioned over and over again.

3. **Mental stimulation**: Men want a woman who can carry on a good conversation. They like to be mentally challenged and love a topic that will engage their imagination. They are tired of the normal, safe dialogue and are looking for something that allows them to fantasize and go "off-roading" mentally.

4. **Adventurous**: This was a big one. Men love women who will hike, bike, bowl, ski, go to concerts, sit on a mountainside watching the sunset, hit the haunted houses at Halloween, camp, fish or just create something fun and surprising to do. Boredom kills, fun thrills.

5. **Supportive**: 87% of the men in the survey said they valued a woman who supported his dreams, sports, careers, friends, and lifestyle. They wanted someone who "had his back".

6. **Has Her Own Interests**: The guys said a woman with passion about life is a huge turn-on. They loved a lady who had hobbies, friends, a career she loved, and was passionate about things that enhanced her life. The opposite of this was someone who was content to sit at home and live vicariously through TV and movies. Many of the men said they enjoyed

learning something new from their girlfriend's list of interests.

7. **Playful/Feisty**: A woman who would tease with them, bring a little girl zest to the equation, sassed them back, was playfully physical and just loved being a woman was a huge magnet. Being hugged, kissed, stroked and nibbled on was obviously adored by these guys. They loved the woman taking the initiative in a playful, confident way.

8. **Enjoys sex**: There were a lot of complaints about women who did not seem to enjoy intimacy. According to the men in the survey, making love to a woman who obviously just wants to get it over with, or who is merely going through the motions is hardly a turn-on. They wanted a partner who enjoyed sex, brought variety and surprise to the love making and was the aggressor at times. Having her initiate sex made these men feel desired.

9. **Maintains the Mystery**: Oh how men love mystery! It came up time and time again in the answers from the 98-question survey. Men still love the chase, earning a woman's time and attention, not knowing what she is thinking or what's coming next. It kept them guessing and coming back. The flip side was the girl who chased them; texted, called or emailed them too much; talked incessantly; and was always available and too clingy. Several men even mentioned women they lived with leaving the bathroom door open while they used the toilet, cut their toenails or shaved. They said it was a turn-off

and the women needed to leave a little more mystery when it comes to their bathroom habits.

10. **Flexible**: Women who got upset over a change in plans were listed as high-maintenance. Men preferred women who could change gears and still have a good time. Inflexibility fell under the Drama Queen mantle.

Those are the top 10 most-desirable attributes listed in the survey. Many of them have subtitles such as spontaneous, fun, etc. Men also said they appreciated a woman with a good head on her shoulders who wasn't drowning in debt or constantly in one crisis after another. A sense of humor came up often as well. The guys said they love a quick wit, a woman who will engage in "verbal volleyball" with him and tease him in a playful way. I thought it was interesting that a woman's physical appearance did not fall inside the top 10 most-desired traits. Taking good care of herself was mentioned, but actual physical traits were way down the list.

Dust off that toolbox and see which tools could use a little tending to. We all have areas that need attention. Always put your own stamp on it. It's your unique personality and skill set that will make you shine.

Chapter Nine
The 10 Biggest Mistakes Women Make

Is it just me or should this whole female/male thing be a lot easier? We are the only two genders in the entire homo sapiens species and yet we still don't seem to understand the differences of each, or what makes them tick. It makes me wonder if animals have this problem. Do you think the male lion knows instinctively what his mate wants from him? Does he ever mess up and get sent to the dog house (well, lion house in this case)? Every breathing creature on this planet seems to migrate toward a mate. Some primordial urge causes us to seek out our soul mate. It's as instinctual as geese flying south for the winter.

Then why do men and women make so many mistakes when it comes to dealing with each other? I believe it's for one simple reason: WE ARE TREATING EACH OTHER IN

WAYS THAT *WE* RELATE TO AND UNDERSTAND, AND IT JUST DOES NOT WORK!

If you are looking for a nurturing, happy, positive relationship with that man across from you (or at the amusement park, behind the cash register at Happy Mart, seated down the aisle on the subway, or just in your dreams at present) then you need to stop making the mistakes that drive men away. Stop thinking that you should relate to him the way you relate to women. It does not work, has never worked and will NEVER work!

Here are the Top Ten Mistakes women make when dealing with men:

1. **Complaining constantly**. This is a gigantic turn-off to men. Many said they were tired of women who were always grumpy (hence the "moody" nickname so many of us get saddled with) and complaining about everything from a fight they are having with someone, to things that are broken around the house. Chronic complaining can become a habit. It becomes a worn-out form of communication after a while. Over time, most women don't even realize they are doing it. One of the reasons complaining can become second nature is we tend to "vent" to our girlfriends who are only too happy to "vent" right along with us. Women like gossip, men don't. Women like complaining about the men in their lives, men don't dis to other guys. For a woman, complaining is an outlet. To a guy it's a red flag that this woman will never be happy with anything he does for her…ever!

If you feel you have stumbled into the insidious complaining mind-set...stop now! Seconds before we say something we form the thought in our minds. Cut it off before it escapes your lips. If it's a complaint, don't do it! You may be surprised how often in a day you complain about things.

This was a habit I had. And when I say habit, it was just that. I had slipped into the "I need to complain about this and get someone to commiserate with me, fix it or just let me vent." The man I was dating at the time would sit and listen to me, time after time. I could see his body language signal that he was tired of the whole thing: his nostrils would flare slightly, his eyes darted, he took deeper breaths, or fidgeted in his chair. If he tried to change the subject to something more positive, I felt hurt and that he didn't care about me.

My 20 year-old son even saw this unattractive trait in me and decided to help me out. When he heard me complain, he simply said, "Negative, Mom...negative." I stopped immediately. He was a big help in getting me to see how negative I was being. I even started putting a smiley face on my calendar for the days I made it through without complaining. I began to see a more positive me and people around me began responding. They called me more often, sought out my company and commented on how they loved my new happier outlook.

If you are guilty of seeing the negative side of life...and letting everyone around you know it, try turning it on its ear and begin appreciating life—and him. Employ an "Attitude of Gratitude."

2. **You don't appreciate him for what he does**. This was such a big topic that the men in the essay felt the

need to write follow-up paragraphs about it. Many of them felt saddened, dismissed, angry and ready to walk away due to this one factor. "Why would I want to keep trying to make her happy when it is never enough, and never appreciated?" was the common refrain. The men who did receive appreciate comments, hugs, and reinforcement went the extra mile to do it again. If it was to bring flowers, mow the lawn, get an angry bill collector off her back, fix a lamp or bring her lunch to her workplace, it only took a heartfelt "Thank you!" for him to want to keep making her smile. He felt like a million bucks and she kept receiving the things that made her happy. Pretty much a win-win. As you can see, this is the opposite of complaining.

Why does this seem so foreign to women? Don't we want the same recognition for the things we do? How often have you complained to a friend "Do you think he even notices or cares that I pick up his dirty socks or make sure his dress shirts are back from the cleaners? Heck NO!" Or, "I'm done making him a nice dinner only to have him wolf it down and get back to the game on TV. No "Thanks, Hun, that was great", just gobble it down, and leave me with the dirty dishes."

We all want to feel appreciated. The sad truth is that we often withhold praise as a means of punishment. It's a passive-aggressive game where no one wins. "He hurt my feelings yesterday. Why should I thank him now for simply changing the oil in my car? Isn't that his job?"

Please be careful with that. It's how vines of contention enter a relationship and choke the life out of it. Experts on my talk show were adamant about this topic. Be the one to start the "Appreciation Game". One small comment from you can break the ice and get the ball rolling in a positive way. It is miraculous how this can change a bad relationship into a good one. Be the bigger person and go first. If you have been warring for a while, he may feel you have ulterior motives at first, so be patient. Make your comments sincere. A man who has been shot down for a long time may be battle weary but he will come around if you are consistent. He may be waiting for the other shoe to drop and if you do go back to belittling ways, he will probably go behind his wall and stay there. Start looking at him through the eyes of appreciation and you will see all the little things he is doing to try and get through life the same as all of us. The person who tells him he is doing great will win his heart.

3. **Being Passive-Aggressive**. This one drives men crazy. You're upset. He asks "What's wrong?" you say, "Nothing." Do you hear that sound? It's men all over the world pulling their hair out. This is not the way men communicate with each other and it makes them insane. If a guy has an in issue with something another guy has done, it is put out there on the table so that it can be resolved. " Dave! You just drank the last beer! What's up with that?" Direct and to the point. Now the offending Dave can apologize, defend his actions, or hurriedly produce more beer. The point is, the communication is open. When women play the "I'm not going to tell you, you will have to guess" game, it is not fair and most of all, it completely shuts down the communication channel. Men hate this, repeat, *hate this* trait in females. They are not mind

readers and they feel manipulated. They are now in the position where they have to sit and wheedle it out of you, jump through hoops to make you happy, or feel guilty for something they didn't do, or have no idea that they *did* do it. It's obvious you're upset. So now what do they do? After a while a man will quit trying to get through to you. Again, it is not how men communicate and he doesn't like playing this game.

Women do this a lot. I have been guilty of it; I'll lay odds you have as well. Withholding sex is another form of the passive-aggressive game. You aren't dealing directly with the underlying issue, but you are making your feelings known through your actions, not your words. There are a million little ways we think we are letting him know we're upset without being mature enough to just come right out and say it: we make sure we aren't home when he gets home so he will worry where we are; we don't talk to him…some times for days; we deliberately "forget" to do something for him we promised we would do; we bang pots and pans around, slam doors and hang up on him… Do you see anything productive coming from this? How can any solid foundation be laid when the relationship is built on quick sand?

Another version of the passive-aggressive move is **hinting**. Boy, do men detest hinting. It is for the same reasons mentioned above. When was the last time you heard a man hint to another man about something he wanted to get across? "Hey Joe, did you see that new commercial about Man Up deodorant? I'm thinkin' of tryin' it out. What do you think?" Noooooo… If he feels his buddy's hygiene is lacking, he will simply say, "Joe, buddy…you smell. Invest in some deodorant, man!"

This is how men communicate. It's direct and uncomplicated. It's how they are wired. While hinting may seem like a kinder, gentler way of getting what you want, it does not work with men. And since he is not programmed to pick up on those oh-so-subliminal messages of yours, you often feel he doesn't care about you when the reality is he probably didn't get it at all! Again, stop dealing with males as if they are your girlfriends. Use your words to tell him what you want. Stop sending smoke signals and then getting upset if he didn't get the *Indian Guide to Campfire Message Recognition.* Talk to him on his terms. You will be happier, and he will be relaxed and ready to fulfill your wishes, if they are within reason.

4. **Bad Timing**. We talked quite a bit about this one earlier in the book. Men put this in their top 10 mistakes women make because it causes a lot of undue stress in a relationship. Men compartmentalize. It's really very simple. Let him finish one thing before you ask for his time or attention. We keep thinking we can get our way and have our needs met on our terms. Has that worked for you? He may stop what he's doing and help you out or listen to you, but he will feel thwarted and edgy. This is not how he goes about doing things. You are forcing him to play by different rules. If this seems one-sidedly in his favor, ask yourself this—"Do I want him to be happy to help me, or just get my way?" Unless it's important, let him finish what he was doing, and this may mean letting him watch the final five minutes of overtime in the Super Bowl.

Men in the survey repeatedly mentioned that women have a poor sense of timing when dealing with men. They force men to sit down and talk to them, knowing he was just about to start a project, jump in the shower, make a 9:00 tee time, or fix a lock. They said if women would just let them know that they have something they want to talk to them about when they have a minute, it will make the guy more likely to be at ease and ready to listen when he comes to you. He has checked something off his list and is more relaxed. And isn't that want you want? His full attention?

This isn't just big guys we are talking about here. If you have sons, watch what happens if you interrupt a video game, his homework, a project or anything else he is involved in. It will not end well. Give him advance notice that you need his time soon, and he will be more likely to comply. This works well with needing a phone call from him as well. Texting that you need a few minutes puts him on notice, and he can finish up what he was doing.

As mentioned, I have four grown sons, three of whom are married with small children. Their lives are hectic. I sometimes miss the frequent phone calls I used to receive from them. Rather than employ the quilt trip, which never works and makes everyone feel badly, I have learned to give them a quick text…infused with humor:

A recent text to one of my sons: "Hello. Allow me to introduce myself. It is your mother. You may remember me. I went through 9 hours of labor to bring you into this world, attended all your basketball games, bought you $140 Air Jordan shoes, washed your roommates' boxer shorts, and let you tease me mercilessly during holiday feasts. I figured you were missing me terribly by now, so I thought I would beat you to it. I love you and miss talking to you. ☺"

He texted me back within three minutes with an "LOL!" and "I love you, Mom. I'll call you tonight after the kids are in bed, OK? Hope all is well." And he did call that night at 9:30.

It was a great conversation that lasted quite a while. I felt connected to him and loved; he felt unhurried and able to give me his time.

Giving him his space falls under the timing category. If a man is in a bad mood, he will go inside his head to work it out. This is another area in which men behave very differently from women. "We do not want to talk it out!" was a common remark men made to me. "It may work with you and your girlfriends, but if you push a guy to talk when he is upset, it will backfire on you." Let him have some room to "percolate" and resolve things in his mind. Let him know you are there if he needs to bounce something off of you. This shows your confidence in him that he can handle it, but that you are interested in hearing what's bothering him.

5. **Being jealous**. Men are going to look at other women. If he doesn't he may be more interested in men. This is not a slam to you or his desire to be with someone else, it is just that visual thing men do. Women who respond with over-the-top emotion to his appreciative glances at the female form are headed for trouble. Now if he is leering, or making a point of extolling another woman's virtues, then you have a right to point out that he is causing some unloving feelings in your department. But a man's casual glance at a woman walking by is normal.

I dated a gentleman for a while that gave the term "wondering eyes" a whole new meaning. He would turn his head all the way around to watch a hot babe go by. Finally, I calmly asked him how he thought I felt when he made such a point of checking out a girl's departing backside. He was surprised I brought it up. It had become a habit and he said he meant no disrespect to me. To his credit, he reined it in, and I let him know I understood a man's wiring to appreciate curves and femininity. To underscore my security in that department, I would comment on another woman's appearance from time to time, mentioning her great figure or lovely hair. He appreciated my understanding of men, and I felt less jealous.

While painting wall murals at a huge residential construction site, I got to know a lot of the technicians and builders as we were all there for over a month creating a lovely 14,000 square foot home. Two of the electricians befriended me and I enjoyed their humor. One day the two came to where I was painting. "Becky…you're a girl," one of the men named Dave said to me. "Uh…thank you," I said, uncertainly. "Go ahead, Scott, tell her what you did last night. You need a woman's point of view," Dave said to his buddy who was shooting daggers at him. It was clear Scott was not as amused by something he had done the previous evening as Dave was.

"Oh for Pete's sake…," Scott began. "My wife and I were out to dinner and this really hot blonde walked by. I turned to look at her as she walked away. When I looked back at my wife, she was sitting there with her arms folded and a sour expression on her face. I said, "Honey…it's a guy thing. Just because we see a Ferrari doesn't mean we think we are ever going to own one."

I cringed. Dave was doubled-over laughing and Scott was looking miserable. Hoping to redeem himself, Scott continued, "So she says, "Oh really? Well if that's a Ferrari, what does that make me???!!!" So I said what I thought was a compliment, "I think of you more like a Ford truck...you're dependable."

At this point, Dave has lost it, and my facial muscles are in spasms from trying to control my laughter. All I could think of to say was, "How is that couch working out for you, Scott?" He got mad and walked off, with Dave (in tears) following after him.

While this tale was to underscore how men can overdo the "checking out the chicks" thing, just know that men dislike overly-jealous women. It does not make you come off as secure and confident. A woman who does have a healthy self-esteem will kick a guy to the curb if his attentions to other women are hurtful or manipulative, or if she knows he's cheating on her. Some men will try and make you jealous, and you don't need that either.

On the note of cheating, if a man does talk to a woman in front of you, odds are he is *not* cheating with her. Men are not going to be that obvious. So allow him to have a little space here, show your confident side and keep it all within reason. If he is being too overt, call him on it in a calm and respectful way. If he continues, knowing it is bothering you, then you don't need him around.

Forms of jealousy men brought up were their wives or girlfriends getting upset if they talked to another woman, glancing at women, mentioning a pretty girl in a movie or magazine, or commenting on one of her girlfriends. Women who snooped through a man's emails, texts or phone contacts were women men tended to get rid of. Being questioned about why they were late from work, asking who they were talking to on the phone, and other acts of jealous insecurity were huge turn-offs.

Allow him to be a guy...within reason here. Give him the same privacy you would demand, and if you feel you are unreasonably jealous with your man, look to yourself to see if your sense of security is intact. If not, work on getting a healthy self-esteem. It's one of the most-valued and attractive traits men see in a woman.

6. **A woman who doesn't take care of herself.** I feel this concern's flag can fly over both the male and female camps. No one wants to be around a person, especially one they are involved with, who has poor hygiene habits, has gained an unreasonable amount of weight, sits around in tired or stained clothing, or has simply quit trying to look their best for you. You feel as if they don't care what you think of them at this point, and you aren't worth them looking nice for you anymore.

   Where men are concerned (being the cute little visual creatures that they are), this is a big turn-off area. If their wife or girlfriend begins letting herself go, it will affect his feelings of attraction, and possibly affection, toward her. If the romance has died off, this may be one of the reasons. Women, and men, tend to relax a little after they feel they have "bagged" their prey. Actually, this is the time to ramp it up a little. When familiarity seeps in, it takes extra effort to keep the flame burning. Men are highly susceptible to the female form, especially if it is accentuated in clothing that makes it seem feminine, sensual, and the opposite of what a guy would look like.

Many men complained that their wives starting borrowing their sweatshirts, t-shirts and even their boxer shorts as a short-cut to dressing for a day around the house. While there are times a woman in a guy's dress shirt or tank top can look sexy, men gravitate with their eyes, and physically, toward a woman who plays up her female-ness. Keep your nails looking nice, shave your legs, comb your hair, put on some perfume and change it up a little. Being seen in the same robe day after day was a turn-off men mentioned.

7. **She has no life of her own**. Men are most attracted to a woman who has her own outside interests, friends and passions. Guys fear a woman who makes him her entire world. To him, this means she will need him to fulfill her needs, make her happy, be there constantly, give up his own interests to be with her, and basically give this woman a reason to get up in the morning. No man is going to don his red cape and fly off to rescue a woman who is clingy, needy, and well…empty.

Again, men and women differ somewhat here. Women may love to feel a guy has built a life around her. We've dreamed of the Prince and the castle since we were little. But for men, the freedom to run off with the Knights, slay a few dragons, drink some grog and eyeball a few wenches, tickles his fancy as well. Freedom is a big deal to men. The nesting instinct may be there, but not to the degree it is for women. His hard-wiring is to protect, provide and preserve. (And here, preservation includes continuing the family line, which equates to his sexual drive.)

8. **She doesn't understand men.** This was an umbrella statement that covered several areas. One of the main traits men mentioned was women giving men love in a way that appeals to a woman, but not necessarily a man. For instance, women typically love to receive flowers or have a man fix a problem for her. To her, this makes her feel loved. If you give flowers to a man, he will probably appreciate the gesture, but it won't do much to stir his emotions. Offering to help him fix something might send a signal that you don't feel confident he can do it on his own...not a good thing! Do you see the difference?

A man may feel loved by a woman when she gives him physical attention, such as hugs, kisses, massages or sex. Making him his favorite dinner, foregoing dinner out so that he can watch the game, or other gestures that show you have his interests at heart are signs of love to a man. If we remember to watch and listen to the things he responds to, and keep doing them, we will be miles ahead in understanding men and making them happy. As one man put it, "Getting a tie for Christmas may make a woman think she is upgrading our wardrobe, but if you want to see him light up, give him something that appeals to the little boy in him or a hobby he loves (tickets to a car show, an addition to his coin collection, an archery kit, Kung Fu lessons, etc.) Again, make it specific to what you know will make him smile and feel you really "get him".

Other grievances fell on this door mat. Basically, they were these:

- She makes fun of me, thinking it's cute.
- She buys me clothes she thinks will look good on me, knowing I don't wear that stuff.
- She keeps forcing me to go to movies I hate. Men will compromise on this, but just know, we are pretty much hoping your girlfriends want to see this movie with you.
- She talks…and talks and talks. This is such a downer to men. We just don't talk as much as women do, or feel the need to. One guy described it as "verbal vomit". It can be overwhelming to men and they will avoid it if they can. Several guys in the survey brought up feeling like Archie Bunker in the popular *All in the Family* television series when he is mimicking hanging himself, playing Russian Roulette with a gun, or stabbing himself in the heart as Edith blissfully babbles on ad naseum about some trivial subject. Work on keeping it succinct. Save the "scenic route" for your female contemporaries.
- She pushes me to share my day with her. Guys like to leave their work at work. We don't want to rehash our day, unless something important happened we are proud of, or an occasional need to vent about the boss or a jerky co-worker. Let us unwind and forget the 9-5.
- Don't belittle our athletic ability. "Some women feel they are being helpful by pointing out what they see us doing wrong on the court/field/alley. Nine times out of ten, we know we screwed up. We're hoping you didn't notice." Having a

woman be your armchair quarterback will not earn you points, and he may stop inviting you to come watch him play.

- If we want your help, we will ask for it. "Don't hover. Don't offer to help us. Yes, it's male ego. We don't like it when our buddies do it, and it's worse when the woman we are trying to impress does it. Even if there are 17 parts left over after he fixes the TV set, bite your lip and tell him you appreciate him tackling the job. Which is more important, his feelings of self-worth or your need to watch *Gossiping Housewives* tonight?"

- Don't put down his friends. He chose his friends. Your poor opinion of them is an indirect critique of his judgment. A man will often continue hanging out with guys he may know are not good for him in an effort to maintain his freedom if you keep harping on about them. Men aren't stupid. They won't continue doing things they find unpleasant. Give him his space…and trust his instincts.

- Stop being our mother! This was a very big issue for men. They felt smothered. It felt condescending with a total lack of faith on their girlfriend's or wife's behalf. Women who took a cigar away from him, told him to go get his glasses, reminded him to get a jacket because it was going to get cold later, forced him to eat Vegan when he craved some protein, altered his appearance, tidied up his man cave, and on and on.

This brings us to our next mistake, but possibly the most-important:

9. **Stop trying to change men!** I am going to be straight up here...this is more prevalent with women than men. Women tend to fall in love with a man's potential. They see a "fixer-upper" and list the things they would like to change about him to make him perfect. The problem with this mind-set is two-fold: 1) He will resent your need or desire to change him. Let's face it; it's an insult to tell another human being they need to change to fit your criteria. The male ego is sensitive about failure in any area, and implying or out-and-out saying he is not measuring up in an area is a slap in the face. The famous saying that says "Women marry men hoping they'll change; men marry women hoping they won't" is amazingly true. The groom hopes his bride will remain the wonderful, sweet and beautiful woman he married for the rest of their lives. She is already sizing him up to see what needs to be done to get him to fit into the Prince costume she has picked out. 2) Women who think they can change a man are in for a rude awakening. If the flaws you see now bother you, then walk away. Many a woman has entered into a relationship thinking that a flawed man will change for her. She will be the one to save him from his bad ways. If women understood that this is doomed to failure, it would save them a lot of headaches.

I have a friend who was dating a man with severe anger issues. She thought if she loved him enough, appreciated him enough and showed her support he would change. She was convinced her love would "save him". She poured her heart and soul into this guy and hung in there through four brutal years of his yelling, raging, belittling and humiliating her before she finally gave up. The adage that says "most people don't tend to change" is a true one. It usually takes a major turn of events for them to have a wake-up call. People with addictions are especially hard to change. If you can't accept a man at face value, it will be fairer to him and to yourself to pass him by before vows are exchanged.

10. **There's no fun/adventure anymore**. We covered this category quite a bit in earlier sections. Men will give up their hard-earned freedom for a woman if they feel the marriage still offers him fun, adventure and some space. This does not make him self-centered. Many men take on the responsibility of husband and father with remarkable aptitude and love the roles. But as we mentioned, if he feels suddenly trapped by a female who is calling the shots, locking out his friends, dictating his clothes style, eating habits and putting the kibosh on outside activities, you are going to see a mighty unhappy guy.

I have noticed another big difference here between men and women. Most men encourage their wives to get out and enjoy themselves. Perhaps part of it is to have a little space for himself, but it is primarily because he likes to see her happy. Women, on the other hand, have a more difficult time giving the "thumbs up" to their boyfriends or hubbies to go out without her and have fun. A lot of men told me they saw this inability to send him forth into the world for fun and frolic as controlling, fearful and clingy on the part of the woman.

Another comment made often was that suddenly life got too serious. "I get that there are bills to pay, kids to raise and work to be done, but it seems like all we talk about are those things now," one man said about married life. "Can we still be romantic, laugh, be spontaneous and have some fun? Does it all have to be so serious and heavy?"

You can find the balance between responsibility and fun. It may take some effort, but it will be soooo worth it! Even setting one night a week as date night can do wonders. It will rekindle your feelings for each other, get you out of the house and remind you of what you enjoyed doing during your dating phase. Remember the power of boredom and monotony to choke the life out of a relationship? This is how you nip it in the bud. Keep the surprises, adventure and fun coming!

Those are the top ten main mistakes women make when dealing with men. So, what happens to the woman who possesses the traits men *are* looking for? Very often, she ends up on a pedestal.

Chapter Ten
Deserving of a Pedestal

Do you think the notion of men putting a woman on a pedestal is old-fashioned or setting women back 50 years? Would it surprise you know that of 2,000 men surveyed in the past four years 78% said they want a woman "worthy of a pedestal." They were done with the Drama Queens, male bashers, couch potatoes and Sugar Babies. Today's man is looking for a woman with a kind heart, and an adventurous outlook on life. They are applauding and admiring the career woman, the independent woman and the lady with a bagful of interests. And for good reason...

The enormity of men complaining about dealing with women with entitlement mentalities is staggering. Males are, quite frankly, sick of jumping through hoops to make some female happy. They are hoping for a woman with a life of her own, filled with pursuits and happiness. Is that so hard to understand? Do you want to hitch your wagon to a guy who is perpetually moody, depressed, out-of-work, boring and thinks a great night out is a beer and WWF?

After interviewing both men and women for my self-help books, and teaching women how to have abundant lives for the past 39 years, it is apparent to me that men have simpler needs. If you throw something at this book, IPad, computer screen or smart phone face over that last sentence, I'm sorry…it's true. You take a close-up look at any relationship and you will see men putting out more effort to make the woman he is interested in smile—not all men, but the huge majority.

Am I saying women don't try to create romance or do things to make him happy? Absolutely not! It's just women are more complex than men. We worry more, obsess over trivialities more, and second guess information more frequently. And, unfortunately, we are harder to please in most areas.

How often has a man done something nice for you and the thought of "well, it wasn't exactly what I wanted, but it was nice of him" run through your head? Perhaps the restaurant, movie, gift, flowers, card or home fix-it project didn't measure up to your expectations. Did all our efforts to become equal with men put us on a throne instead of a pedestal? According to the men out there, they are ready to throw in the towel.

- Warrin*, 42, psychologist. "If I had a nickel for every male client who sits in my office and complains about the woman in his life demanding more than he can produce, I could retire. It's sad to see these guys beaten down when they are giving it all they have."

- Mikal*, 33, computer tech. "I quit dating women who feel a guy should be drug around by some ring in his nose. Why can't girls just be happy? So many are grumpy, angry, depressed or demanding. To find someone who loves their life is pretty rare."

- Randy*, 58, theology professor. "I've lived a good many years on this earth. I've raised three daughters and been married for over 30 years. I will say here and now that men's needs are pretty basic. We just want to know we are appreciated and loved. That's pretty much it. Throw in some surprises and color us happy."

- Douglas, 49,* mechanical engineer. "I saw a relationship documentary that compared men to dogs. It showed how a dog reacted when he had his stomach scratched, was taken for a walk, fed and taken care of. A "Good Dog! Good Boy!" was met with tail-wagging and tongue lolling. The dog was always happy to see his owner come through the door. It was unconditional love. I would have to say, this scenario is not far from the truth. Hug us, get us outside, take care of our needs as you would want yours catered to, and love us unconditionally. Men really don't need more than that…other than the appreciative "Good Boy! Well done!"

- Ken*, 24, graphic design. "I don't know of a single friend of mine who won't go the extra mile to make his girlfriend or wife happy. It's always on our minds. When she's happy, we feel we are doing a good job in being there for her. Her happy face lights up our day and we will keep doing things that show us that beautiful girl we fell in love with."

- Rashis,* 35, engineer. "I would have to say I meet more unhappy women than not. There seems to be a "men owe us" mentality. I'm not sure if there are a lot of abused women coming out of bad relationships, or just a lot of women still feeling they need to make a point, but it's not opening a door for men to walk through. It's slamming it in their faces."

- Dave*, 39, financier. "I'm the luckiest guy in the world. I have buddies wanting to beat me up they are so jealous about the great wife I have. She is always upbeat, positive and happy to spend time with me. There is no judging, snide comments or trying to run my life. She sees our marriage as two people who were lucky to find each other and spend much of their lives together. She still enjoys pursuits she had before she met me and said once "It's ludicrous to think that just because someone marries you he needs to change his world and give up things he enjoys." We all have black days, but she keeps it in perspective and tries to find the best in the situation. I am her Hero. And I try every day to be worthy of that."

- Robert*, 51, bank manager. "If women knew how much men love it when they are happy, it would show them a side to males they don't know about. Men…good men…are still old-fashioned in wanting to provide her with a great life, less stress, and happiness. I think a lot of guys would still put their coat over a puddle for a woman, but today's woman would toss it back in his face."

We've shown what men are wanting in a woman throughout this book. To be deserving of a pedestal in a man's eyes is pretty simple. Be happy, be positive, appreciate what he does for you, show some independence and have interests of your own, be affectionate and playful, and stop looking at him as if he is the enemy. Today's man wants what you want: a romantic relationship, open communication, adventure, love and kindness. 95% of the men in the survey said they would commit, or have committed, themselves to a woman if they feel/felt they are looking at a lifetime of two people being there for each other and enjoying their days.

Part III:

TODAY'S VIEW

OF ROMANCE

Chapter One
Online Dating

The world of online dating has infiltrated the romance department like a juggernaut. It is an indicator of not only a society dominated by high tech and fast track solutions, but also a pronouncement on how the lives of men and women have changed. Our lives are busy, sometimes isolated, and the norms of clubbing and bar hopping are not the desired go-to havens for finding dates they used to be.

Enter computer dating. Within minutes of logging on to any of the prolific relationship sites on the Internet you can peruse hundreds of photos and profiles of the people looking for a date, a relationship...or ... a scam. If you have an hour or more to spare, you can stroll through *thousands* of smiling faces from all over the world. Sounds wonderful? It can be. It requires certain knowledge of how the whole thing works. According to *Statistic Brain*, these are some of the statistics:

Online Dating Statistics	Data
Total number of single people in the U.S.	54,250,000
Total number of people in U.S. who have tried online dating	41,250,000
Total eHarmony members	15,500,000
Total Match.com members	21,575,000
Average spent by dating site customer per year	$239
Average length of courtship for marriages that met online	18 months
Average length of courtship for marriages that met offline	42 months
Percentage of male online dating users	52.4%
Percentage of female online dating users	47.6%
% who say common interests are the most important factor	64%
% who say physical characteristics are the most important factor	49%
% of marriages in the last year in which the couple met on an online dating site	17%
% of people who believe in love at first sight	71%
% of women who have sex on the first online date	33%
% of people who date more than one person at a time	53%
% of sex offenders who use online dating to meet people	10%
What's Most Important on a First Date?	
Personality	30%
Smiles and Looks	23%
Sense of Humor	14%
Career & Education	10%

Girls Prefer:

Nice Guys	38%
Bad Guys	15%
Blend of both	34%
Any man I can get	6%

Guys Prefer:

The modern career girl	42%
The girl next door	34%
The "Hottie"	24%

Women lie most about: Weight, Physical Build, Age

Men lie most about: Age, Height, Income

It's apparent from the above statistics that personality and common interests trump looks.

It is also obvious that there are a lot of people misrepresenting themselves in their profiles. Caution is indicated.

Before we talk about creating the perfect profile, I would like to warn you about the dark side of online dating. This is very real, and can be very scary. There are married men, men in other relationships, scammers, "broken men" (men with some very dangerous personality disorders), women haters, and players. These people hide behind the safety, and anonymity of a computer screen to approach women they wouldn't have the courage to in "real life". Even the men who are not in another relationship may just be hitting on you for fun—for the sheer joy of seeing if they can get a woman to flirt with them. Not all men on dating sites are there for the wrong reasons, but many are. Here are the warning signs:

He's in a hurry!

Someone on a dating site that is married, in a relationship, or wanting to scam you in some money deal will try to pull you away from the site as fast as possible. Married men don't want their profile visible for too much time for obvious reasons, ditto for a guy dating someone else already. The scam artists will do the following:

Scam artists will post a profile, hit as many women as they can in an email or a wink, or just by parking there in the hope you will approach them as they are usually very nice looking, and then take their profile down, usually within 3 days after posting it. Their agenda is that you will email them back in a hurry. Then they send you an email saying they don't like coming onto the site all the time (or their membership is about to expire) and it would be easier if you call them or email them at their personal email address. They are in a hurry to get you away from the dating site where they can take their time talking to you in private emails or on the phone, and because they will be jerking their profile down as quickly as possible..

Next, they will start sending you very long, romantic emails. They feel the longer the email, the more flattered you will be that they took so much time to tell you their heartfelt desires and how much a great relationship would mean to them. Do you know why the letter is so long and detailed? Because it was a great one-time investment for this guy. He has copied and pasted that letter into dozens of other letters that went out to other women he hooked from the dating site.

Now you are corresponding back and forth. You may even be talking on the phone. You will start to notice something fishy…or "froggy." His letters are very generic. He rarely answers a question you posed to him in your last email. Your name may not even be on the letter. It may be a generic greeting like "Hello Beautiful," or "Hello Gorgeous." If you read the letter carefully, you will see there is nothing specific to you. This letter could have gone out to any number of women. He plies you with all the romantic things he is capable of and how he longs for a perfect partner.

He will keep this game up for a while, sometimes as long as two months to get you good and invested in him. He is now telling you he loves you. He has canned answers all ready to go for statements you may make like, "This seems too good to be true," to which he responds immediately with, "People who say things are too good to be true, don't trust they are worthy of something wonderful." He has now pricked your insecurity and even made you feel slightly ashamed for not trusting it. He may bring it up before you do, sensing you are hesitant about how fast this is happening when you haven't even met him. These guys are very, VERY good!

Finally, after he has you hooked, here comes the pay-off for him. He will have some emergency come up where he needs you to wire him some money. $10,000 is a usual sum. During your emails and phone calls this guy has weeded out of you how well you are doing financially (usually in a manner so expert you don't even realize what is happening).

A friend of mine emailed and spoke on the phone with a man for five weeks she met online but never in person. During a phone call one evening she mentioned to him that he sounded a little "down." He brushed it off by saying he didn't want to burden her. When she persisted, he finally said his car repairs had come to much more than he expected and he was now without transportation as it sat at the mechanics awaiting him to come up with some cash. My friend is no dummy. She saw through it but wanted to make sure. She asked him if she could help in any way. He kept saying it was "not her problem"...pause. Finally, he agreed to let her help and asked her for $5,000. Although she was mad and knew he was just another online scammer, she decided to see how far it went. She agreed to send him the money. He said he would send her an account to wire the money to. Instead of agreeing to those terms, she turned the table on him and said, "You know...it would be so much easier for me to mail you the money. My bank is clear across town. What's your mailing address?" There was a huge pause on the phone line. Finally he said (with a tinge of anger in his voice) that he was out of town and not at his home. He said a bank wire was the only way to get it to him. When she insisted that she mail it to wherever he was, he disappeared. She never heard from him again.

I do not advocate toying with these guys if you suspect them of playing you. They can be dangerous. They may have found out things about you during your conversations to where he now knows where you work or live. Please...just walk away knowing you are more knowledgeable and savvy about the dark side of Internet dating and won't fall for it again.

Don't look back...just RUN!

What can you do to make sure you are dealing with an On-line Toad?

If they try to get you away from the site in the first email, say something like this, "I appreciate your interest but I prefer to get to know someone a little better before giving out my personal information." (By having you use *his* private email address, or *his* phone number, he now has yours, hence the need for caution.)

Play it coy and ignore the contact information he just gave you and simply ask him some innocent questions, such as "You mentioned golf in your profile. Do you play often?" "How long have you lived in California?" If they don't write back, they see you as a waste of time, while they are trolling fast for targets. They may send you a quick answer or two if they think you are worth it, but they will bring up again that they prefer for you to contact them via their phone number or personal email. Repeat the above until he gives up. You can push the envelope and say "I prefer to meet someone in person to see if there is a connection. How do you feel about that?" If it's a scam, he will disappear. If he says "Yes," keep him talking to you for a while before you meet him to make sure he is legit! Always meet at a public place but, again, MAKE SURE HE IS NOT A SCAM ARTIST OR A PLAYER!!! There are dangerous people out there. Error on the side of caution and get to know someone before you go out on a date!

If someone who is a perfect '10' contacts you and it seems fishy or "too good to be true" due to what he has written, give it a day or two before you respond. Go back from time to time during those couple of days and see if his profile is still there. If it has been pulled, he was a scam artist or player. If it is still there on day three, go ahead and answer him, but check back from time to time to see if he disappeared. Even if he isn't a scam artist, there are married guys and men with girlfriends winking and flirting online just to see if they can get a pretty girl to flirt with them. Take your time. The bonus side to that is that the legit men like a challenge and if you don't come off as eager, you are ahead of the game.

BEWARE THE PREDATOR TOAD

Here is a sample email from an online Predator Toad. These men are usually looking for money.

Sample Scam Artist Email:

"Hello Lovely!

I can't believe what an amazing profile you have! We have so many things in common. Your smile just leapt off the page at me. I could get lost in that smile! Do you have a lot of hobbies you enjoy? What is your favorite movie?

I am looking for the last first date. I want to find my soul mate and be in a loving relationship where we value each other and plan for the future. I want someone who is happy having my strong arms around her and loves to see my face light up when I see her. My parents had a loving marriage of 40 years and that's what I want. All of my friends are married and really happy and I find myself eager to spend quality time with the girl of my dreams. After reading your profile, I think that girl could be you. Do you want those things? Are you looking for a man who will treat you like a queen and protect you from all the bad things in the world? Do you like a romantic man who will draw you a bath, complete with candles and scented soaps and have a fluffy towel ready for you? Did I mention I can cook? Lol.

I really want to talk to you and see where this might go. I am not often on this site, so if you would, please email me at my personal email address, John Doe at Losers.com, that would be great and I can answer you faster. Or, if you're brave (wink) you can call me at 555-307-8888.

Can't wait to hear from you, precious girl!
Eagerly,
Dimitri

Critique: You will notice that there is nothing about your profile's interests mentioned. He may have read it looking for the women with higher income brackets (hint: don't post your income level on your profile), but he is sending the same letter to every woman he hooks. Another common thing is the use of an exotic name like Marco, Dimitri, Dominic...not always, but more than you would think.

Yes, he asked some questions, but watch. When you write him back, he won't address them. If you say something like, "I love to golf, do you?" He won't answer that question. He will derail you by going back to his romantic dreams for your future with him (a letter he is sending to 10 other women at the same time. That's why he deals in generalities).

Note the generic greeting. Gorgeous, Beautiful, Lovely, Sweetheart...take your pick. If you do write him back and he ignores your questions to him, or the answers you provided to his questions, ask him why he didn't answer or

comment. Personally, I don't suggest you give these guys two seconds of your time, but it is a way to see if they are scammers or for real.

Please be careful. These players and scammers are increasing online. Again, take your time; don't give out personal information about where you live, your birth date, your work place, etc.

CREATING A GREAT PROFILE

As we can see from the statistics in our online dating table there are a lot of people online searching for "true love", among other more devious interests. The key to garnering more winks and emails is to create a profile that stands out from the rest. By the time a person has read ten or more profiles they all begin to look the same. Judging from all the people who list one of their interests as "a walk on the beach", there are tons of sunburned daters out there with sand between their toes. "A glass of wine in front of a romantic fire" was listed so often that I can only guess the liquor stores and gas companies are rubbing their hands together.

The point is this: If you want to show from the get-go that you are unique, create a profile that underscores it. Here are some ideas for stepping away from the crowd:

- **Don't tell...show!** This works in creating a novel, and it bodes well for the profile. What this means is rather than say "I like snow skiing", write "Fresh powder on a bright Colorado morning will see me first in line for the lift." There is action here and a better sense of your personality. Instead of "I'm an interior decorator", try "The thrill of designing creative environments is a passion of mine." This is infused with energy and we've talked about how important it is to have passions in your life.

- **Just the Facts Ma'am!** Men are not like women when it comes to information. If they see a profile that is 13 paragraphs long, they won't even pause to read the first several lines. It screams "This woman is verbose and probably will be on a date", and it may signal being desperate to impress. Keep it simple and engaging.

- **Show your funny side.** Everyone loves a sense of humor. It is listed over and over again on a man's list of preferences when it comes to finding a female that lights up his life. Sprinkle some humor throughout your profile. For instance, if you golf, you might say "I adore playing golf. Even driving the cart is fun, although my license was suspended in several counties." ☺ (The smiley face is important here.) Don't be afraid to show your playful side.

- **Be upbeat and positive**. I cannot tell you how many profiles begin or end with a list of things they don't want. The negativity screams "poor past relationships" and a person looking for the worst in people. We all have a dirty laundry list but airing it online is a huge red flag. Stay positive. Listing such things as "No smokers, players, guys over 60 or short men" will not win you any favors. Profiles show these stats anyway, so why hammer it home here? Men are particularly sensitive to "man-haters" and "male bashers" so go easy on the deal breakers. He will find out soon enough what your likes and dislikes are...if you make it to that first date.

- **Liars Beware**! Online daters have had it up the wazoo with dishonest profiles. This is just not the way to start a potential relationship. And from a man's point of view, it's more than just feeling disheartened when he meets a woman who does not resemble the photo she posted, or has lied about her interests and other things. For him, it also affects his wallet. He just paid for a date with someone who essentially scammed him. Don't think your personality will outweigh the fact that you were evasive with your information or photos. Some men may even retaliate with anger. I know of some personal friends who spent months emailing and talking to a woman before meeting her only to find she weighed over a hundred pounds more than she presented, or lied about other pertinent information. One man, who had corresponded with a woman for *six months* due to it being a long-distance acquaintance, told her he was specifically interested in someone athletic and slender due to his obsession with sports, and she led him to believe she was what he was looking for. When he met her, she admitted she was not interested in hiking, camping, scuba diving, zip lining or all the other activities she had professed to love. She was also very out-of-shape and looked nothing like her photos which were a good 15 years old. He was so heartbroken, and disillusioned from the lies that he quit online dating and has never looked back. This is not just the females fibbing online; a large portion of men are "padding" their profiles as well.

- **Spell Check Please**. Men and women discarded profiles based on the prolific spelling or grammatical errors. While that may sound picky, misspelled words and getting creative with your syntax can signal to another person that you may not be as educated as they are hoping for. Polish your profile. Have a friend look it over for you if you need to. Fresh eyes can be a lifesaver.

- **Current photos/smiling photos**. While a lot of us feel we still look like we did ten years ago, a newcomer will be seeing you through the eyes of discretion. Because photo fraud is so prevalent on dating sites, most people meeting you for the first time may be a little jaded. Keep your photos updated. Show yourself being active. Men gravitate to photos that show you involved with life, especially outdoor life. Smile! 90% of online daters felt a magnetic attraction to a smiling face over the serious pose, or provocative pout. As we've touched on in this book, men are hoping for fun and adventure. Show it in words and photos in your profile. Post some full body shots as well.

- **Leave some mystery.** A profile is a great place to leave a "hook"; something that will intrigue him and push his finger toward that wink button or email feature. Statements such as "This is a brief snapshot of myself. To be continued..." Or, "Warning: Contents have been known to be addicting." Don't list all your interests, hobbies or career resumes. Make him want a first date to learn more about you.

Warning! Don't do the following when filling out your profile:

- Don't list the name of your business or work place.
- Don't get too specific about your home or area where you live.
- Don't list places you tend to frequent such as "that little coffee shop at 4th and Main."
- Don't show photos that might inadvertently show your house, or house number in the background.

- Don't show photos of friends and family unless they are okay with it.
- Don't list your income level or mention you are a CEO, drive a Maserati, etc. Some scammers are looking for women with money.
- Don't show revealing photos of yourself. It sends one message, and it will attract the men looking for that one thing. Be conservative. I know women who have gotten unappreciated comments simply because she posted a swimsuit picture. Err on the side of mystery.
- Obviously, don't list your personal information such as your email address, phone number or address.

When it comes to creating a dynamic profile, show the guy a glimpse of someone interesting, playful and fun with whom he can picture a lifetime of great experiences. Check out the competition to see what others are writing and note the ones that stand out.

When sending him a dating site email, keep it short. Many of us feel so excited about getting a wink or an email from someone we are interested in that we jump in with both feet and go overboard to impress him. It's as if we feel we have this one chance to prove to him how desirable we are before he vanishes into the ether. It can backfire on you and cause him to disappear as your desperation spills out across the page in black-and-white. A good rule of thumb is to follow his lead. If his email is a simple "Hello, how are you?", answer it with "I'm enjoying summer. How are you?" (Enjoying summer shows him your positive, upbeat side and sidesteps the boring "Fine".) Answer his questions in a simple, playful way without going overboard on the "cutesy". Ask him questions in return. Sometimes we forget this is a two-way communication. Avoid drilling him like a Marine Sergeant about his interests. Keep it light. Give him the impression getting emails is nothing new to you but you are happy to engage with him in some short exchange of information.

A Word about Emails/Phone Calls and Texts:

If you begin communicating with a man on a dating site, and it doesn't seem to be going anywhere, I would give it a few emails back-and-forth and then let him know you are too busy for an online email relationship. You can do this nicely. There are a lot of men simply looking for a woman to talk to online. If your goal is to have a first date with this gentleman to see if he interests you, then there comes a time to let him know that.

You (in an email after you've corresponded for at least three or four times): "You seem really interesting and I've enjoyed emailing with you. I do prefer talking to someone instead of emails as it's a much better way to get a sense of them, don't you think?"

See what he says. Leave it just that simple and short. His answer will tell you where he thinks this is going.

Another effective course of action is to use distance rather than words. Don't answer his next email in a hurry. Let him wait a few days and wonder if you're coming back. It will create a sense of urgency on his behalf. Another form of this is to end your email leaving him with lots of empty days coming up without hearing from you, such as saying "I hope you have a great weekend/week." If you have been emailing back-and-forth every day, he just got the message this has become tiring to you and you may be moving on. He will more than likely ask you out if he has the confidence, or is interested.

Letting someone take up your time with endless emails doesn't show a woman with a busy life of her own. And it can point to someone who may be married and just wants a female pen pal to play around with. It may also be a scammer trying to reel you in through tons of emails until you feel a bond with a man you have never even met.

This logic also applies to copious phone calls or texts without the man ever getting around to asking you out. Nip it in the bud. You have better things to do.

Just be careful, use your common sense, and never let a man pick you up at your residence or work on a first date! Be judicious about who you give your phone number or personal email address to. Let him earn the right to have access to you. It will set you apart from the eager females hoping for a date…any date!

Read Between the Lines.

Here is a quick list of translations for online dating references:
- His age range for women: If his date preferences are ages 10 years younger or more, and none are his age or closer, he is looking for someone to make him feel younger, or look younger. Or, he may still want to father children.

- Children living at his home will mean you will not have total access to him on weekends or holidays.
- If his dog(s) is/are in 80% of his photos, or listed throughout his profile, you can expect Fido to be along on many of your dates, or in your lap while you are visiting at his house.
- Many, many men online pepper there photos with pictures they have taken of oceans, flowers, mountains, etc. There are a lot of amateur and professional photographers out there. While he is hoping you will admire his talent, it doesn't really give you a glimpse of *him*. You may need to ask for a few photos of him after you have corresponded a time or two.
- If someone is evasive about the question where it asks him to list drinking or smoking preferences, it's a pretty safe bet they are a smoker or drink more than just "on occasion." This is your call.
- Men who list all the things they are *not* looking for have been burned before and have a fairly negative outlook on dating. It could spell trouble.
  - A lot of men will put higher incomes than they really make on their profiles knowing a high percentage of women are looking for affluent. Just know that going in. They may also fib about their age, weight, height and show deceptive photos. I was surprised at how many men showed themselves leaning on a private plane or Corvette when they didn't own it, or they once did but were now driving a VW. I personally don't look at a guy's Material Meter. Just know that what you see is not always

what you get. False Advertising abounds on dating sites.

- If religion is important to you, note that preference category.
- If he has tons of photos of himself involved in sports, hiking, travel and camping, and you are not interested in anything that requires losing your heels, then don't waste his time. He is not going to give all that up for you. Vice versa, a guy who comes off a couch potato will probably not get all jazzed up to suddenly change his lifestyle to join you in extreme sports.

You can become quite expert at reading between the lines on profiles if you will take your time and ask yourself "What is he really saying here?"

75% of men in the survey said they prefer a quick email from an interested woman over a wink. They felt winks were lame and too passive and left to him to do all the work.

Online dating can be a good thing or a disappointment. Just be careful and go slow. You will probably have to kiss a few toads before you find your Prince.

Chapter Two
Today's Dating and Marriage Environments: How Our Expectations Have Changed

I would like to preface this chapter by showing you how we as men and women have changed when it comes to our roles in society, and especially inside a relationship. Very often the media has its finger on the pulse of society and reflects back to us through television, movies, art, music and the written word where, and who we are in a particular generation. Just for fun, take a look at women's changing roles as viewed through the camera lens of TV and film.

Let's see how Disney's princesses evolved over the years. It is quite revealing.

Snow White and the Seven Dwarfs appeared on the scene in 1937, and was, in fact, Disney's debut film. She was depicted as a frightened woman lost in the woods who ends up cooking and cleaning for seven bearded miners while waiting to be rescued. In 1950, *Cinderella* hit the screens and even though 17 years had passed since Snow White bit the apple, not much has changed. Here, our princess warms her tootsies by the hearth while dreaming of meeting her prince, which she finally does. He places her on his horse and they ride off into the sunset toward a fairytale castle. *Sleeping Beauty* took being rescued to a whole new level in 1961. She simply lay back on satin pillows and waited for that life-altering kiss.

Then the 80's rolled around and things began to change; in the real world and in the media. Disney's princesses evolved right along with women's changing roles. *The Little Mermaid* debuted in 1989 and just look at our heroine now. Ariel is a feisty, determined, rebellious little aquatic princess with a mind of her own. Rather than waiting to be rescued to get the life of her dreams, she goes after it, sacrificing whatever it takes to get there while leaving behind security and safety. It is our first sense of the princess taking charge of her destiny. She wins the prince, but it was through her efforts rather than his, in fact she saves his life along the way.

In 1991 Disney took it up another step with *Beauty and the Beast*. Here we have Belle, an educated woman, impatient and unaccepting of the traditional female role model of wife and mother. She is feisty, confident and determined that there "must be more than this provincial life." When her father goes missing, she saddles up and rides off into a winter storm, facing hungry wolves, a forlorn castle and a towering beast. Here our princess has become the rescuer as she trades her life for her father's and earns him his freedom. Big difference from the earlier princesses who waited for the man to come riding up on his white stead with promises of love ever after.

Princess Jasmine glided onto the scene in *Aladdin* in 1992, and while presenting women with an impossible figure to live up to, she showed her spirit, confidence, independence and spunk by turning down the suitors who were not to her liking, and finally running away from the palace in an effort to gain freedom. She chooses a man on her terms and teaches a few males along the way that women aren't to be trifled with.

Pocahontas upped the ante of the independent female role in 1995. She defied her father's insistence that she marry someone who would keep her safe and protected, and went out in search of adventure and following her dreams. She was instrumental in saving her people's lives and those of the "white men". A strong woman is once again portrayed as the rescuer instead of a victim.

In 1996 *The Hunchback of Notre Dame* showcased a woman of questionable background and put her in a hero position as Esmeralda displays courage, compassion and integrity. Here is a gritty performance where basically she takes "no crap" from religious heads or anyone else, and empowers the life of an exiled hunchback named Quasimodo.

Following close on the heels of these female warriors comes *Mulan* in 1998. Family expectations, traditional female roles of wife, mother and dutiful daughter are flaunted, as this brave young woman goes off to battle in an effort to save her father and her country. To the extreme of impersonating a man in order to defend honor and right, she risks her life and saves the day. The men in the story take a back seat to her heroics.

The Princess and the Frog in 2009 depicts today's version of the determined entrepreneur as Tiana doggedly goes after her dream of opening her own restaurant. She has no time for frivolity, men or obstacles. The fact that she has to go through a "green period" does nothing to daunt her dreams. And in this scenario, the guy joins *her* vision of success and comes onboard.

Tangled filled the theaters in 2010 with long hair and big dreams. While Rapunzel is not the dashing heroine depicted in earlier films, she is determined to discover what waits outside the tower walls. She saves the hero's life several times throughout the movie, showing cunning, compassion and street smarts, until she finally claims the crown she was born to wear.

Frozen debuted in 2013 and depicts strong female roles as two sisters tackle life on their own terms. Again we see independent, confident women who brave the elements and deceit to conquer fear and obstacles.

If you look at the evolution of these animated princesses, along with the changing roles women portray on television, you will see the female's steadily changing of the guard throughout the past 70 years. Suffragettes, women's rights, and the Feminist Movement all made their message felt as the media began changing how women were depicted.

Take the television shows of the 50's: *Leave It To Beaver, Father Knows Best* and *Dennis the Menace*. The role of the female was to dust, deep-clean, diaper and defrost, all while wearing a starched dress and a strand of pearls. The trend continued as the 60's brought us *Bewitched, Green Acres, Lassie, Ozzie and Harriet, The Andy Griffith Show, The Donna Reed Show,* and *The Dick Van Dyke Show;* the only difference was women were wearing slacks and showing some spunk. Even *The Munsters, Addams Family, The Flintstones* and *The Jetsons* depicted traditional family roles of the stay-at-home mom while the men went off to work and brought home the bacon…or T-Rex burgers.

If you fast-forward through to *All in the Family, Married With Children, The Simpsons, The Bill Cosby Show, Everybody Loves Raymond* and other gender-defining sit-coms, you will see a major change in the female role. Women were talking back, holding down jobs, touting women's equality, and making Tang Sandwiches instead of the traditional pot roast and potatoes (or tossing the apron to the man as she headed out the door). Today's female roles include CSI agents, forensics experts, medical examiners, doctors, lawyers and police officers. Many TV shows and movies of the 21st century portray single, divorced or widowed women taking on the world, kicking butt and taking names.

While our view of women and their gifts to society have changed, the fundamental needs of a relationship still hold to many of the basic needs between the sexes. Men still want to feel needed, and women still want to feel loved. We may have gone from hand-written love letters to abbreviated prose via text and email, but there is still that underlying need to connect to another human being and feel valued.

Do men want women to go back to the barefoot and pregnant mentality of long ago? Heavens NO! Today's man is very turned on by the independent, confident, goal seeking female with passions, dreams and determination all her own. What the men in the survey did say vehemently was a wish for a woman who still got in touch with her feminine side and let him still fulfill his role as a man in other areas. The hope that women could have it all without it meaning emasculating men to get it was very prevalent. And after hearing women denounce "the new male" as too passive, too sensitive and not "edgy" enough, it sounds like we have some reshuffling of the cards to take care of.

Men just want to feel that attraction to a woman who is all woman (and that includes heading a corporation or winning Gold medals) and get back to the courting, flirting, passion and energy that comes from two sexes creating some friction. This "one size fits all" generation has taken away the male/female mystique and left us with a generic blend of confused genders and frustrated expectations. When we started creating perfumes and colognes that could be worn by either sex, I wondered what was coming next.

If we get back to accepting and appreciating the differences between the sexes, and realize we are hard-wired for certain dispositions for a reason, I believe we will all be happier and more fulfilled. We will stop looking at the opposite sex as the enemy camp. We will embrace what we've learned, and earned, through the passing years and hopefully bring those new insights to a relationship. Lots of men love to cook and lots of women love to march off to the office. There's nothing wrong with that. The problem lies in the inflexibility to still put something feminine next to the attaché case, and something masculine next to the apron. We can have it all. But progress doesn't mean needing to annihilate the foundation it is built upon.

IN A NUTSHELL...

With all the pushing and shoving, cutting away and stitching back together, is it any wonder there are some pretty confused men and women wondering how to make it all work?

As shown in the chart for online dating statistics, over 41 million people are on dating sites looking for love. What does that tell us? To me it means there are a ton of people out there who still believe in romance and who believe life is better shared with someone special. Love springs eternal! So does hope—even in the face of confusion and frustration. May I postulate a solution for the unhappy women out there?

What if we look at the man we are dating or with whom we've exchanged vows and realize he is just like us. We've hammered home the differences between the sexes in this book, but what about the similarities? Men are human and fallible, just as women are. They have fears, needs, desires, hopes and dreams. They are hoping for the happily ever after just as much as we are. When they stumble they are hoping you didn't notice, or love them enough to allow them to save face. If their day was hard, they are hoping for someone to hug them and give them that boost that sends them out the door to face the jungle again. They cry over sad situations and stand in awe at the birth of their child.

We are all susceptible to criticism. It hurts. It affirms our biggest fear: "I am not perfect. How can I be loved if I am faulty?" To love someone is to let them see us at our most vulnerable. And that stirs up all kinds of insecurities.

My mother taught her models a very poignant truth: "You can't give away what you don't have." You can't give love if all you have in your heart is hate. You can't be happy for another if you have feelings of inferiority where you are secretly hoping for another's failure. You can't support, uplift and empower another if you are wallowing in self-hatred and fear.

All too often when we feel the need to attack another and demean them, it is because we are feeling fear of some kind or a need to hurt. People with healthy self-esteems never feel the need to pull another down. They want to share their happiness and lift the other person up. It is only those who are feeling a lack within themselves that go after another human being in hopes of feeling bigger by making the other person appear smaller.

My point is this... If you are looking at the man in your life and feeling a need to point out his flaws, miss-steps, shortcomings and annoying habits, does that say more about him, or about you? Does your need to be right, vindicated and controlling highlight an underlying fear that perhaps you know you aren't measuring up, or the need that the situation must be perfect?

Psychiatrists will tell you that if there is something about someone that sends you over the edge, nine times-out-of-ten it is because you feel a "hook" to a similar feeling about yourself. It may be subliminal and deeply buried, but it's usually a trait you don't admire in yourself, and so the need to extinguish it in another. His laziness, anger, lack of empathy, procrastination, etc. may be triggers that set you off because you recognize those tendencies in yourself, or they may be unresolved issues from past relationships, including those with your father or an important role model. Either way, if you feel an unreasonable emotion about some trait or another exhibited by someone else, he/she may be holding up a mirror to something needling you deep inside.

All I'm saying is our need to punish or belittle someone close to us is not coming from a healthy place. And very often it is coming from fear:

- Fear that his ignoring your wishes at the moment is a direct affirmation that you are not worthy.
- Fear that an argument or pulling away signals the relationship is over because it is now "not perfect."
- Fear that the inability to communicate means he doesn't love you.
- Fear that others must see your relationship as wonderful. If not, then you have failed.
- Fear that his unhappiness with something you've done means you are not measuring up. Perhaps he even regrets being with you.
- Fear that you have failed…as a person, a friend, a wife, a daughter, etc. Failed…failed…failed.

- Fear that misunderstandings and seeing things differently means you made the wrong choice in a partner and now you are trapped.
- Fear that any cracks in the veneer could mean you may be looking at living life alone.

If you look at these fears you will notice one underlying problem. They are all erroneous. They are packed with insecurities, most likely from childhood. Fears of abandonment, isolation or simply being in an uncomfortable situation can surface in an instant from their storage area deep within your brain.

A person coming from a secure and confident place would see these situations differently. They would know an argument was just that. Two people who may be overly-tired, stressed or just misunderstanding each other needing to air their viewpoint. It does not signal the end of the relationship. It can be a way of opening the door to understanding and better communication. Be more nervous about the relationships who don't feel safe enough to vent or bring up an issue.

Someone with a healthy self-esteem will not see another's actions as an affront or desire to hurt. They are just human beings struggling through life with the rest of us. If their viewpoint is different from ours, it's supposed to be. They are not us. They don't come from the same background, experiences and needs. We allow them to be themselves and embrace their differences rather than fear or condemn them. A person coming from a core of self-respect will also shut out the opinions of the masses and rely on their own judgment. Too many relationships have been riddled with holes from the shots taken at it from outsiders. It is not their business. And often they are coming at it from their own fears and insecurities.

So...in a nutshell, men and women alike are hoping that first date is the start of something wonderful. Men who lay aside their precious freedom and carry their selected woman across the threshold are excited about sharing their life and creating wonderful memories. Both sexes are still interested in romance, the kind they see in the movies. That castle in the clouds is still something they believe they can attain if they will just relax, support each other, be a best friend, lover and companion. One man from the survey summed it up nicely.

Darin* 45, electrical engineer. "If women understood how much a man wants that fairytale ending as well, I think they would put down the artillery and relax into being with us as our partners, not as the adversary. We love women. We love their softness, their childlike love of life, their compassion, empathy, curves, kisses and the gentleness they bring to our lives. We don't feel whole without them. And we would do anything to make their lives rich and happy."

What's In Your Future?

I predict an amazing future for you! It is totally unlimited! Filled with the possibility of fulfilling everything on your wish list.

Start with yourself, just as we did in the beginning of this book. Work on the areas that are hanging you up and causing you unnecessary misery. When you find yourself through self-discovery, it's an amazing feeling. When you can embrace that incredibly wonderful person you see in the mirror and stop being so hard on her, you will see doors open all around you. Erase the parts of your past that aren't serving you now. Become your best friend and biggest supporter. Develop a healthy self-esteem (and it can be re-invented!).

Only then can you enter into a relationship and bring your best self to the equation. You won't feel the need to take a man and recreate him like modeling clay until he fits your mold. The need to belittle, demean and punish won't be there—those insidious traits that have sent more partners to the relationship graveyard than anything else. You will have your own life filled with passions, interests and goals that will keep your days brimming with happiness, even when he is off pursuing a few of his own. You will go into those first dates brimming with confidence and a realistic view of it all.

When you realize your hands are on the steering wheel, it releases the fear that life is buffeting you around like a rudderless ship at sea. You will begin calling the shots. Other's opinions of you will be filed under the "take it or leave it" category. You will see accomplishments pile up, friends gather around you, your health improve, bank accounts fill and adventures begin. Your positive thoughts will pull more good things into your world. The Law of Attraction is real, and it works. Read some of the books I list in the Recommended Reading section that have helped so many people live lives of abundance. It is all within reach…you just have to say "Yes" to the Universe.

Troubleshooting Men is just one part of building a great life. Troubleshooting YOU will guarantee it's a jaw-dropping one.

And best of all…you will have an amazing future! ☺

Recommended Reading

Excuse Me, Your Life is Waiting. Lynn Grabhorn

The Lies We Believe. Dr. Chris Thurman

Self-Esteem. Mathew McKay, Ph.D. & Patrick Fanning

Self-Defeating Behaviors. Milton R. Cudney, Ph.D & Robert E. Hardy, Ed.D.

Feel the Fear and Do It Anyway. Susan Jeffers, Ph.D.

Simple Abundance. A Daybook of Comfort and Joy. Sarah Ban Breathnach.

When Perfect Isn't Good Enough. Martin M. Anthony, Ph.D. & Richard P. Swinson, M.D.

Getting the Love You Want. A Guide for Couples. Harville Hendrix, Ph.D.

The Power of Intention. Dr. Wayne W. Dyer

About the Author

Rebecca F. Pittman is an author who defies genre norms. Her fields of interest vary from researching and writing about the most-haunted venues in America, to helping people in the creative arts arenas start their own businesses. *Troubleshooting Men, What in the WORLD do they want?* is a labor of love and a tribute to her mother, Collette Wells who spent her life helping women discover their core of excellence by creating a life of abundance.

Ms. Pittman designed and created *Troubleshooting Men* the website in 2012, a forerunner in its innovative use of a panel of men answering women's questions in every area of dating and relationships. It spawned a popular television talk show by the same name. She conducted a relationship survey of 2,000 men in an effort to help men and women better understand each other. Helping women through motivational speaking, seminars and books like these are her way of giving back and encouraging others to go beyond ordinary.

Her latest book, *T.J. Finnel and the Well of Ghosts* is Ms. Pittman's first novel. It is Book One of a 5-Book Series in the Juvenile Fiction market.

Rebecca makes her home in the beautiful foothills of the Colorado Rockies where you will find her golfing and boating, or hanging out with her family and friends every chance she gets.